Praise for The White Mo

"Dan Szczesny's *The White Mountain* is an exceptional book and an unforgettable ode to a peak so near and dear to all of us who live year-round in the shadow of New Hampshire's Mount Washington. His writing deftly captures the spirit, the allure, and the fascination we have with the Rock Pile, while also reminding us of its storied past and humankind's enduring bond with this true giant of a mountain."

—*Mike Dickerman, coauthor of* 4000-Footers of the White Mountains *and editor of* Mount Washington: Narratives and Perspectives

"There is an expression in architecture, 'function follows form.' But what if the form is the highest peak in the northeast? Over the course of a year, Dan Szczesny was able to take his time, get to know Mount Washington and follow that peak's progeny—poets, painters and hard-scrabble New Hampshire natives whose stories all begin in the shadow of the mountain. Then, with the help of Dan's curiosity, experience as a journalist and the gift of time, we get to follow those who stay and those who move away, but like a family, every character carries with them a piece of the mountain's DNA. I have lived in New Hampshire for nearly forty years, but in *The White Mountain*, I am seeing Mount Washington for the first time and am beginning to realize what I have missed."

—*Arnie Arnesen, politician in recovery and host of* The Attitude *on WNHN 94.7*

"Mount Washington is more than punishing temperatures and fog that blows sideways. In *The White Mountain*, Dan Szczesny parts the curtain of intrigue and shows you the heart and soul of the people who have found inspiration and self-discovery there. Surprising and fun! And a cool cat named Marty, who may very well hold more of the mountain's secrets than he's willing to share."

—*Mike Morin, columnist, speaker and broadcaster, and author of* Lunch with Tommy and Stasia: TV's Golden Age of Candlepin Bowling

"This is a book for those who love to explore, not only our sublime northern landscape but the cultural mindscape inspired by New England's most iconic mountain. I can't imagine a more amiable or knowledgeable companion on this literary ramble than Dan Szczesny. He is graced with a hiker's inexhaustible drive, a reporter's eye for story, and a poet's way of seeing past the surface of what's before him. He has written *The White Mountain* as a celebration: come and join the party!"

—*James Patrick Kelly, lifelong hiker, author,*
and winner of the Hugo, Nebula, and Locus awards

"Dan Szczesny writes about his relationship with Mount Washington not with the voice of the conqueror but with the voice of a seeker. In a compellingly modest style, he illuminates the history, lure, majesty, cruelty, and beauty of one of the world's most fascinating mountains. He scales it while reading poetry; he paints it under the tutelage of artists; he tells funny and poignant stories of others who have hiked it. His view of one of America's most enduring natural monuments changes him, and perhaps his book will change its readers as well."

—*Craig Werner, Associate Professor Emeritus of English,*
Buffalo State College

"When we seek to learn about a mountain, what we find is that the mountain often teaches us about ourselves. Dan Szczesny's yearlong quest leads him to find the quirky, the obsessed, and sometimes the tragic characters whose lives were shaped by Mount Washington, while attempting to understand what draws him to the peak. Part thoroughly researched historical fact, part colorful and funny tale, and part poetic memoir of a year spent under a mountain's spell, *The White Mountain* masterfully takes readers to this intriguing place and leaves them longing for their own year of adventure there."

—*Mary Emerick, author of* The Geography of Water *and*
Fire in the Heart: A Memoir of Friendship, Loss and Wildfire

"Mount Washington may be the Rockpile, but it's also a cultural phenomenon. In *The White Mountain*, ride in Dan Szczesny's pack with him for a year and see all the ways Mount Washington's extreme beauty and ferocious weather have changed everyone who comes in contact with it."

—*Christine Woodside, editor of* Appalachia *journal*
and author of Libertarians on the Prairie

"*The White Mountain* flows effortlessly, leading its readers through layers of history, people, and personal reflection. Dan Szczesny's keen sense of curiosity and mindful storytelling enabled me to see the fabled rock pile from a different perspective and both appreciate and re-appreciate it in ways I never thought possible. A highly recommended read for hikers, history buffs, or anyone else who simply loves a great story."

—*Matt Landry, author of* Learning to be Human Again
and Forward, Upward, Onward

"Who else but Dan Szczesny could plunge into the lore and lifestyle of New Hampshire's highest peak in such an original way? Dressed as Walt Whitman, he struggles up its road while reading from *Leaves of Grass*. Getting into the heads of artists, he tries painting the mountain's wide profile. Beyond the affectionate portrayal of New Hampshire characters and the quirky historical tidbits, there's a broader message in *The White Mountain*: Live exuberantly, learn creatively, bond with the landscape."

—*Betsy Woodman, author of* Jana Bibi's Excellent Fortunes,
Love Potion Number 10, *and* Emeralds Included

"Dan Szczesny is in a lifelong love affair with mountains and high places. He's not particular; any will do—from small ones with views to Himalayan giants. In this book, *The White Mountain*, he focuses on just one: Mount Washington, the magnificent pile of rocks crowning New Hampshire's White Mountains. He's cooked for the summit observatory crew; introduced his infant daughter, Uma, to its alpine tundra; and even hiked up the auto road, dressed as Walt Whitman, reading poetry. Don't ask. It's a love affair, and it doesn't have to make sense. But it does have to be beautiful, and it is."

—*Willem Lange, writer, storyteller, and host of New Hampshire Public Television's* Windows to the Wild

THE **White Mountain**

REDISCOVERING MOUNT WASHINGTON'S HIDDEN CULTURE

Dan Szczesny

HOBBLEBUSH BOOKS
Brookline, New Hampshire

Although all the events depicted in this memoir are true, some have been consolidated or the time line moved for clarity. No names have been changed, historic or current. Everyone knew what they were getting into and kindly agreed to be a part of this project.

Chapter 4 of *The White Mountain* appeared in excerpted form in the Winter/Spring 2018 edition of *Appalachia* journal. Various excerpts appeared in different form in *AMC Outdoors, Good Men Project, Manchester Ink Link, The Concord Monitor* and *In Depth NH.*

Composed in Bembo Book with Mr Eaves Sans display at Hobblebush Books (www.hobblebush.com)

Printed in the United States of America

Cover and chapter illustrations by Kat Maus (www.katmaushaus.com)

All other photographs by Dan Szczesny

ISBN: 978-1-939449-17-7

Library of Congress Control Number: 2018944956

HOBBLEBUSH BOOKS
17A Old Milford Road
Brookline, New Hampshire 03033
www.hobblebush.com

Contents

To my father,
Joe Szczesny

Foreword

There are many ways to climb Mount Washington—hiking trails, the auto road and, of course, the Cog. Go ahead and build it if you can, the New Hampshire Legislature scoffed when Sylvester Marsh proposed it in the 1850s. You might just as well build a railway to the moon. He went ahead and built it.

How many millions have ascended Washington by train, by car, and on foot since Darby Field made the hike in 1642? How many paintings have been painted? How many photos snapped? How many books written?

A heck of a lot.

I've been telling stories about this rocky old place for twenty-five years. I know a good story when I see one. And so does my friend Dan Szczesny. He tackles the formidable task of writing a book with something fresh to say about the most famous of all the Whites. I didn't know what to expect from Dan's book—folklore, history, hiking, geography, geology, wildlife, wind, weather? What could he add to a subject explored so thoroughly by so many others for so long?

A lot, as it turns out.

He brings something special to the page—himself. Through his wide, wise eyes readers get an unexpected perspective on a mountain with more history than you can shake a hiking stick at.

The White Mountain reminds me of the haunting images of Richard Moore, a photographer from Deerfield. Moore calls his photographs "twice seen" and creates them by superimposing new images over vintage ones—a landscape, seascape, or streetscape. Moore's photographs show how things change and how they don't. Same with this book. Dan digs deep into what was and superimposes what is. He spends time on the mountain in all seasons with all kinds of people. He travels far from the mountain in search of parts of the story never told before. He writes the story and he is the story.

It's Mount Washington "twice seen."

On Alton Weagle Day climbers set bizarre records in the spirit of Alton Weagle who hiked backwards, barefoot, blindfolded, and pushing a wheelbarrow full of sugar (not all at the same time). Asked why, Weagle said he liked to do things that no one had done before. Dan dressed up as Walt Whitman and read poetry all the way to the summit. Readers climb with him. He is Dan, he is Weagle, he is Whitman, he is some tuckered at day's end.

The White Mountain is informative, funny, and full of fascinating characters. It is also deeply personal. When Dan introduces his three-year-old daughter, Uma—a collector of pebbles—to the Rock Pile, oh my heart! To Uma and her dad, everything old is truly new again. The wonder never ends.

In this part of the world, Washington is THE mountain. It is beloved, respected, feared, and familiar. In *The White Mountain* Dan Szczesny bushwhacks a fresh, new, wonder-filled trail.

Rebecca Rule
Northwood, New Hampshire
February 2018

Introduction

As part of my research for this book, I spent a week in April cooking for the meteorologists who live year round atop New England's highest peak at the Mount Washington Observatory. I'm a terrible cook, but I had help and guidance from a longtime volunteer and restaurateur by the name of John Donovan, a character in his own right who you'll meet in the pages of this book. Our strategy for keeping those scientists fed was pretty simply—John told me what to do, and I did it.

In April, winter still churns at 6,288 feet, which meant I was able to experience firsthand the enormous changes in weather that occur every day at the summit, home of some of the world's most unpredictable weather. From the spectacular rime ice that formed in delicate tendrils off the weather equipment to the freezing rain, from winds that neared one hundred miles per hour and shook the living quarters at night to a midnight sky that brought the Milky Way seemingly within arm's reach.

And after, when I finally got back down, unshaven, wind-burned, my head and heart deeply affected by the epic stay, the first question I was most often asked was: Did you meet Marty?

Marty the Cat is the observatory's mascot, and he's lived atop New England since 2009. He's the latest in a long line of kitties dating back to the 1930s that have called the mountaintop their home.

No amount of wicked weather (the observatory holds the record, at 231 miles per hour, for highest land speed wind measured by man), environmental science, engineering, or contributions to outdoors culture can ever measure up to the daily goings of the summit cats.

The lesson that I quickly learned as my year exploring Mount Washington went on was that the things I thought this book would be about—weather, geology, history—took a back seat to the less heralded events and people that have created the mythology and culture behind one of the most popular places in the world. And make no mistake, the connections to Mount Washington extend worldwide, are generations deep, and speak again and again to the artistic urge not to best the mountain, but to better ourselves.

In 1859, a New York City-born Unitarian minister serving as the pastor of Hollis Street Church in Boston published a book called *The White Hills: Their Legends, Landscapes and Poetry.* Thomas Starr King, already one of the most famous preachers in New England when the book came out, was among the first to begin to approach Mount Washington and the White Mountains of New Hampshire with something more than fact or fear. Inspired by men like Ralph Waldo Emerson, Starr King gazed up at the northern mountains and saw the metaphysical reflected back at him.

His writing, in turn, has inspired poets and artists, myself included, to feel the mountains first, to connect with them emotionally. In one of his sermons, Starr King asked, "What would a soul be with no pure delight in the beauty of the world?"

Then, in his book, he writes:

A visit to New Hampshire supplies the most resources to a traveler, and confers the most benefit on the mind and taste, when it lifts him above mere appetite for wildness, ruggedness, and the feeling of mass and precipitous elevation, into a perception and love of the refined grandeur, the chaste sublimity, the airy majesty overlaid with tender and polished bloom, in which the landscape splendor of a noble mountain lies.

So, in setting out to write about Mount Washington, I took Thomas Starr King's approach: find the heartbeat in each adventure, delve deeply into the sublime connections to the land, and explore the greater purpose—spiritual, transcendental, sacred—of that one hill.

Though my research began prior to January 1, 2017 and extended beyond December 31, 2017, over the course of that one year, Mount Washington became my obsession; the shadow of that mountain seemed to follow me everywhere I went. No corner of New England, and indeed many distant parts of the country, went untouched.

In Manchester, where I live, I tracked down the history of a lawyer who donated his land atop a different, smaller mountain so that early scientists could test whether or not it was even possible to live and survive atop the mountains during the winter.

In Buffalo, New York, I walked along the river where the soon-to-be founder of the most famous railway in the world made his fortune, and I toured that city's remaining mill silos with a man suffering from loss and finding solace in the proud industrial history of his city.

In Stark, New Hampshire, I followed in the footsteps of the man whose very existence revolved around bettering himself on that mountain and whose mother left an indelible mark on the landscape of the North Country.

In State College, Pennsylvania, I walked alongside a ninety-seven-year-old athlete who has tested the limits of human endurance on Mount Washington by running up her a dozen times.

For every stone overturned, every question asked, every historic string pulled, newer and more surprising doors opened. My job as the year went on was to simply try to follow the trails. But like branches of a vast, ancient tree, all too often I had to pick a route and stick with it, follow it to the tip of its branch. So many stories. So many memories. So many places and people the mountain touches.

Whether you are a regular hiker of Mount Washington or are lucky enough to live in a place where you can sit on your back porch and watch its summit, or whether you have never been to New Hampshire and have yet to experience the top of any mountain, my hope is that you'll find connection, as I did, in the pages ahead.

For I also discovered, as many before me had, that this mountain offers solace and reflection as well. During a year when the challenges of being both a dad to a toddler and son to a dying father tested my patience and endurance, I sought comfort in Mount Washington.

And Mount Washington delivered me, redeemed me and became my prophet, and I became its storyteller.

This mountain—Washington—is many things: a testing ground for athletes, a muse for artists, a reminder of our mortality, a reason to exalt in our gods. But most importantly, to understand why we are drawn to such a place is to understand our own humanity. After all, in the end, we have been coming to her summit for nearly four centuries, and throughout that history Mount Washington has never been anything but a pile of rocks.

But it's a pile of rocks that has reflected our aspirations and culture, has inspired genius and caused tragedy. This place has created heroes and brought love and passion to a wide swath of people who looked up into the sky and saw more than rocks. They saw life.

I found a little bit of all of that on the mountain during my year at her side, and I found that off the mountain as well. I discovered that once the mountain touches you, it changes you. No amount of miles that fate puts between you and the hill can ever change you back.

In the end, I hope you'll find inspiration in this journey, find hope in the direction simple geography can provide and, if you haven't already, find your own Mount Washington wherever you may be.

Finally, I did find Marty, comfortable and content on a top shelf in what the scientists up there call the weather room. He's older now, more settled in his place in the annals of Mount Washington lore, less likely to feel the need to show off or perform.

I scratched his black whiskers under his chin while outside a vicious storm rattled the observatory windows. But Marty had seen it all. He just lifted his head, gave me a stretch and yawned before drifting back to sleep.

That's what happens when you find your happy place. It becomes part of who you are.

Mount Washington did that for me. I hope you're able to find a place to give you that as well. Perhaps this book—perhaps the story of this mountain—will be a place to start.

Dan Szczesny

Manchester, New Hampshire

January 2018

CHAPTER ONE

Treads of the Coach

In Which the Author Begins His Journey
by Facing Down a Nor'easter at 4,000 Feet

The snow comes down in thick waves, wet and heavy, dripping from my
eyelashes to my cheeks in cool, streaking drops. Here at 4,200 feet, surrounded by the mid-sized pines and scrubby, snow-covered krummholz
of Mount Washington's eastern flank, the wind is mild.

But behind me, farther up the mountain's auto road, out there
where there's nothing but air and ice—where the air becomes pure and
vicious—I understand there is a storm, a miles-long blanket of wind,
howling, somewhere up there, in a place where there is only white, and
distance deceives your own feet and balance.

It is February on the highest mountain in the Northeastern United
States. This morning, a great nor'easter—a sloppy, dripping sheet of a
storm—overtook the White Mountains. The storm feels more like walking through slushy ice cubes than a proper snowfall.

It is February, there is a storm, and I am alone on one of the most unforgiving mountains on Earth.

There are no mountains in New Jersey, where I lived before coming to New Hampshire in 1998. There are no mountains in Buffalo, New York, where I'm from and where I grew up. I remember the first time I drove through the White Mountains in the winter, on my way to Montreal. I couldn't understand how I was going to be able to drive through those ice-encrusted monsters.

Ours are just little hills compared to some of the ranges around the world, but my heart leapt the first time I saw the snow caps along Franconia Ridge, the wide near-half circle of Mount Eisenhower's enormous summit, and the shimmering tips of the Observatory and summit buildings that look like rocket ships set against a deep azure sky there on Mount Washington, our state and region's high point.

And as life and my work as a journalist pulled me deeper into the politics, culture, and the outdoor hiking and climbing community that thrives in the state and in the White Mountains, a few things began to take focus.

The first is that Mount Washington, for all its tiny height of only 6,288 feet, casts a long shadow over every aspect of life in New England. Few mountains, if any in the world, save perhaps Mount Everest, or Fuji, or Olympus, have such a long, rich, and controversial history as this one. And few have such a long list of casualties.

Since 1849, about 150 souls have been lost on the Presidential Range, but that casualty rate—about one death a year—has stopped no one from coming. In fact, the number of visitors are going up. About 250,000 humans tag the summit of Mount Washington every year. They ride cars, motorcycles, bicycles, trucks, and shuttles up the auto road. They climb aboard the Cog Railway and chug their way up. They hike in all weather, in all seasons, over a variety of trails and terrain to get there. They strap skis to their backs and climb up steep ravine walls to glide back down. They stay overnight in nearby Appalachian Mountain Club huts where they have dinner and breakfast before facing the exposure of the Presidential Range to get to the summit.

Scientists come in helicopters, snowcats, snowmobiles, and in the early days, even piper cubs, to work at the observatory, museum, or radio buildings. Others work in the concession, cafeteria, or gift shops.

Tamworth, New Hampshire, writer Russ Provost worked on the top of Mount Washington during the summer and fall of 1963. He ran the snack shop at the Cog Railway hotel called the Summit House. His first day working atop the mountain was the first time he had ever been up, and like so many before and since, he looked out at the rolling hills and was enthralled. Back then, workers lived up top and had one day a week off. Russ picked Thursday as his off day because that was the evening that weekly square dances were held at the old Huckins Barn in his hometown.

Once, he recalled a challenge issued to him and his friend Jerry by a Cog Railway driver that if the boys could beat the train down on foot, the engineer would buy them ice cream sundaes at the station below.

The boys made it by tearing down the tracks, gripping steel and soot-encrusted rocks to keep them on their feet. Along Jacob's Ladder, a steep section of the tracks that crosses a gully, the boys ran straight across the span, the Cog fast on their heels. They made it but just barely, the ultimate train dodge. Filthy and exhausted, they claimed their prize.

"Racing the Cog down Mount Washington was a pretty amazing, some would say stupid, feat," Russ told me over a cup of joe at a Concord coffee shop, his eyes gleaming when telling the story of his youth. "But it was not until the next day that I realized just how foolish it was."

That next day was his first day as a senior at Kennett High School in Conway, New Hampshire. And by mid-day, Russ could barely walk.

"My thighs hurt so much when climbing the stairway that I needed to hold the railing and take one step at a time," he said "Later in the day I was coming down a flight of stairs when I noticed Jerry going up, holding the railing and taking one step at a time. We just looked at each other and laughed."

A half century later, Russ tells this story with conviction and pride, of moments on that holy place burned forever into the human he became. Years after his summer at the top of New England, Russ would travel to Nepal and write a book about it.

This mountain. Ask anyone who has been in its sphere of influence. When you come back down, you're different. Mount Washington changes you.

I pause for a moment, there under the blanket of snow, to listen to the silence. I know the wind higher up the mountain is howling like wolves to the moon. I know how it feels to be in wind like that, the ice beautiful and harsh, the air scratching any uncovered flesh as surly as if you ran a piece of sandpaper over it.

I'm glad I'm down low on the auto road, under the torrent, in that peaceful place where I can hear my heart beating under my Gore-Tex jacket, where each breath of cool air fills me with life, where the muscles in my legs and the bottoms of my feet strapped to my snowshoes have their own pulse, straining, ragged, and primal.

Though my study of Mount Washington began on the day I drove through Crawford Notch and caught my first glimpse of the summit and continued over the course of many years, many summits, and many sore muscles, this day, here in a storm in deep and heavily falling snow, is really the beginning of my journey.

I've long believed that the pull of this mountain, the inextricable urge to sit atop her summit, has existed in some long dormant human gene embedded to explain our own existence—to bring meaning and direction into lives often compromised by the unhealthier aspects of modern life.

To understand us is to seek a power greater than us.

The naturalist and writer Peter Matthiessen, in his classic book *The Snow Leopard*, writes specifically of the draw of mountains and the irony of seeking wisdom from them: "The secret of the mountain is that the mountains simply exist, as I do myself: the mountains exist simply, which I do not. The mountains have no 'meaning,' they are meaning; the mountains are."

In other words, Mount Washington has no opinion of us, takes no sides, exists (or didn't) regardless of her history and stories. Like all mountains, she relaxes in time content in the complexity of her simplicity.

And we swarm over and around her, ostensibly to pursue a connection to the natural world. But in reality, *we* are the riddle that needs to be solved. And we've created whole industries of mythology, science, the supernatural and folklore to thrive under the not terribly benevolent Mount Washington master.

For 350 years, Europeans have explored, settled, abused, and died at the altar of this mountain. And before that, New Hampshire's native peoples called the mountain by a variety of names: *Waumbik*, or "White Rocks" to the Algonquians and *Agiocochook*, or "the place of the Great Spirit" to the people who lived in the region, the Abenaki. The story told by Europeans is that the native dwellers didn't dare summit the mountain for fear of upsetting their gods—a convenient "truth" for merchant and ferryman Darby Field of Durham, New Hampshire, who in 1642 summited the mountain, becoming at least the first European to do so.

Whether Darby made this harrowing journey (he climbed the mountain twice within a year) to enrich himself with what many at the time believed were rare jewels and crystals at the summit, or as a bargaining chip in negotiating for land with the Abenaki, is beside the point.

In retrospect, it's clear that the mountain immediately became a magnet and place of mystery and fascination. Before the country was even a country, the myth of Mount Washington was already a century old.

My initial goal in this journey of discovery was to experience the mountain, first hand, in every possible way. Over the course of 2017, from January 1 to December 31, I would participate in every event, race, and happening that took place around Mount Washington. From the foot race to the huts to the Cog Railway, from bird watches to flora explorations, from the hikers to the tourists to the environmentalists to the teachers. If it was happening on that mountain, I would be part of it.

But it didn't quite work out that way. What I hadn't anticipated was that Mount Washington wasn't really the star in this ages-old play. That distinction belonged to the people looking up at the mountain and seeing infinity reflected back into their eyes.

Mount Washington doesn't exist in a vacuum. The mountain is part of the Presidential Range, a nineteen-plus mile long crest of mountains that form the highest peaks in New Hampshire. The primary peaks in the range—Washington, John Adams, Jefferson, Madison and Monroe, Eisenhower and John Quincy Adams—are named after United States Presidents. The range is a significant watershed, with separate drainage via the Saco and Androscoggin rivers into the Atlantic Ocean on the coast of Maine, and from the Israel and Ammonoosuc rivers into the Connecticut River and down into Long Island Sound.

Weather-wise, the range is merciless—a training ground for climbers looking to cut their teeth on extreme weather while preparing for K2 or Everest. The range's convergence near three major and regular storm tracks provide constant and erratic weather.

The Mount Washington Observatory still holds the record for the highest surface wind speed ever observed by man—231 miles per hour on April 12, 1934. Eighty-three years later to the day, I would find myself living atop the summit in the observatory on the anniversary of The Big Wind, bunking in a guest room named after Alex McKenzie, one of the weathermen atop the mountain that day.

The legacy of the mountain and that range were well established by the time of the wind record, but it's anyone's guess what northern New Hampshire would have looked like had it not been for the view from the top of a tiny, 2,037 foot mountain in the wooded southern section of the little North Country town of Lancaster, NH.

It was there atop Prospect Mountain that a U.S. Representative from Massachusetts built a summer estate with a view of the Presidential Range and decided it might be a good idea for the government to own and manage those mountains.

Ostensibly, when John Wingate Weeks began drafting what eventually became known as the Weeks Act, the idea was to protect watersheds as natural resources and to improve fire control between federal and state authorities. In 1910, wildfires in the west killed eighty-five people, destroyed three million acres of timber and put the U.S. Forest Service over a million dollars into debt. At the same time, logging and commercial development was sweeping through Northern New England and the federal government owned nearly no large tracts of land devoted to conservation.

The Weeks Act changed all that, and changed the direction of conservation, development, and tourism in New Hampshire, creating the modern landscape that exists today and supercharging the climate for tourism. And without tourism, northern New Hampshire would basically be the trees you have to drive through to get to Canada.

The trees that I'm walking under occasionally shed huge clumps of snow, a signal, perhaps, that the storm up high is beginning to snake its way into the lower heights. I begin my four-mile hike down, my whole body sluggish from being away from the mountains for so long. My daughter, Uma, was born just fifteen months ago after a harrowing delivery, and most of last year had been spent as a stay-at-home dad. And although the baby loves the outdoors and adores being in a backpack, big mountains like Washington have eluded me, and now I was paying for my neglect.

Further complicating my generally limited head space, my father, now eighty-nine, had begun to show signs of wear. After bouncing back from a series of health-related setbacks over the last couple years, my sister and I feared this latest decline might be his final one.

Since moving from the flatlands to New Jersey all those years ago, this terrain had signaled peace and connection for me—a way to unlatch from the shackles of concrete and congestion. Since my first 4,000-foot mountain summit—Cannon Mountain in 1998—I had slowly returned again and again to this forest, earning my place in the Appalachian Mountain Club's 4,000-footer club by hiking all forty-eight peaks in the state over 4,000 feet in height. I tagged the high points in twelve states, spent a week in the Grand Canyon, hiked the Centennial Trail in the Dakotas, and hiked fifty-two mountains in fifty-two weeks with my then nine-year-old foster daughter. And in 2010, I somehow managed to marry the woman of my dreams first atop Mount Lafayette here in New Hampshire, then in Kathmandu, and for our honeymoon, trek to Everest Base Camp.

A four-mile hike down a snow-covered road ought to be child's play. But it's not. I feel fretful and uncertain of the journey ahead of me, worried that this mountain won't allow me to tell its story. My foolish thoughts are interrupted by a gust of wind, the frigid air brushing my cheek as if telling me to just go, just walk, and let the mountain ease my mind.

The storm I'm hiking in is named Niko, and it formed as a great Alberta Clipper coming down from the Midwest and the Ohio Valley before sweeping up into the Whites and making landfall as a nor'easter on Mount Washington this morning, only a few hours prior to my trek.

For decades, an eccentric fellow from Brunswick, Maine by the name of Edgar Comee waged a fruitless battle against what he called "cruddy local news anchors" to unravel the word *nor'easter* and call the storms what they are—*northeasters*. Over the years he sent out thousands of ready-made blue postcards to media outlets, professors, and anyone else he heard misusing the word, finally gaining the attention of the *New Yorker* in 2005.

"The use of *nor'easter* to describe a northeast storm is a pretentious and altogether lamentable affectation, the odious, even loathsome, practice of landlubbers who would be seen as salty as the sea itself," Comee's cards read. "You will of course accept my view in this matter in good part and will never again use *nor'easter*, at least in public, and thus oblige."

Edgar's efforts, of course, have been fruitless. And he was working against hundreds of years of usage. The first recorded use of the term "nore" in regards to points of the compass happened 420 years prior to the Mainer's campaign. The English playwright John Lyly used the term in his 1585 play, *Gallathea*, an early version of comedic cross-dressing gender story lines with the young Gallathea having to pretend to be a boy in order to avoid being sacrificed to the god Neptune. Shakespeare himself borrowed heavily from the play to create *Twelfth Night* and *As You Like It*.

And the specific usage of "nor'easter" pops up in 1836 in a translation of Aristophanes. So had Edgar survived to this day, I'm sure he'd be horrified to hear those local newscasters breathlessly talking up Nor'easter Niko, their green screens swirling with cheerful reds and blues signifying the storm's impending wrath.

I lift my head to the nor'easter, let the snow kiss my eyelids, and begin my journey.

The Mount Washington Auto Road is not a technical or difficult route to follow. Billed as America's oldest man-made attraction, the 7.6-mile road to the summit opened in 1861. In many ways, the road was an afterthought, a profitable way of driving tourism into the eastern section of the mountains from the little northern town of Gorham. In 1851, a rail line had opened, connecting Montreal, Canada, to Portland, Maine, and as long as folks were coming through Gorham, they may as well stop and stay at the railroad-owned grand hotel there, or travel on the railroad-built road to the foot of the mountain, and what the heck, the railroad thought, why not build a toll road to the top while we're at it.

It's easy now, to take a road—even one to the top of a mountain—for granted. But consider: back then, the nearest supplies were miles away, all that rock and gravel had to be moved by cart and hand. Black powder was used, and all the blasting holes were drilled by hand. And even in the mountain's terrible weather, men worked ten- or twelve-hour days and lived in primitive shacks.

The very first motorized ascent was undertaken in 1899 in a Stanley Steamer by none other than Freelan O. Stanley himself.

A road to the top or near top of a mountain is not new to today's adventure tourism industry. New Hampshire, Vermont, and Maine all have popular mountains you can drive partially or all the way up—Mounts Kearsarge, Mansfield, and Cadillac, respectively. The highest drivable road in the world is on a double-peaked volcano, Uturuncu, in southwest Bolivia at a top elevation of 18,923 feet.

In America, Mount Evans near Denver is the highest mountain road in North America, peaking at 14,130 feet above sea level. Mount Evans has ties to the White Mountains in a most interesting way. Originally, Evans was named Mount Rosalie, after the wife of the famous landscape painter Albert Bierstadt who, in 1863, became the first known person to summit the mountain.

In the fall of 1869, Bierstadt, who grew up in New Bedford, Massachusetts, spent six weeks in the White Mountains, sketching and making studies of what would become his largest painting of an Eastern subject. That subject, of course, was Mount Washington. The painting, now in the Chrysler Museum of Modern Art in Norfolk, Virginia, is called *The Emerald Pool* and it is six by ten feet.

The painting's focal point, the Emerald Pool, gives the work a more secluded feel, while the towering, rugged peak of Mount Washington in the background lends the work an air of danger and mystery. Mystery indeed, because in reality, no part of the summit of Mount Washington can be seen from the Emerald Pool. No matter. Bierstadt's painting would travel the world—New York, Paris, Philadelphia, San Francisco—and become a catalyst for opening the doors of tourism to the Whites.

In a few months, if I managed to get down off this mountain, I would be taking landscape painting lessons from a master, trying to recapture the Hudson River School of art in modern times.

For now, though, despite its modest position among the mountain auto roads of the world, Mount Washington's wide, beautiful, snow-packed thoroughfare was testing my endurance.

A few hours earlier, on the way up the mountain, my SnowCoach driver, Ernie Mills, rattles off a series of factoids about the road and the fairly amazing shuttle that's taking us up to 4,200 feet. I learn, for example, that there are 122 culverts on the road.

Gregarious and funny, Ernie is a tall man with a penchant for chatter. He doesn't talk *at* the coach riders, he wants to talk *to* us; asking folks where they are from, opening them up, making them less nervous about driving up a mountain in a storm.

Besides being a longtime navigator of the turns and bends of the Mount Washington Auto Road—Ernie has worked for the road off and on for thirty years—he's also a photographer. Much of his work deals with outdoor wedding photography or above-tree line sunsets. But some of my favorite work of his exists at the junction of nature and technology. A favorite shot is one of an enormous tanker truck working its way around a bend to deliver fuel to the summit.

"Hope you're able to keep your fear of heights in check today, folks," Ernie says as we rumble along. "I know I've tripled up on my own meds!"

As it turns out, there's no reason to worry about heights as the storm prevents us from seeing any real views, but the four-wheel drive Chevy SnowCoach is a master work of engineering. The auto road owns three coaches, which in reality are souped-up shuttle vans, but instead of normal wheels, the coaches have treads, like a tank—snowshoes for a truck. Ernie estimates that the snow on the road he has driven over has been anywhere from one foot to five or six feet deep.

To a passenger who has never driven one, the coach, with its treads plowing through drifts and ice, feels deeply unsettling. It rumbles and growls; the vibration chatters teeth and unsettles stomachs. But to Ernie, that rumble is music to his ears.

When we got out at 4,200 feet—about the halfway point of the road—we were above tree line and the wind and snow made it impossible to see anything. But somehow, Ernie managed to turn the coach around, get us facing back down the mountain, and I took my leave.

Now, as I snowshoe past the marker signifying I have only a mile to go to get to the bottom, I begin to fall into a comfortable rhythm, half stepping, half sliding on the hardpack created by the coach's treads. Being here in the snow, on this mountain, begins to feel proper.

And my thoughts turn to what lies in store for me in the months ahead. Soon, I'd be packing my bags to spend a week at the summit, exploring the observatory, learning about rime ice and weather, and most importantly, cooking for the meteorologists. I wonder if there would be a way to use Ernie's coach to bring pizza to the top.

I would also be part of a team helping a ninety-seven-year-old ultra-athlete run to the summit. I'd interview one of what the AMC calls an "original hut girl." (Until World War II, women didn't work at the huts, but that changed when the men were gone.)

I'd travel down to an even older observatory, the place where early Mount Washington weatherman learned their craft and where the famous Big Wind anemometer was built.

I would dress like Walt Whitman and attempt to become the first person to climb the mountain while reading poetry, and I'd attempt to track down the family of the man who held the most records for setting ridiculous records.

I would drive up in a Mini, take part in a steampunk festival, and pay witness to a wedding at the top of New England. I'd pick dandelions at the summit for the state.

I'd travel to the only town in New England named Mount Washington and explore why a tiny rural community in Western Massachusetts calls itself the Town Among the Clouds.

And I would show my two-year-old daughter the wide, brown summit sign that has attracted people for over a century from all across the world, and I'll trace her tiny fingers along the etched letters and see if she feels the strength and energy I feel whenever I do the same.

My search to find the soul of Mount Washington would also take me on an unexpected journey across the country. From Buffalo, where the founder of the Cog Railway made his fortune, to State College, Pennsylvania, where a ninety-seven-year-old athlete shared his secrets, to Porter, Maine, where a tough thru-hiker staked her claim on New England's highest peak, I would search for the heartbeats that pumped the lifeblood of this mountain. I would be invited into the homes of retirees and athletes, soldiers and historians, celebrities and archivists. The more I dug into the story of the mountain, the further and further away I would find myself being pulled. And the closer and closer I came to understanding that—with all due respect to Mr. Matthiessen—this particular mountain lives and breathes in the memory and blood of those who identify with her.

It's not just hikers or climbers. Mount Washington's influence crosses cultures and ideology, art and economics, and in some cases, time itself.

In writing this book, I would learn how to paint, to cook, to identify clouds and read the sky. I'd try to walk on the summit in eighty-five mile per hour winds. And I would sit near the summit during long summer days watching hikers, drivers, and railway passengers alike step up to that summit sign, hands shaking, and lay their fingers upon the wood—some for the first time, some for the hundredth, always smiling. I would watch children who had climbed up and children who had ridden up buy chili and candy bars at the concession, then run to the vast windows in the cafeteria and stare in silent wonder, watching the weather change over the Northern Presidentials.

I would go to towns like Groveton, Keene, Manchester, Conway, Concord, Lancaster, and Stark and sit in the homes of people whose tether to the mountain extends back generations. I would watch the eyes of grandchildren tear up when talking about their ancestors' connection to the mountain.

A sixty-six-year-old man from Maine would die on Mount Washington in a few months, near a place called Lion's Head—perhaps one of the finest spots on the mountain, within sight of the summit.

And in that same year, I would watch two people, one in a t-shirt that looked like a tuxedo and the other wearing a bright green tutu, join hands, pledge their love to each other and say, "I do" on that mountain. (State park officials estimate that there are ten weddings a season during the summer on Mount Washington.)

There are environmental purists who would like nothing more than to see the railway and road obliterated from the mountain, along with every stitch of wood, concrete, and brick from the summit. Some hikers climb this mountain only once and then refuse to return, unwilling to wait in the same line as a tourist who rode the shuttle. Other hikers come back over and over, relishing the summit's chaos, people watching before finding their own secluded spots to reflect.

As I write these lines, the debate rages about whether or not to erect a hotel along the Cog tracks just above tree line. In the end, those who oppose the building and those who support it do so because the mountain means something to them—something deeply rooted in their sense of ownership to the natural world.

Many have never been there. In one case, I would accompany a group of veterans to the top—older, tough-as-nails men of the greatest generation. One lived his whole life twenty miles away, and from the back seat of a shuttle, he openly wept the first time he gazed upon the Great Gulf Wilderness from above.

All this is to say that the story of Mount Washington, the real year in the life of the culture, history, and significance of this place, relies not on rocks and water and weather, but in the deep memories and experience of all the people who have borne witness to the sacredness of the mountain over the years. The story of the mountain is everywhere—in the wind-burned cheeks, rough hands, and thoughtful eyes of everyone who has come into contact with her.

In fact, as the year went on and it became apparent how deeply felt was the mountain's influence, I simply began to ask everyone I met, "What memories do you have of Mount Washington?" Every single person had a story, either about themselves or someone they knew or something they read that peaked their interest. After asking that question, I'd inevitably have to put aside ten or fifteen minutes to hear a story.

There is a particular curve on the auto road, near the bottom, that I like, especially on the way down. The road begins at an elevation of 1,565 feet, and from this curve in the road, the tree line opens up and you can see a perfect view of the valley below—the road curving down, past the toll booth and general store, over the metal grate and out to State Route 16. And across the road, the Great Glen Base Lodge, Outdoors Center, and home of the auto road are clear. At this point in the road, you are still a good three-quarter mile from the bottom, but it's the first time that civilization intrudes on a road hike. In the summer, you'll be passed by hundreds of cars and hikers. But in the winter, in a storm, until now, the day has been just the sound of my snowshoes against the white and the whisper of the mountain's breeze. And now I can finally see the valley, and the faint outlines of the buildings and roads through the heavy flakes.

It's also at this moment that I hear the familiar rumble of a SnowCoach. I step off the side of the road and before long, a coach rounds that curve and comes growling up. It's Ernie! He's on his way back up for his second trip of the day, carrying another coach full of the curious and the daring, another group of folks going up into a nor'easter on the flanks of Mount Washington.

Ernie pulls the coach over and rolls down the window.

"Having a good hike?" he asks.

The wind blows snow into the coach, and I can see Ernie's passengers wiping the moisture off windows to see why he's stopped. Some eye me with suspicion, like maybe I'm part of the wildlife. Certainly, there can't be anybody outside walking around in this.

"Been nice," I say. "Feet hurt a little, been a while since I've done this. I'm surprised you're going back up. It's a little crazy up there."

He laughs and slaps his hand on the snowy door. "She can handle it. Want people to get their money's worth!"

And with that, the coach jerks forward into the blowing snow. I watch the taillights disappear into the white.

In a few months, I'll have a conversation with Ernie that will change the way I think of my first driver up the mountain. Turns out, that season would be Ernie's last as a driver. He'd hang up his treads and hit the road, becoming an adventure photographer, sending glorious photos of Midwest sunsets back to his social media feeds.

Then, in October, only a couple months before I interviewed him, Ernie was diagnosed with Bell's Palsy.

"Boy, I didn't see that coming," Ernie says, talking to me from a location in Indiana where he's waiting for one of those glorious Hoosier sunsets.

It's been nine months since our drive. "It's been interesting, I guess the eye issue has been difficult more than anything."

Just that morning, while trying to shoot a sunrise, his eyes had begun to water, making it difficult to capture the scene. Bell's Palsy is a type of facial paralysis that results in an inability to control the facial muscles on the patient's affected side. It can affect eyesight, ability to eat, and in Ernie's case, can cause some difficulty in speaking. Though the cause is unknown, many doctors believe the infliction is viral. The condition often improves on its own, and there are treatments for it. In Ernie's case, he was feeling much better when we talked. Still, as a photographer, the experience left him shaken.

"I'm not the first person to have it, there are others much worse than myself," he says. "You just have to rise above it and just go out there and shoot. Nothing is going to slow me down."

Some of that passion may have come from his dad, an Episcopal minister in Syracuse, New York, where Ernie grew up. The family spent summers in North Conway, where his dad was a fill-in at a church there. So Ernie had plenty of time to fall in love with the White Mountains, and he was nine the first time he hiked Mount Washington.

After a stint as an Army photojournalist and a job doing some broadcast journalism in northern New Hampshire, Mount Washington once again came into focus when he was hired as an auto road driver in the early 1980s.

And thus began Ernie's love affair with a 7.6-mile long stretch of asphalt and dirt.

"Some of us drivers, we had a romance with that road," he says. "That place, the spirit of it all, there was never a boring trip."

Ernie says that when he was shooting up on Mount Washington, in his mind's eye he'd be able to imagine every turn and location and backdrop from his days as a driver.

"I had the kind of access to that mountain that other people only dreamed of," he says. "And my goal when I had passengers in the shuttle or coach was to pass that on, to help people see something I saw and give them an experience most people will never have."

I ask him if he ever had a difficult or dangerous ride up the mountain, and he gets quiet for a moment.

"You know, it's about respecting that place and that road," he says. "I paid attention to the old timers, to what the other drivers said, and kept their words close to my heart."

We chat for a while longer, but it's getting to be late in the afternoon and he's eager to capture the sun's descent. I ask him if he has any advice for someone experiencing Mount Washington for the first time. He doesn't hesitate.

"That place, that mountain, it will turn on you and hand it to you faster than anything," he says. "To enjoy it, you have to respect it."

After my hike, I strip off all my heavy gear, buy a hot chocolate at the Outdoors Center across Route 16 from the auto road and find a seat near the window to watch the snow. Down here in the valley, the storm hasn't reached the same frenzy as up on the mountain. For the most part, I can see across the road, but the mountain itself is shrouded in swirling shades of white.

There is a palpable feeling of excitement at the center. To a place like this, a nor'easter is something to be heralded. Tomorrow, outdoor lovers would descend on the shop for rentals and passes to go cross country skiing, snowshoeing and tubing. The SnowCoaches would be packed, and Ernie would have a very busy day. On the other side of the mountain, winter hikers would be heading up to sit a spell in the sun at Lakes of the Clouds Hut, just below the summit. And in the great Tuckerman Ravine, hikers would strap their skis on their back and make the journey up the head wall, only to head back down again, and again, and maybe even again.

And once again, even in the middle of winter, Mount Washington will be swarmed with humanity. I wander around the center for a while, looking over the old photos—past shuttles, the old hotels, all the vestiges of tourism past. The gift shop sells everything from baseball caps to maple syrup candy.

In the lobby, near the cafeteria and behind a velvet rope, rests a working Stanley Locomobile, the first steam car designed by the Stanley brothers. Back in 1899, Freelan Stanley and his wife Flora drove the car, at an average speed of five miles an hour, all the way up from their shop in Newton, Massachusetts, and then drove it all the way up the mountain, becoming the first to do so. It took them five days, but half the time of a carriage.

The history of the car gets fuzzy and peters out in Philadelphia, until the auto road purchased the car on display from an owner in Pennsylvania whose grandfather had it hanging in pieces in his barn. Is it the original that made that record climb? Sure, says the auto road!

During my year on Mount Washington, celebrity Jay Leno would surprise everyone by duplicating that famous ride.

But for now, my first adventure is drawing to a close. My thighs ache pleasantly, my head swims with visions of the grand adventure ahead. It's time to go before the storm makes it impossible for me to get through the mountain notch and back home. For me, the year is just beginning—my discovery of the mountain is in its first baby steps.

Impassive Mount Washington—as always—just watches, amused.

CHAPTER TWO

Like Noises in a Swound

The Wind, the Rime, and the Cat:
One Week Above the Clouds at the Observatory

If we are to be in clouds, let us be in the blackest, most hopelessly thick mass of clouds,
But if we are to have blue sky, let's have it unobstructed by this damp, messy veil of mist.
—Alex McKenzie

At first, I'm grateful when the snowcat grinds to a stop to allow us to take a break. I need to pee, and I would feel awful being the one to ask them to stop up here in the middle of the white. But then I realize we're sitting above tree line, someplace around 5,000 feet, in a storm, and I can see next to nothing.

One by one, we hop out the snowcat's back cabin door into the wind and snow. There's nine of us back there. Samantha Brady, the retail manager of the Mount Washington Observatory's gift shops—one in North Conway and one at the summit—reminds us to bring a couple packs and make sure everyone has gloves and hats. It takes me a moment to understand she says this because while we are out doing our business, the snowcat is going to roll up ahead a ways to deal with a particularly frightful snow drift.

Should the snowcat—well, there's no other way of saying this—go over, we'd need to be able to get up there, or get down, on our own.

It is April, and I'm taking part in the weekly Wednesday shift change at the Mount Washington Observatory. The auto road is not yet open to tourist traffic, but the observatory is open for business year-round and that means the crew needs to get up and back for their weekly shifts. And this hulking monster of a vehicle is the only thing that can get folks up and back once a week.

I'm part of the volunteer crew going up to learn what it's like to live in one of the most unforgiving places on the planet. Normally, when volunteers apply and are selected for this incredible opportunity, they need to do a week in the summer first. I'm grateful that the observatory has waived this requirement for me under the condition that my volunteer partner is a veteran to this job. In other words, my fellow volunteer, John Donovan, coming up for his ninth duty week at the observatory, is here to look after me, show me the ropes, and make sure I don't break anything. Given that we'll be expected to cook for the meteorological crew during our stay, I'm deeply grateful to have John to lean on because he has experience in the restaurant industry and mainly because I'm a terrible cook.

Beside my initial worries about the cooking and being up there for a week, I'm nervous that the snowcat will go cascading down the side of the mountain. I'm sure it would burst into flames like you see in the movies, leaving us stranded in a storm and below-zero weather and having to deal, most likely, with wolves. And I'm nervous about peeing in a snowbank when I can barely see two feet in front of me. I guess you could say I'm nervous.

But to every other person in that cab, this is just another day at the office.

The snowcat is fine. Everything is fine. The little baby storm we're in barely makes an impression on this crew. John takes selfies with me, and Samantha does headstands in the road, there in the swirling snow. It takes us three and a half hours to go the 7.6 miles to the summit, but that's nothing, I'm told.

Brian Fitzgerald, the observatory's director of education, is along for this ride, and he tells me that there's been days when it takes five or six hours to get up there. Occasionally, it's too dangerous for even the cat, and they turn around or cancel altogether, leaving the team up top stranded for another day. Or another few days if the weather stays bad.

"We have to be flexible," he casually observes, which seems to be a pretty decent explanation for everything that takes place up here.

I know Sam from spending time down at North Conway, at the Mount Washington Observatory Discovery Center, where the observatory offices are. And I know Brian from my time down in Milton, Massachusetts, where I worked as a guide for the Blue Hill Observatory and Science Center.

Like many observers and meteorologists before him, Brian cut his teeth in observatory work at Blue Hill before graduating to Mount Washington. In fact, it's fair to say that Mount Washington's observatory as it exists today owes much of its formation and history to that "little" observatory 175 miles south, just outside of Boston.

There atop 640-foot Great Blue Hill, the Blue Hill Observatory has kept a record of weather observations since 1885, the oldest continuous weather record in North America. In 1886 they managed to send a weather kite to 8,740 feet. And during the Great New England Hurricane of 1938, observers there measured the strongest wind gust ever directly recorded in a hurricane at 186 mph.

But perhaps Blue Hill's most important contribution to its little brother observatory in New Hampshire—aside from, of course, training scientists like Brian—is that the #2 heated anemometer that measured the record Big Wind atop Mount Washington in 1934 was designed and built at Blue Hill.

Meanwhile, the snowcat rumbles and grinds its way to the top. Drifts are managed through a series of push procedures that move the snow off the road and off the mountain. In an interview with *Yankee* magazine, one of the observatory's former superstar snowcat drivers, Slim Bryant, explained that the snowcat driver's job is not to actually plow the road, that would be impossible.

"We're not actually plowing the road, but moving the snow with the least resistance," he said. "That means we're basically creating a new road every time."

I think back to what my SnowCoach driver Ernie Mills said in February about driving atop the snow. Since the snowcat drivers are basically creating a new road to the top every time new snow falls, by the end of winter they might be driving on top of fifteen or twenty feet of snow. In the cab of the heated cat I can feel every twist and turn whenever the driver pushes or moves around a drift. Passengers feel the treads underneath grinding and pulling. We attain the Cow Pasture, a somewhat level section of the road just below the summit, and the wind howls. I try to clear some of the frosty condensation off my window, but there's not much to see outside anyway. The drivers use enormous sticks or poles, some twenty feet tall, clamped to metal road markers to help keep them somewhat on track.

I find it hard to believe that I'd be back here in about 40 days to walk up this mountain reading poetry on Alton Weagle Day.

Inside the snowcat, though, no one seems worried. This machine is one of the toughest in New England. It weighs eighteen thousand pounds. For comparison, your standard neighborhood garbage truck is slightly lighter. The snowcat is half the weight of a Greyhound bus.

The plow that's smashing down the drifts is sixteen feet across and can push left or right.

The snowcat roars up the mountain on a 275-horsepower engine. That's about the same horsepower as Steve McQueen's Ford Mustang 390 GT 2+2 Fastback in the movie *Bullitt*.

Finally, the snowcat uses about twenty-two gallons of diesel per round trip.

She is a blistering, powerful, merciless machine—a giant white and black heavy metal beast named a Bombardier. But when the mountain is in a foul mood, even the snowcat is not enough to tame her. Not today, though. Mount Washington is a bit cantankerous this morning, but it's nothing this team hasn't seen before.

As we pull up near the summit, members of the down-going crew are waiting for us. There's a couple hours of crossover between the two crews, starting with unpacking the snowcat's gear and supplies and repacking trash and more gear for the way down.

Once unpacked, the two crews converge in the main kitchen area for a lunch of sandwiches and salad that's been laid by the down-going volunteer crew, something John and I will repeat a week from today. Sam and the IT guys head up to the gift shop to make some upgrades to the registers there and at the museum, and the observers begin to store their gear and coordinate the shift change.

Meanwhile, John gets right to work. Our first order of business is to confer with the down-going volunteers and get a sense of what food is in the fridge and coolers. Just off the kitchen behind the living room is a large walk-in pantry with floor-to-ceiling shelves of canned and dried goods along one wall and two enormous freezers along the other. John's done this many times before, and we're lucky this week: there's no Edu-Trips of commercial trekkers expected during our week. That means John and I will be cooking for five.

He spends a few minutes looking over leftovers in the fridge, then checks each freezer, reaching in and pulling out a variety of frozen items: a package of sausage, a turkey breast, some fish fillets, some packages of frozen vegetables, mushrooms, and other odds and ends.

I've known John through social media and his yearly observatory hiking fund-raisers. He's a big man, fearless and affable, quick with a joke and has a light-hearted attitude. But the one thing I learn very quickly about him is that he takes his role as the chef for the observers seriously.

"Look, these are guys who work hard, twelve-hour shifts," John tells me, pawing through some canned cranberry and applesauce. "At 6:00 p.m. when they come down, they are hungry and they are going to eat a lot. The price of us being up here in this unbelievable place is that we make sure food is ready for them when they get here."

John announces that we'll have chicken parm subs for dinner that evening and that there's more than enough turkey, bread, mushrooms, and stuffing to put together a Thanksgiving feast later in the week. This after only ten minutes of taking inventory.

"How would you like to work this together, Dan?" he asks. "Let's take a minute to develop strategy on how we'll work in the kitchen."

"How would a strategy of you telling me what to do and me doing it work for you?" I ask.

John gives me a big grin and clasps a meaty hand on my shoulder. "This is going to be a great week!"

Once the kitchen is settled, we drag our gear into our bunk rooms. The observatory living quarters would not be considered expansive were there fifteen or twenty people staying the night. For only five of us though, the space is enormous. There are four bunk rooms. Three of them have space for four comfortably, though you could cram more in there. One of the bunk rooms is exclusively for the observatory crew and has an inside door in order to give the night shift observer a little more quiet and privacy during the day.

Each bunk room is named after one of the original observatory founders. My room, as it turns out, is named after Alex McKenzie.

I unpack my duffel and hang up some of my winter gear. I want to have my heavy pants and fleece at the ready for outside trips. I have goggles in case the temperature outside really drops, and I'm hoping it does. And I brought a set of micro-spikes for my boots; they're basically tiny chains with sharp edges for walking on ice.

For kicking around inside, I have fleece pants and a couple flannel shirts with wool socks. I brought a sleeping bag, but there are blankets here and I doubt I'll need it.

I've got some snacks for myself to munch on through the week—wasabi peas, peanuts, and some jerky—and I've brought some candy for the crew. Just as I'm wrapping up, Brian pokes his head in and asks me if I'd like to sit in on an observer shift change meeting. Turns out that the departing crew and arriving crew meet in the changeover to talk about weather patterns—past and upcoming—maintenance issues, broadcasts with the Discovery Center or schools down below, and other miscellaneous checklist items.

It's a kind offer, and I take a seat as far in the back of the small conference room as I can find. I'm acutely aware that though the directors and front office managers wholeheartedly approve of my being here and writing about the experience, the everyday observers—the ones up here doing the actual work—are the people who will have to deal with me, and all the questions, video, and pictures that would be coming. In other words, I don't want to get in anyone's way. Yet.

Believe it or not, even at the top of New England, work meetings are fairly perfunctory and not terribly exciting. There is a moment when I perk up, though. Turns out that Marty the observatory cat and mascot "writes" a weekly column about his experience at the top, and the observers go round and round about who is going to "help" him write the column that week.

Since literally the first days of the observatory all the way back to 1932, there have been observatory cats living up here. In nearly every case, the cats have become the rock stars of the observatory, earning a fan base, pictures, and many columns of ink in various newspapers and books over the years writing about their exploits.

From 1995 to 2002, writer and teacher Eric Pinder worked as an observer at the observatory. He wrote a book about his experience as an observer, *Life at the Top*. But his kids' picture book on Nin, Marty's popular and mischievous predecessor, really brought the summit mascots into the popular imagination.

Illustrated by T. B. A. Walsh, *Cat in the Clouds* follows the adventures of Nin as she travels to the top of New England and discovers that home can be a place above the clouds.

Marty was up here somewhere, but I'd have a whole week to find him. For now, I had another cat to catch. My ride was leaving.

I say my goodbyes to the crew going down, including Brian and Samantha, toss on a heavy jacket and make my way up to the observatory deck where I can watch the snowcat slowly move away from the observatory loading dock and begin the long ride down. The baby storm that accompanied us up here remains, a gray and dreary mist holding its position at the summit, making it cold but not freezing.

I watch the snowcat grind its way to the service road on the other side of the ice-encrusted Cog Railway platform and hang a sharp left to begin its route down. Even over the wind I can hear the crunch of the snowcat's treads, the low growl of its motor. In a few seconds the cat moves out of sight.

I listen to engine grind from somewhere behind a blanket of mist and then, slowly, the sound fades into the void and I'm standing alone on the deck, my ride gone for the next week. There's no views, there's no sound but the wind. My nose starts to feel cold.

Dinner prep is waiting for me; we have salad and chicken parm subs to make and hungry observers to feed.

My first morning begins with a powerful lesson in humility from the universe.

A knock on the door of my bunk room jolts me awake. It's Caleb Meute, the night weather observer. His shift is 6:00 p.m. to 6:00 a.m., so it's early.

"Sunrise in ten minutes," he says cheerfully.

My room is warm and my legs are sore from tromping around the mountain the day before. Sadly, I am still unaccustomed to the rigors of snow adventure. It takes me a couple minutes to orient myself. Morning is here, very early. I'm on top of Mount Washington. It will be very cold outside.

I drag myself out of bed, my head a mix of drowsy muddle-headedness and excitement, and pull on my heaviest gear. There's a monitor in the living quarters on a wall near the dining room table, which I glance at on my way out. The temperature is 17°F, practically a heat wave for this morning in April.

The weather tower on the western side of the observatory is basically the staircase that leads to the living quarters, weather room where the observers work, and the outside deck. If you continue up the metal spiral stairs you'll come to the top of the tower where smaller, steep stairs will lead you to the outside deck. Rungs along the outside of the tower will take you to very tip top of New England. That's one of the places where observers must come out in all types of weather to check the equipment.

I climb up one flight to the thick metal door that leads to the deck, slip on gloves and a balaclava, and shove the bar up and out to push open the tower door to my first morning atop the Rock Pile.

I am immediately assaulted by reds and yellows. The wind pushes me sideways as I step outside, and I stop and take a deep breath to try to focus on understanding what I'm seeing.

It is as if the eastern horizon has cracked open, an enormous seam extending from the northern horizon to the southern horizon. Above and below the sun rising over the Carter Range across the valley are clouds. A flat line of clouds are above our heads, and a rolling line of undercast cloaks the mountains at about five thousand feet. The result from where we stand is like the sun has become a giant orange egg spilling color against the clouds. It is like the air itself is red and pink.

I have been a witness to the sunrise in many places on Earth. I've watched undercast from the tops of mountains. But this is new. I stand still for a few minutes, afraid to move, afraid to let the landscape know that I'm now part of it, like if the sun was made aware of my tiny presence, it would shut off. I can hear my own breathing, coming fast. My eyes begin to water.

"Not bad for your first day, huh," Caleb says, breaking me out of my reverie. John's up there as well, part of our little crowd at the eastern rail of the deck watching this light show parade.

I look back at the observatory tower and Tip Top House; the summit buildings are bathed in such a deep hue of pink it's like they are painted that color.

And to the west the tips of the mountains along the Franconia Ridge poke out from the undercast. I was married up there, atop Mount Lafayette.

I join the men at the railing, and we all watch in silence for a few minutes, the colors and shades changing, an organic landscape. The undercast rolls like a river, up over the valley, pouring down into the Great Gulf.

There are seven billion souls on this planet, but only four of us bear witness to this display.

"Give me the splendid, silent sun," I whisper to the horizon, a quiet prayer from Walt Whitman and words I'd be repeating in a few weeks as I walked up this mountain. "With all his beams full-dazzling."

Caleb points to a cluster of puffy clouds far in the western distance. "A storm is coming," he says.

I hope so, I think. I hope a storm comes and blows. I hope the bad weather is as bad as this sunrise is good. I want it all.

In the summer, especially on holiday weekends, walking through the observatory visitor center can be as chaotic as being in the mall on the day before Christmas.

The Mount Washington Auto Road shuttles and Cog Railway engines are chugging full speed ahead. The auto road itself is open to traffic. Perhaps there's an education trip or two in attendance. Adding to the mix are hikers with days off, coming from the surrounding Appalachian Mountain Club huts—Lakes of the Clouds, Madison Hut, or the Joe Dodge Lodge. And then there are the day hikers, those hearty souls popping up to the top of New England to tag that summit sign, often deeply frustrated to have to wait in line behind tourists to do so.

There are two gifts shops, the observatory museum, tours of the observatory itself, the post office, a hikers' lounge and changing area, and a concession that serves what you might expect—hot dogs, pizza, candy. (Even now I contend that nothing is as delicious as a bowl of chili at the top of Mount Washington after you've spent six hours climbing the mountain.)

But in the winter, with the tables and chairs folded and put away and everything shut down, the main hall of the visitor center is an eerie and mesmerizing place. John and I walk through the mezzanine, our footsteps echoing off the empty space. Outside, that little storm Caleb warned us about has begun, expected to last into the night—a wet, slick, sopping mess of a blow. I'd decide tomorrow whether to go out.

For today, we are taking an afternoon constitutional.

The observers have dragged some exercise equipment out into the open space, along with a ping pong table.

We stroll down to the museums and walk through with only some natural light from above. The original anemometer that measured the Big Wind is here on display, the brass device shimmering in the dull lights. Back up top, John cracks wise about Mountain Mike, a giant wooden totem erected by the park service and placed out near the summit during the summer—a tourist draw and the focus of many, many smartphone photos. Mountain Mike wears old time hiking shorts and a red stocking hat. He has enormous well-worn boots and is holding a long, hiking staff—The Paul Bunyan of Mount Washington.

"I've been told we look the same and we tend to dress the same. This guy, he cracks me up." John points to a long, deep crack in the wood that extends from Mountain Mike's chin down to his waist.

For somebody who is that quick with a pun, John takes the job of chief cook and caretaker of the observers deeply and personally seriously. Much of that attitude comes from John's own journey to the top of the mountain and his designation as one of the top fund-raisers and cheerleaders of the observatory.

Born in Boston, John's love of cooking came from his father. John would sit at his family table on Sundays watching his father cook the basics—home fries and scrambled eggs, hash and fried bologna—split among his family of seven.

Later in life, John took a job as a bouncer for a local country and western-themed nightclub and began working his way through the ranks—bartender, cook, manager, general manager and then finally investor.

He eventually moved to Cranston, Rhode Island, where Italian food flourishes and where he now works at the outdoor outfitter R.E.I. Two careers—cooking and hiking—both coming together at the summit of Mount Washington.

"I love interacting with the observers and with guests, making them feel like they are sitting in my home kitchen getting a timely hot meal made with love," John says without a hint of cynicism. "I love the challenge of drawing back the curtain and creating meals with what's there, from my food-based knowledge."

And he's good at it. Over the course of the week, besides the chicken parms and turkey dinner, I'd help John make three cheese mac and cheese dishes, lasagna, and chicken pasta. The observers on my shift work hard and are all young men with big appetites. They are also well mannered. I'm convinced that they would eat anything that was put in front of them, but that wouldn't be good enough for John.

When he says "made with love," there's a tangible aspect to his volunteer work, both in terms of a passion for food as well as an awareness that his reputation as an unofficial face of the observatory among the hiking community has meaning.

He's one of the most vocal unpaid salesmen the observatory has, but his journey to get here is credible.

About ten years ago, John was in a rut and looking for hobbies for people older than fifty to get healthy again and reconnect with the natural world. He had climbed Mount Washington in college, and that trip had never left his mind.

He learned about an annual fund-raising event the observatory sponsors called Seek the Peak, a day when the hiking community from around New England and beyond descend on Mount Washington for an all-day hike-a-thon. Hikers go up in teams or solo and raise money for the observatory.

At fifty years old and weighing more than three hundred pounds, and not having hiked in years, John signed up. The result was, perhaps, not unexpected . . .

"It was an epic fail. I felt horrible and didn't even come close to making it up the mountain," John says. "I immediately went on a huge diet and decided to share my progress on Facebook so people could follow. The next year, when I touched that marker at the summit, I just started crying. Since then, I've been among the top ten fund-raisers in the country."

I planned on being at the top later that summer for Seek the Peak, and looked forward to seeing John touch that marker again.

I ask him what it is exactly that keeps bringing him back to this mountain, to this place, and he thinks for a long time before repeating a variation of a feeling that I hear again and again throughout the year: slow down.

"Smell the air, enjoy the birds; when you walk through an alpine garden, it smells like a Christmas tree lot," John says. "I can sit up here among the rocks, listen to the land, have the sun in my face and just know I'm the only person in that spot at that moment."

There are two types of geography: the physical place—the rocks and dirt and wind—and then there's the geography of the soul, an internal place of mindfulness. Sometimes, if we're lucky, we find those two geographies in the same place. Sometimes, that place is the top of a mountain, cooking for scientists.

How remarkable that this can even happen, that eggs can even be scrambled and cakes baked in such comfort. Such was not always the case.

For the longest time, it was thought impossible to survive at the summit of Mount Washington over the winter, and for good reason. But climbers, businessmen, and scientists kept trying. It wasn't about securing the funding. By the mid-1800s there were plenty of outfits, public and private, that would gladly give financial assistance to such an endeavor.

But no one wanted to be the sponsor of a winter expedition where everyone froze to death.

It wasn't until 1869 when a prominent Manchester, New Hampshire lawyer by the name of William Little found himself in the position of being able to make a deep and historic contribution to Mount Washington history. Though he didn't know it at the time.

A well-read man with deep connection to the burgeoning city, William's law office sat right on Elm Street in a building called the Merchant's Exchange. He was only a few blocks from the train station and right up the street from Manchester Locomotive Works, which had just begun producing newfangled engines for something called the Sky Train—a cog-driven locomotive that took passengers to the top of Mount Washington.

William had a hobby, which he talked about at parties and social gatherings to anyone who would listen: meteorology.

At one of those gatherings, William bent the ear of a young but eager scientist who happened to find himself in the post of New Hampshire's assistant geologist. That scientist was a fellow who went by the name of Joshua H. Huntington, a name today that is synonymous with what is generally accepted as the most difficult non-technical hiking trail in the White Mountains and the Huntington Ravine the trail scales.

William learned that his new friend had been trying to secure the mountain's Tip Top House for a winter scientific expedition, but the owners didn't believe that anyone would survive.

As it happened, William owned a chunk of property in Benton, New Hampshire, that included the summit of Mount Moosilauke. William immediately offered Joshua Huntington free use of the stone hotel at the top of Moosilauke, Prospect House, for a full winter expedition—the first time a science expedition stayed at that sort of elevation through a heavy winter and a trial run for getting an expedition up Mount Washington.

The winter test at the top of Moosilauke was a success. Using the photos, notes, and information gathered from atop that mountain, Huntington was able to take a team up to the summit of Washington in 1870, the first time a scientific team spent the winter up there. It could be done.

The observations and photography from these early excursions captured the interest of the United States Signal Service who set up and maintained a weather station on the Mount Washington summit until 1892. But it would be four more decades until a dedicated handful of sturdy mountain men decided that the highest mountain in New England needed a permanent observatory to challenge the snow and ice.

Ice is a paradox. Terrifying and exhilarating. Loud and deadly silent. It can mesmerize. It is art. It is the final ring of Hell according to Dante. My guess is that back in the 1870s, most of the men up here during the winter would refer to *The Divine Comedy* to explain what they witnessed.

However, I prefer Samuel Taylor Coleridge.

Caleb was right a couple days ago. A storm moved in overnight, a quick flash of thunder, snow, and rain and sleet. This morning, the mist sits heavy on the summit, ghostly. Everything—every building, piece of equipment, sign, railing, window, deck, rock, railway track, and tower— every single inch of every single everything is covered in rime and ice.

The rime flints off every available surface, even the ground. The chains that hold the signal house to the ground are so encrusted, I can't get my hand around a link. The summit sign is gone under the ice. The precipitation collector is under ice. There are no rocks, only ice.

And it's quiet. All sound relates only to ice—flakes tinkling in the slight wind, the crunch of my spiked boots against the ground, my breath, which from under my goggles looks hard, like it's halfway to ice. There are one hundred shades of white.

I wander down off the deck, doing a circuit of the summit. Visibility is, perhaps, twenty feet. In some cases, the ice on the side of a wall, or railing, blends so perfectly with the misty air that it's like an illusion; I have to reach out and touch a rock to know that something is there. That or trip over it, which I do several times because the ground is that way as well. White. Ice.

And for the first time since I read *The Rime of the Ancient Mariner* back in college, I finally, like a flash of lighting, understand the one word in that epic poem that has perplexed and befuddled me for decades.

Swound.

I am in daze, in a dream world. I am hearing noises in a swound.

Coleridge's 1798 masterpiece tells the tragic story of a mariner's journey. At first, the voyage goes well, but a vicious storm drives the ship into Antarctic waters and into an ice jam:

And through the drifts the snowy clifts
Did send a dismal sheen:
Nor shapes of men nor beasts we ken—
The ice was all between.

The ice was here, the ice was there,
The ice was all around:
It crack'd and growl'd, and roar'd and howl'd,
Like noises in a swound!

The word "swound" means the act of fainting, like a swoon. But to Coleridge, the proximity of the ice, the sounds it makes—wild and raw like an animal—creates a moment of fear and disorientation. The mariner is sliding into a dream atmosphere, the ice serving as a metaphor for the unknown and the unconscious.

This is similar to what a mountaineer might experience in a white out—the very air, perhaps gravity itself, submitting to vertigo as the ice groans and the sheen becomes indistinct and shapes undefined. Being here is all so beautiful—hazy and comforting. I reach one of the benches near the Tip Top House and sit on the ice, watch the ice, listen to the ice. How easy to close my eyes here, to take off my goggles and let the ice caress my cheek. How simple it would be to surrender to the swound.

But then, who would make the stuffed mushrooms for John's Thanksgiving dinner tonight? Who would open the cans of cranberry sauce?

I was determined to not let John down. I break free from the siren song of the ice and head back to the tower. Over my shoulder, the ice growls.

Later, stuffed and happy, the crew settles down for a post-meal movie in the rec room of the living quarters. The observatory living quarters is basically one big room, with the kitchen and pantry on one end and bunk rooms along another wall. But the main space is the sitting area. Well worn couches and easy chairs, comfortable and soft, rest in a half circle around the room. Against the far wall is top-to-bottom, end-to-end, bookcases full of research folders, novels, Mount Washington history, DVDs and other knicks and knacks. The TV sits in the middle of the collection. This evening, the wind down movie is Mel Brooks' *Young Frankenstein*, a classic comedy that somehow seems the perfect companion to wolfing down the remainder of John's brownies.

As the evening turns to night and the crew laughs and jokes to unwind, I begin feeling that all this is surreal—that in eighty-five years, the observatory has gone from a barely functioning, freezing wooden house held to the earth by chains, to essentially a high-end hostel, secure, well-outfitted and safe. While the dedication and work ethic of the observers has always been beyond question and the technology is top of the line, as it was back then, I wonder if those early observers and visitors had any idea or hope that this place would become what it has.

Some of that answer can be found in a curious book that I find tucked in a corner of the bookshelf.

Self-published in 1994, only three years before he died, *The Way it Was* is a collection of journal entries, observations, statistics, and photos compiled and written by the man whose name graces the bunk room where I sleep.

Alexander Anderson McKenzie II was born on October 2, 1908 in Albany, New York. And while all the stories of the four founders of the current iteration of the Mount Washington Observatory are worthy of their own books (in fact, one of them—Joe Dodge—has that) it's Alex's journey to the top of New England that sparked the most interest for me.

His story seems the most far-fetched and unlikely, his background so unrelated to the work he eventually became known for. While the other men in that original crew groomed personas of tough, wilderness mountain men, Alex stood out as a man of letters. He seemed gentler than the rest.

His book is filled with remarkable passages about the philosophy of place, thoughts about food and the spirit of exploration. He lays out a regimen on how to be both a good man and a healthy man. Macko, as Joe Dodge called him, was a poet.

For example, on Wednesday, September 12, 1934, between log passages about ignition systems and storage batteries, Alex seems to be responding to someone's belief that he is a believer in "moderation of all things."

"That philosophy interests me little in actual practice," he writes. "Let us either be one thing or another. It is such a spirit that pushes through the causes it espouses, the spirit that wins battles. One can seldom find success in life until he backs some cause completely, insanely, and to the end!"

Another fascinating passage comes on March 17, 1935, when Alex writes about his work ambition, but begins to consider, literally, the meaning of life.

"To fight nature hand to hand is just as thrilling a struggle as the accumulating of dollars. To fight her on the battleground of science is almost as good." He continues, "All in all, even if I can never become rich, I shall feel happier and more successful if I can succeed along these general lines."

Therein, I suppose, is the tie between the two men. Their ambition extends to their landscape, their passion is up there, in the clouds. Joe didn't care that Alex had an English literature degree, or that he read poetry, or that he had a delicate soul. Joe needed a radio man, someone to connect the huts, to improve communication with Blue Hill and Pinkham Notch. Joe did see a poet, but a poet of science and technology. Alex was the best at what he did, and Joe knew it, even if it would take a couple years for Alex himself to figure that out.

And speaking of Joseph Brooks Dodge, any discussion about the Appalachian Mountain Club (AMC), the White Mountains, or the Mount Washington Observatory between the years of 1922 and 1973 begins and ends with the "The Mayor Of Porky Gutch," Joe's name for Pinkham Notch back when he ran the White Mountain roost.

Born in Manchester-by-the-Sea, Massachusetts, Joe ditched high school at seventeen. Wanting nothing to do with his family's lucrative furniture business, he joined the Navy, becoming a radio operator in the submarine service. He came back in 1922, argued with his brother about attending college, climbed into a Model-T pickup and drove north, and that's where he stayed.

The short version of Joe's White Mountains footprint is this: Within a couple years, Joe was responsible for the sixty-seven-mile burgeoning hut system in the Whites. He refurbished some and built a bunch of new ones from scratch. Between 1927 and 1931, it's estimated that Joe's teams used their backs, burros, and a tractor to haul more than two hundred tons of material into the mountains to create the current AMC hut system. He nicknamed the AMC lodge in Pinkham Notch Porky's Gulch because of the porcupines, he said. Today, it's the Joe Dodge Lodge.

Whole books have been written about the toughest son of a bitch ever to set foot on White Mountains rock. The legend of Joe Dodge runs so deep in White Mountain culture it's challenging to parse truth from fact on occasion. What is fact, however, is that by 1932, Joe's grip on his White Mountains empire was so established, no one got a job in the mountains without the explicit approval of Joe. In fact, despite all his other duties—search and rescue, trail engineering, hut master, bear wrestling—Joe personally interviewed everyone looking to set foot in his mountains.

And that brings us back around to Alex McKenzie. What interested me the most was how Alex the poet found himself on the radar of Joe the taskmaster.

Alex graduated from Dartmouth in 1932, but more important than his degree in English was his participation in the legendary Dartmouth Hiking Club. Upon graduation, he didn't become a writer or a teacher; he hefted a backpack and walked to Pinkham Notch where he interviewed with Joe to become a hut croo member.

Back in Albany, when he was growing up, Alex lived next door to a radio hobbyist and became interested in the electronics of the day. That was good enough for Joe, and soon Alex was working on stringing together radio blocks for the AMC huts.

A few months later, Alex once again found himself in the right place at the right time when Joe's pick for a radio man for the new observatory, Al Sise, bailed at the last moment. There was no one else but Alex to take his place, and when Joe asked you to do something, you did it.

By fall of that first year, Alex found himself in the role—along with Joe, Bob Monahan and Salvatore Pagliuca—of one of the four founders of the Mount Washington Observatory. When Joe asked him in August, only two months before the observatory opened, Alex had only made his first trip to the summit two weeks earlier.

Eighteen months later, Alex would be on the summit as the observatory shook and the fastest wind speed ever recorded to that point, 231 miles per hour, bore down on the young radio man. A few years after that,

Alex would marry Joe's longtime Pinkham Notch secretary, Barbara, and set off on a post-observatory career that included FM radio, MIT and blueberries.

Near the Maine border, up by the picturesque Crystal Lake, living at the end of a pitted, hard pack road, Alex McKenzie's son, Ken, is following in his famous father's footsteps.

Ken, like Alex before him, is a blueberry farmer.

"He never wanted to be known as a founder of the observatory," Ken tells me over coffee at his home. Outside, winter has already landed in the mountains, the back roads slick with a dusting of ice and snow. The lake this morning, right outside Ken's living room window, is calm like blue glass. "He always said he just happened to be there when the observatory formed."

Five months after my week at the observatory, Ken invited me to tiny rural Eaton to show me the place where Alex truly felt he belonged. Since 1948, the family has been making gourmet Wild Mountain Blueberry Jam, harvesting three hundred acres of blueberry fields along the slopes of 1,647-foot Foss Mountain. Up at the top of Foss is the tiny cabin Alex built and where the family would spend their summers.

"My dad bought one of those Radio Shack Tandy computers and hooked it up to a solar panel so he was able to work while we were up there," Ken says.

Often lost in the history and adulation surrounding the observatory's four founders is the fact that Alex wasn't a meteorologist or an observer. He was a radio man and later a master electrician and transmission expert.

Between 1940 and 1945, Alex worked for MIT's Radiation Lab, an elaborate microwave and radar research facility that was at the cutting edge of electromagnetic and microwave physics. Half of the radars deployed by the United States military during World War II were designed at the facility. Several of the physicists that worked at Rad Lab went on to work on the Manhattan Project.

Ken brings out a plate of doughnuts, makes sure I'm settled, and leans back in his chair. He designed this home, where he lives with his wife, and plowed out the lengthy driveway himself. A long entrance hall leads you past a small kitchen area before the corridor opens up to a grand two-story living room with a fireplace and mementos of the mountains on the walls and bookcases. Above the table where we sit, Ken has hung two antique long rifles, which he says were gifts from friends. Ken's home is a couple miles from his father's cabin at the top of Foss.

At seventy-two, Ken is one of the youngest seventy year olds I've ever seen. He's wearing a Mount Washington Observatory fleece. He has a high forehead but still has a full mane of hair—not all of it white, either—unlike his father, who in some pictures appears to be balding in his twenties. His thin white beard is well trimmed and close to his face.

Whether or not Alex found his passion in the observatory is debatable. What's not is Ken's pride and interest in his father's accomplishments. Ken digs around in a cardboard box—one of those legal ones with handles— and gently places a stack of photos, correspondences and miscellaneous paperwork from his father's life before me.

It's a treasure trove of Mount Washington history: original photos of Alex and his crew at the observatory dating back to the beginning, shots of Alex hunched over a radio during storms, pictures of the men horsing around and teasing each other, like outtakes of the pictures you can see in the museum collections.

One black and white photograph shows a supply train of old pickup trucks, the kind of truck with the wooden rails on the flatbed. It looks like the trucks have stopped at what is now the five-mile turn on the Cragway. Winter is close, hasn't yet arrived, but it's cold. In the back of the last truck in line sits Alex McKenzie in a heavy peacoat and what appears to be a beret. He's propped on top of a pile of boxes destined for the summit.

"My dad told me that was the final supply run in October 1932," Ken says.

"Seriously, this picture is of the founding of the observatory," I say. The observatory was officially re-established on October 15, 1932.

Ken nods. I flip the photo over. The watermark reads "Winston H. Pote, photographer, Swampscott, Mass." Pote is, perhaps, the most celebrated of the early Mount Washington photographers. Later, I discover that Ken's original image was published in a 1985 Pote book of early Mount Washington photos.

"Yeah, that guy, Winston," Ken says. "My dad says you couldn't shake a stick up there without hitting Winston or one of his cameras."

There's some paperwork about Alex's life after his stint at the observatory on Mount Washington. He went back up for a few years, working alongside Edwin Howard Armstrong, the developer of FM. Alex helped Armstrong conduct field tests of this new, unknown FM technology from the top of Mount Washington.

In 1954, after a fight with his wife, Armstrong committed suicide by jumping out of the thirteenth-story window of their apartment in Manhattan.

"Working with Armstrong had been a high point of his life," Ken says. "Dad came home devastated on the day Armstrong committed suicide."

Ken hands me a framed sketch of his father, a black and white profile drawing. Alex is young, his curly hair a mess, intense concentration in his eyes.

"That was sketched by Arthur Griffin on the night before the Big Wind," Ken says casually.

My eyes grow wide. "Are you kidding me?"

Ken just smiles. Joe Dodge liked to invite guests up to the observatory for overnight stays in those early days, even if Dodge himself had no plans on being there. One of those guests was the famous *Life* and *Time* magazines photojournalist Arthur Griffin. The Griffin Museum in Winchester, Massachusetts, opened in 1992 and has become a showcase for rotating exhibits from famous photographers.

Griffin just happened to be staying at the observatory on April 11 and 12, 1934, and was one of the civilians present for the record-breaking wind.

"I think this sketch was used in *Life* magazine, maybe," Ken says. "I'm not really sure. Nice likeness though, right?"

I try to imagine the scene around that sketch of Alex McKenzie, what must have been happening, the sound of the wind, the cold and chaos of the ice and snow. And there was Alex hunched over his radio equipment triangulating weather information coming from Blue Hill, the Cog Railway Base Station, and Joe Dodge down at Pinkham Notch. Into the early morning as the observatory shook and groaned, Alex kept himself awake by chatting with other ham operators.

And at some moment during that famous night, Arthur Griffin took pencil to pad and drew the profile of Alex McKenzie.

"Why did he draw him?" I ask. "Why not just take a picture?"

"Maybe the light wasn't good," says Ken. "Maybe he was scared and needed to do something to calm himself."

"Was your dad scared that night of the Big Wind?" I ask.

"Oh yeah, but it wasn't something he talked about publicly," Ken says. "He felt that it was the massive amount of collected and frozen ice along the observatory walls—not the chains—that kept the building from blowing away that night."

I reflect again on that sketch; a handful of men in the raging wind, huddled inside a tiny wooden building held to the mountain by chains and ice, snow blowing in through seams in the doors and windows. And there was Alex, doing his job.

"Hey," Ken says, like it's an afterthought. "Want to see Dad's cabin?"

I very much do.

To reach Foss Mountain, we need to drive around the lake and though downtown Eaton, which consists primarily of three things: a general store that also serves as a post office, Camp Waukeela (a summer camp for girls established in the 1920s), and the Little White Church.

From the east side of Crystal Lake at a small beachfront picnic area, the Little White Church on the other side of the lake is one of the most photographed images in New Hampshire. Tourists come specifically during leaf-peeping season and sometimes have to wait in line in their cars to get that picture.

Built in 1879, the church was the meetinghouse for a particularly New Hampshire-specific religious group known as the Free Will Baptists. It was founded in New Durham, New Hampshire, by a former Calvinist, Benjamin Randall, and Eaton had three congregations practicing around the little lake by the mid-1800s. Randall would literally carry followers from the coast on horseback and on foot to several towns in the area where they found quick acceptance in the more rural parts of the state. Along the more progressive Seacoast they were considered a fridge denomination at best, and were sometimes called Randallites. But in Eaton, their emotional, evangelical ways thrived.

Preachers weren't allowed to write down sermons. They had to speak from the heart. Music made from wooden instruments were forbidden, as that could cause listeners to break out into a dance, which was also forbidden. Nonetheless, the concept of each congregation having the free will to pick a community path that worked for them was new, and it helped both attract the rural farmers who lived in these areas and also dovetailed nicely with the sharp independent streak prevalent in Northern New England. By 1882, twelve churches in New England alone had been founded.

Today, the little white church is literally called the Little White Church, purchased by Eaton around 1945 for $1 to become the Community Church of Eaton, and governed and maintained by an association as a nondenominational place of worship of which anyone could be a member.

Just past the Little White Church, Ken turns his pickup truck right. We circle around the north side of the lake and drive right past that lovely, popular view.

"The problem is that there's a summertime guy who comes out here and parks his trailer right down there," Ken says, shaking his head. "Ruins the view. We have to do something about that soon or people are going to stop coming."

We continue up into a section of Eaton called Snowville, a village that no longer formally exists, and drive past Snowville Cemetery, where Ken's parents are buried. Nearly as soon as we hit the thin dirt road that leads up to near the top of Foss Mountain, Ken shakes his head.

"I don't think we're gonna get up there today," he says.

The road is not maintained and is already slick with ice. As we get high, the snow gets deeper and even Ken's four by four begins to slide. So we turn around. Not today.

"Is it nice up there?" I ask.

"Oh yeah, he loved it, we all love it," Ken says. "From the cabin, there's a perfect view of Mount Washington."

Even though Alex worked for MIT and accomplished other prestigious things after Mount Washington, when he retired, he made sure the front window of the cabin he built had a view of the mountain. He literally spent the last years of his life in the shadow of Mount Washington.

We stop at the post office on the way back to Ken's. Only about 350 souls call Eaton home, so the post office is small and looks like it hasn't changed a bit in one hundred years. It takes up one wall of the general store, with rows of post office boxes on either side of a large window. The store carries Ken's blueberry jam. The postal clerk and Ken know each other, and they exchange pleasantries as Ken collects his mail.

As we pull up to Ken's house and I begin to gather my things to take my leave, I ask him how important, ultimately, Mount Washington was to his father.

He thinks for a moment and says, "Hang on a sec."

He goes back into the house and comes out with a small box, which he hands me. I open it to discover a Purple Heart medal.

"I was wounded in an ambush in Vietnam," Ken says. "My time there was only one year of my whole life, but it was the most memorable. Not the best, but the most important. I'd compare that to the five years my father spent working on Mount Washington. It's something he never forgot."

Instead of going straight home, I drive back into town, past the Little White Church, past the post office and the lake, and pull over next to the cemetery, which is small, maybe a hundred stones. Ken mentioned that his parents are near the back, so I head there. The sun is just beginning to move down behind the hills, and the air is wet and cold. My breath swirls in my face as I look for the marker.

I find the gravestone of Alex and his wife Barbara near the back, under a grove of trees. A weeping willow is etched into the stone. I hear a rustling sound to my left and am surprised to find myself looking into the eyes of a cow, only a few feet away behind a wire fence. I was so intent on finding the grave, I didn't realize the cemetery abuts a cow pasture.

"Hi fella," I whisper.

But the cow just stands and stares, like he's a sentinel, like he's protecting the observatory founder.

Alex lived to be eighty-nine, but even well into his eighties he practiced a routine the observers at the top of the mountain still talk about.

Every day, whether up in his cabin or in town, Alex would contact the observatory with the weather conditions where he was. Every day. And they would tell him what the conditions were at the top of the mountain. Observers up top would often debate who would speak to the founder, all of them wanting to have a chance, never missing an opportunity.

"Whether they actually did anything with that information, I have no idea," Ken told me. "But they never missed an opportunity to talk to him. There was a connection between him and the observers."

Alex died on December 13, 1997. On April 12, 1998, on the sixty-fourth anniversary of the record breaking wind, Alex McKenzie's ashes were scattered in the gusts at the summit of Mount Washington.

Wind is everything.

Snow is just frozen water. Rain is just wet clouds. Heat is energy. But add wind to the mix and you get gales, gusts, cyclones, hurricanes, squalls, blizzards, and tornadoes. It is the wind that howls through the woods, causes the trees to groan. The wind is like a freight train. We ride the wind and are bowled over by it.

At the observatory, wind is what shakes the oven hood at night, what rattles the tower doors. In the summer, wind caresses your hair and lends urgency to your step to find more of it to keep away the insects. In the fall, wind riles the trees, sends cascades of orange, yellow, and red leaves drifting in waves of colors. In the winter, wind causes frostbite, makes your eyes water, and creates delicate rime sculptures from the air's moisture.

Wind is complicated. Technically wind is a difference in atmospheric pressure, air moving from higher to lower pressure areas, causing differences in wind speed. The rotation of the planet, the poles, the equators, and friction all play a part in the wind dance of our planet.

Nearly every ancient and native mythology involves a wind god, often more than one. The Greek wind god Aeolus lived on the floating island of Aeolia and was visited by Odysseus and his crew in *The Odyssey*. In ancient Egypt, the wind god Amun fused with the sun God, Ra, to become a king among gods. To the Abenaki, Wadzoosen is a great eagle that flaps his wings to create wind. And the Hindu god Rudra, often associated with storms and usually translated as "the roarer," is the most terrifying of them all, usually leaving the devastation of hurricanes in his wake.

In his debut novel, *Hear the Wind Sing*, the Japanese classic novelist Haruki Murakami writes of the power of the wind:

> The wind has its reasons. We just don't notice as we go about our lives. But then, at some point, we are made to notice. The wind envelops you with a certain purpose in mind, and it rocks you. The wind knows everything that's inside you.

Up here, the wind is a constant companion, the wind is noticed at all times. The observers are slaves to the wind, pray for it and to it.

Even in the observatory's moment of greatest triumph on the day of the record-setting wind, as founder Sal Pagliuca climbed to the roof to knock the ice off the anemometer, he imagined himself the powerful Polyphemus, channeling the Greek giant son of Poseidon to do battle with the wind and get to the roof.

"I thought of mighty Polyphemus as the wind was furiously blowing my parka out of my storm pants," Sal wrote in the logbook that night. "The hood was on my face, almost blinding me."

The wind has meaning here, like a character in a never-ending story of life and death. Wise observers treat the wind with as much respect as they treat the mountain. To not do so could result in unfortunate consequences.

And today, this afternoon, Saturday, April 8, I'm hustling to pull on my very heaviest winter gear, my heart beating like a drum under all the Gore-Tex. The summit conditions monitor in the living quarters has just registered a wind gust of 110 miles per hour with a regular wind speed of eighty-five miles per hour. That is the equivalent of a Category 1 hurricane. The temperature is holding at 11°F with a wind chill of -19°F.

This is my window, the coldest and windiest it's been since I arrived. The wind is giving me my wish. I need to walk outside in a hurricane.

John is waiting for me. "Let's go!" he says. He's done this many times. He's still excited. The observers are excited. I imagine this never gets old.

We climb up the spiral staircase in the tower to the deck level, my legs feeling the weight of my gear. I'm wearing heavy wool socks, thermal underwear top and bottom, and eight hundred-fill down snow pants and parka. The heavy bolted door is rattling.

I slide a balaclava on my head, put a stocking hat over that, and slip on my ski goggles. The idea is to make sure every sliver of skin is covered and there are no seams for the wind to shimmy through. I slip on my gloves and we're ready.

John brings up the bolt of the door, pushes it open and we step out into the maelstrom.

Directly outside the main door is a V-shaped steel corridor, like an atrium before going out onto the deck. The corridor keeps chunks of ice from crashing onto observers as they come and go from the tower, and also gives them a (somewhat) protected space to reach the instrumentation boxes fastened to the side of the tower to get their readings. Under the metal awning, it's cold and the wind is howling, but we're able to at least stand and talk. From this vantage point I can even slip off my gloves in order pull out my phone. I hand it to John so he can take a video of my walk.

I step out beyond the atrium and it's like someone shoves me from the left. Those first couple steps are about getting used to how this feels. John's advice was to walk in baby steps to maintain balance, and that's what I do. I keep my head down and away from the wind, for now.

Just outside the tower entrance is a maintenance shack. The wind powers across the deck from west to east, and the shack wall reduces some of the wind's force, so getting to the end of the shack is not difficult.

Beyond that, it's white. I hunch my shoulders, make sure my goggles are secure and step out onto the wide-open deck. The wind hits my back, and I nearly pitch forward. I'm too high. I scrunch my boots into the hard pack and do a quick 180 to face the wind head on.

It's like being punched in the stomach, like there is a harness around my waist and shoulders pulling me backward. I've been in places where a surprise gust was strong enough to topple me. I recall a hike on Mount Jefferson years ago when we could hear the gusts coming over the rocks, like a freight train, and we'd have a couple seconds to get a grip and plant our feet before being hit.

Back in 1934, Sal said that as he climbed to the roof of the observatory to knock ice off the equipment in those two hundred-plus mph gusts, he was certain that had one hit him from the front instead of pushing him against the building from the back, he would have been blown off the mountain.

Standing in only a third of the wind he experienced, it's easy to understand why he'd feel that way, but most meteorologists agree that would not have been the outcome. Though what most likely would have happened would have been just as fatal.

"The winds on Mount Washington are a straight line, so they won't pick you up unless you are shaped like an airplane wing," observer Adam Gill tells me later. Adam is part of the team with me up here. He's the youngest and by far the most eager of the observers to experience extreme weather. "The winds will just push you around like a tumbleweed."

Down in Manchester, WMUR meteorologist and kids' book writer Josh Judge agrees.

"There are always a lot of factors involved like wind speed and weight of the person, direction of the wind," he says. "Normal hurricane-force winds don't really pick people up, they knock people down."

But two hundred-plus gusts aren't normal are they? Surly, Sal would have flown a little bit?

Both Josh and Adam give me a tornado lesson.

"The only winds that really pick people up are from tornadoes because those winds are rapidly going up," says Josh.

"Tornadoes have a vertical component to the wind as it is associated with the updraft of a thunderstorm, so that can lift a person and keep them levitated," says Adam.

And even then, both weathermen agree that the terminal velocity for a tornado to lift up an average sized person would be about 120 mile an hour sustained winds. That's approximately the wind speed used in recreation vertical wind tunnels that are becoming popular among adventurists.

Sal was faced with a record wind, but a gust. Would he have been flung from the roof into the air and into the Great Gulf? No. But his fate would have been the same, as the gust most likely would have knocked him off the roof and sent him tumbling across the ice and rocks. And even if that didn't knock him out, walking back in two hundred mile per hour gusts would have been impossible.

Standing here in only eighty-five mile per hour winds, I can't even begin to imagine how nearly three times this must feel. I've shuffled maybe ten feet out onto the deck, my head down, arms in front of me to keep them from flapping. This feeling is all about pressure. There's pressure on my shoulders and head, as literal a feeling as if someone was standing in front of me pushing. I'm certain that if I just stood up and let go, I wouldn't go tumbling, but I'd certainly be knocked down.

My goggles are beginning to frost up. For a split second, I think of taking a glove off to wipe them, then check myself. *Don't be an idiot*, I think. My black parka is starting to coat with rime ice, long white streaks along the front of my parka chest and arms. There's enough moisture in the air that I can stand here and watch the rime form on my body.

If I stood here long enough, I'd turn into one of those rime sculptures that forms on trail signs or on the weather equipment, long tendrils of snaking ice, delicate strands collecting on my fingertips and off the top of my head—an organic testament to living air.

A tiny blurb of fear forms in the pit of my stomach, which feels foolish. John's right there twenty feet away from me. The observers do this all the time; they make videos for school children. But perhaps this is a reflexive fear, some instinctive fight or flight response to experiencing this for the first time.

My body doesn't know I'm safe. It just feels what it feels. What if I was caught in this on the ridge, miles from a tower door? Is this what the beginning of panic feels like, that moment before making a fatal decision? That instant right before so many hikers and climbers become a statistic?

I shut my eyes and count to three and take a deep breath, willing my brain to assure my body that everything is fine. That in fact, I should be enjoying this.

When I open my eyes, my goggles are nearly entirely iced up. Time to try one more thing and get out of here. I bend my knees and push my head and shoulders into the wind. Then, like I watched observers do, I spread my arms out and jump.

For a moment, the wind lifts me. I can actually feel the lift, the vertical. In the video of my "jump" it lasts half a second, but it feels longer. The wind pushes me about two feet back, and when I land I manage to keep on my feet. That's what I wanted to feel, that split second of air and me above the mountain.

I fight my way back to the steel atrium where John is waiting.

"Cool huh!" he says.

"Cool," I say, out of breath, my black parka white with rime. "Unreal! Let's get back in."

And I hustle back through the heavy door and into the protection of the observatory, most likely a little too quickly.

The next morning breaks clear and calm. The mountain is acting like last night never happened. The sky is nearly perfectly blue. Because of yesterday's wind, the ice and snow lay in crazy patterns, heavy and deep in some places, bare ground in others. Some rocks are scoured clean of the white stuff. Others have massive drifts. It is chaos art.

I use the afternoon to get down off the summit for the first time. I want to visit Lizzie.

There are stories up here, stories about Lizzie Bourne, the first woman to die atop the mountain. Some say they can see her wandering through the mezzanine at night, when the wind howls and the tourists have gone home—her eyes forlorn and distant like the eyes in her painting that hangs near the museum. During the summer, a sign that normally marks the spot of her death is placed over a tall pole atop a cairn right next to the Cog tracks. Cog operators are sure to point that spot out to tourists as they pass on their way up to the summit.

During the winter, though, that sign is brought into the cafeteria and placed next to her portrait. Every evening, my footsteps echoing on the empty concrete, I've walked past Lizzie's portrait and marker. Every night I've waited to feel her presence.

Lizzie collapsed from exposure in a sudden gale mere yards from the summit on Sept. 14, 1885. The mystery and legend of Lizzie has grown over the years, with many swearing the twenty-three-year-old still haunts this mountain.

Summit observers and climbers will sometimes bring down word of seeing a gossamer white cloud rising from that pile of rocks by the Cog tracks, and as the glimmering mist clears the rocks, Lizzie appears in flowing robes and wild hair. The apparition will point sadly to the Tip Top House, then drop to her knees and weep. They say Lizzie's desperate cry can be heard echoing across the Great Gulf.

So, on this clear day, I stroll down to the site of her death, wanting to pay my respects. With the Northern Presidentials as a backdrop, bold and brilliant against the azure sky, it makes me melancholy to think that the girl didn't get to see that view through the fog and mist on the evening of her death.

I am alone. There is no wind. The sound of my breath and the crunch of snow underfoot ring strong in my ears. The pole sticking up out of the rock cairn is encrusted in rime, but as I reach the site, literally the moment I stop, the ice and snow drop off—just slip away like an invisible hand whisking it aside—and the pole stands clean.

I blink. Take a deep breath.

"Hi Lizzie," I say.

A warm breeze brushes my cheek, and I sit for a spell with Lizzie, there on our beautiful mountain.

It is Tuesday, April 11, and that means most of the morning is spent cleaning and taking stock. John and I clean our bunk rooms, take out the garbage, sweep, and make sure the kitchen looks spotless. There's an inventory checklist encompassing both food and supplies so the next volunteer crew will know what they have and what they don't.

The weather the past twenty-five hours has been glorious, clear and warm by summit standards. The result is that it appears to be spring outside. Blues and greens are peeking through the drifts, the distant northern Presidentials have bare spots on their flanks.

I badly want to get out there. John says he has a surprise for the observers to celebrate tomorrow's eighty-third anniversary of the big blow, and I promise him I'll be back in plenty of time to help with whatever that may be.

This afternoon, all I need is fleece pants and a jacket along with sunglasses and I head out. I am able to wear a baseball cap. As I've done every day since arriving, I make a quick pit stop at the summit sign and touch the W. And then I notice them. All of them. They are everywhere, swarming the deck and staircase, sitting on rocks and wandering here and there.

The summit is awash in shredders with snowboards and skiers in brightly colored jumpsuits. They have come up the ravine or the road.

They are flying back down the trails and snow cuts. And there's more—what Joe Dodge would have called "goofers," snowshoers and hikers taking advantage of the warm weather for an out and back to the summit, mostly on the auto road, which is packed with traffic on foot.

After six days of wandering this holy place nearly alone, I feel startled by the activity. I sit on a nearby rock for a bit and watch the energy, the joy of being here reflected in people's eyes. Peace signs at the summit. Insulated bottles of tea and coffee and whiskey. High fives. Someone actually "whoops!" from the road and there's laughter.

This is nice. This is why all this—the road, the trails, the tracks, the observatory—are here.

And I still have an advantage over all these visitors. I don't have to go down tonight.

I head down the road, a tiny breeze blowing, the vivid early afternoon sun casting shadows on the Cog tracks. I have only light gloves, it's that pleasant. After about fifteen minutes I'm passing by Ball Crag, one of my favorite places on the mountain and the site of a famous story of survival.

Only one month after poor Lizzie Bourne met her fate, about one hundred yards from the pointy collection of rocks now called Ball Crag, a young energetic doctor from Boston happened to attend a talk by none other than Thomas Starr King.

The doctor, Benjamin Lincoln Ball, was so enthralled by King's description of White Mountain scenery that he left for the mountains the very next day. From Gorham, he hired a horse, made it to the base of the mountain, and despite the pouring rain and the fact that the doctor had little by way of gear except for an umbrella, he hiked up to Halfway House (then called Camp House) on the auto road.

He tried to make it all the way up but failed due to freezing rain and wind, and came back down to Halfway House to spend the night, determined to go up the next morning. Caretakers there urged him not to go, telling him detailed horror stories about Lizzie's terrible fate, a story fresh in their minds.

The young doctor didn't care and set off the next morning, despite little improvement to the weather. Freezing and exhausted, his legs numb, he managed to make it as far as that jumble of rocks. With night coming on, he crawled into a hole between a rock ledge and some lower scrubs and opened his umbrella to cover the hole. Using his remaining strength, he pulled up brush roots and weeds and piled them on top of his umbrella to create a makeshift bivouac. For sixty hours, Doctor Ball rode out that storm, freezing, wet and starving.

In an incredible coincidence, the first man to find the good doctor was Joseph Hall, the Halfway House caretaker who just a month earlier had the grim job of carrying Lizzie's body off the mountain. Hall helped the doctor back to Halfway House where they first plunged his feet into warm water before putting him on a horse and getting him off the mountain.

Doctor Benjamin Lincoln Ball never summited Mount Washington, the Ball Crag today serving as a reminder of how far he came and how close he was to becoming another careless casualty of the mountain.

Just past Ball Crag, I make a sharp left and head west onto the plateau that leads down to the Great Gulf. There's enough snow to allow me to keep on the rocks and off the vegetation that's peeking through the ice cracks. It is so warm that there are whole clumps of damp or even muddy alpine grass.

I eventually come to the cairns marking out the Gulfside Trail, a magnificent stretch that skirts along side the south rim of the ravine. I rock hop all the way to the intersection of the Gulfside and Westside trails. I turn left on the Westside and pick my way back up to the Cog tracks. Were I to continue on the Westside Trail, I'd go over the tracks and tack along under the summit. The Westside Trail is a bypass.

But instead, I slip off my day pack and thermos and sit back on the tracks to sip some tea. I'll follow the tracks back up to the summit. A father and son hiking team passes by, coming up from Marshfield Station where the Cog lives. The boy must be, perhaps, twelve or thirteen, and it makes me think of my own daughter and wonder if I'll have the stamina to bring her up here in ten years.

I sit at the edge of the Great Gulf Ravine, an enormous, deep chasm that separates Mount Washington from the northern Presidentials.

Darby Field himself, during that first summit in 1642, reported seeing a huge ravine to the north of the summit, though he never ventured down here. In colonial times, the word "gulf" referred to a large ravine or basin. The story goes that it was Ethan Allen Crawford, back in 1829, who was wandering around lost above the clouds when he came to the edge of what he described as a "great gulf."

The Great Gulf doesn't get nearly the credit or the press as its eastern sister ravines, Huntington and Tuckerman. In fact, Joshua H. Huntington himself—the hero scientist who spent that first winter atop Mount Moosilauke thanks to Richard Little, and for whom the Huntington Ravine is named—was far less enthused by the Great Gulf.

He called it the "most monotonous and uninteresting place in the mountains."

Our friend Joshua was correct about a lot of things. About the Great Gulf, however, he was wildly, preposterously wrong.

In 1964, the Great Gulf was designated a wilderness area by Congress, all 5,658 acres of it. The gulf is the largest cirque in the White Mountains. From the head wall, the distance down is between 1,100 feet and 1,600 feet, depending on where you start along the rim. And down at the bottom is gorgeous Spaulding Lake, which drains eastward into the Peabody River.

The lake is named after one of the hardiest White Mountain explorers of the nineteenth century, John H. Spaulding. He first visited the lake in 1853 and then wrote a popular tourist book called *Historical Relics of the White Mountains*. At one time Spaulding was also the manager of the Tip Top House.

From my perch on the tracks, I can look across the gulf to the great Northern Presidentials, Mount Adams in the middle of the three peaks, the mountain where I finished my quest of summiting all of the state's 4,000-footers many years ago. The crowns of the mountains are ringed in white, but as the slope cascades down, wind-scoured rocks shimmer green and yellow and black along the walls. Drop farther into the bowl, and the dark greens of pines shine through, Spaulding Lake just a white, snow-covered blob.

How remarkable to be here today, how impossible the turns of events that had to conspire to deposit me at this moment, in this place, just another pile of breathing stardust at the edge of an ancient ravine, eating peanuts. We walk in the footsteps of those who came before us, we make footsteps for those who will come after us. Make sure your footprints are worth walking in.

My footprints this afternoon barely leave a trace in the hard steel and wood of the Cog tracks as I slowly make my way back to the observatory for my final night.

And John's surprise? He baked a cake. A full on, double layer, jam in the middle, frosting on top, as professional as one could imagine at the top of a mountain, cake. Honestly, I can't recall where he even conjured up the ingredients. To celebrate the anniversary the next day of the Big Wind, in red frosting the top of the cake reads "MWOBS BIG WIND 231," and above that is the logo of the observatory in red. It's like he's a magician, a wizard with a long beard and scrubby bandana.

After dinner, the five of us share that cake after our last meal together. We struggle with leaving some for the crew tomorrow.

Much later, after dishes and clean up, after the lights have dimmed and the day crew is tucked away—and after John has gone off to bed with the proclamation that he wanted to spend some time contemplating life—I head back out onto the deck around midnight for one last look around.

Clouds have moved in so there are no stars. A thin mist has risen up over the deck, giving the tower—bathed in soft white—a hazy, far-away look, like a shimmering lighthouse against a black curtain.

I breathe deeply. Then take another breath. There is barely a hint of wind. I flick on my headlamp and walk down off the deck and up onto the rock pile to the summit sign.

It is midnight. I am alone at the top of New England.

I feel like a sponge, saturated with experience and stories, bursting with the desire to tell anyone who will listen.

I could say, every day for one week, I touched this sign. Every day,

I breathed this air, and I never ventured far from the height. And the mountain gave me everything.

The next day, we get word that the new crew is on their way up, and I set off to pay my respects one final time to the most important creature at the observatory.

On Tuesday, January 8, 2008, New Hampshire held two elections. The first was the National Presidential Election Primary. The other election, though, was the one that actually mattered. More citizens cast their vote in that election than voted for Dennis Kucinich on the Democrat side or Fred Thompson on the Republican side. This election, in which more than 8,000 New Hampshire residents voted, decided the fate of, arguably, the most important non-human in the Granite State.

That non-human, of course, is Marty, the observatory's current mascot cat. He beat out Wilson and Sarah in a three way race to decide which kitty would replace the recently retired Nin. The Conway Area Humane Society helped the observatory in the selection and promotion of the cats. Marty won in a walk-away.

Nin, the famous cat of Eric Pinder's book, was seventeen or eighteen years old at the time, and she went into glorious retirement in Gorham, New Hampshire, moving in with Diane Holmes and Mike Pelchat, longtime and well-known rangers in their own right, at Mount Washington State Park. Nin passed away on July 14, 2009.

Cats have been a near continuous presence at the summit observatory since its 1930s beginnings. At first the cats were mainly strays brought up to perform a bit of mouse catching duty but also to provide some companionship to observers of the day. (Remember, the crew stayed far longer than a week at a time back then.)

Today, it's more of a tradition than anything else, but the cat mascots are also popular with the school groups and tourists who frequent the observatory.

And Marty? Well, the black fuzzy feline is older these days, a bit more stationary than those early years of padding about on the summit grounds. When I find him, he's in his favorite spot, laying on a down vest on a shelf above the main weather center desk, the one where Mike Carmon—the third observer on this crew and the shift supervisor—usually works. Marty's front legs are stretched out in front of him, paws dangling off the shelf. He has long whiskers and white eyelashes and deep green eyes. He is warm and comfortable—a fitting life for such a pronounced and regal mascot.

He's laying up against some logbooks and other communication manuals. Someone has propped up a copy of Pinder's *Cat in the Clouds* next to him. Marty doesn't care; jealousy is below his status.

"Hi boy," I say. "Taking a nap?"

He raises his chin and allows me a moment to give him a vigorous scratch.

People and cats live up here. They live here all the time, every day, in any weather. When you drive down Routes 302 or 2 and see the towers sparkle in the sun, there is someone here. They are a colony, an ecosystem in and of themselves, a brother and sisterhood.

Their work has spanned generations and will soon span centuries. They are record keepers. When they are here, they pay homage only to the changing winds, to trying to predict the unpredictable.

I have watched observers sit huddled before the spinning radar, unblinking, the green screen of precipitation reflecting on their faces and in their eyes.

Behind me, the door to the living quarters opens and John walks past, a duffel over his shoulder.

"Snowcat's here," he says.

I know I'll be up here again, and again, in many ways, but never like this.

"See ya around, buddy," I say.

Marty the observatory cat closes his eyes, tucks his head into his paws and lets out a deep, long sigh.

Extreme Weather is in Their Blood

More about the observers at the summit during my volunteer week

They come from different parts of the country, have different educations, are of different generations and skill sets. But the one thing that unites every observer who has set foot in every iteration of the Mount Washington Observatory since its founding is that they live for another Big Wind.

"Pretty much, you have to love extreme weather to do this job," says observer Adam Gill. "Otherwise . . ." He trails off, shrugs and laughs, as if to say, what's the point otherwise.

The observers are all work during the day, but let their hair down around dinner or during down time in the lounge, casting out stories of playing football in hurricane intensity winds or fighting their way to the top of the tower in the middle of the night to knock ice off the instruments.

A favorite story is that of a lone hiker in the middle of a winter hike, taking shelter in the window well of the observatory's living quarters and relieving himself in full view of the observers sitting in the room below without ever realizing what he was doing.

There have been only a handful of select humans who have done this job since the original four founders. The group up there with me—Caleb Muete, Mike Carmen, and Adam Gill—were the latest in a family of scientists that consider themselves part of the same tribe.

Think of the worst, most dangerous, awful and scary weather you can imagine in your head. The men and women who work year-round at 6,288 feet have been outside in it.

Originally from Southeastern Pennsylvania, Caleb graduated from Millersville University in 2012 with a BS in Meteorology. He worked as an intern for a couple seasons, a typical call of duty at the observatory, before accepting a full-time position. I came to recognize that Caleb was the storyteller and showman of the shift. From a moose that fell to its death from the top of the observatory deck to the ghosts that rattle and bang in the living quarters at night, his head was full of tales, some tall, some funny, all about life at the top. Caleb could hold your ear.

Mike came from Central New Jersey originally, but spent a few years in the flatlands outside Chicago where the storms rage and the tornadoes are a way of life. While everyone else was taking cover when one of those Heartland storms blew through, Mike headed outside.

His interest in extreme weather led him back to the Garden State, where he earned a BS in Meteorology at Rutgers. Like Caleb, he became an intern in 2008 and a full-time observer in 2009. He worked primarily on the night shift for years before becoming a shift leader in 2013.

Today, he's the observatory's education specialist, working with students and handling weather station tours. Mike's the guy who knows it all, has been around the worst of the worst conditions but stays steady. He's the pragmatist, keeping a cool head in the wake of potentially blustery weather, hedging his bets. Mike's the perfect foil for the youngest member of the crew, Adam.

Growing up right next to the Rocky Mountains, Adam's interest in the weather began right there, where the peaks touch the sky. In Colorado Springs, Colorado, Adam experienced it all, from multi-foot snowstorms to frequent baseball-sized hail.

Adam is also the Eagle Scout, and growing up watching documentaries on Mount Washington sparked his interest. He attended the University of North Dakota and completed his BS in Atmospheric Science in 2015. He took a year off and wandered over to New Hampshire to gain some job experience in the place with the worst weather in the world.

Adam has only been on the team for about a year, but he's the most eager, willing to always predict the lowest temperature and the highest wind speed as the observers sit around the table to talk weather. He calls it optimism; everyone else would call it crazy!

CHAPTER THREE

A Gentleman Saunterer

The Life and Times of Alton "Mr. Mount Washington" Weagle

"It is I you hold and who holds you.
I spring from the pages into your arms."
—*Walt Whitman*

If there is a more magnificent early view from near the summit of New Hampshire's Mount Washington than the one from the auto road at the seven-mile post, I have yet to find it. To the north, the great granite mounds of the Northern Presidentials surge up, the plunging Great Gulf giving Mounts Adams, Jefferson, and Madison the illusion of far more height than their humble five thousand feet.

To the south, the Mount Washington Observatory begins to display her summit towers, and the Sherman Adams Visitor Center, with its long open deck, becomes a worthy destination for the weary walker.

I see none of this. I see only words. Specifically these words from *Leaves of Grass* by Walt Whitman:

Scaling mountains . . . pulling myself cautiously up . . . holding on
    by low scragged limbs,
Walking the path worn in the grass and beat through the leaves of
    the brush.

    I take a deep breath and read those words out loud, my right hand holding open my paperback copy of one of the most famous long poems in the world, my left hand holding the wide-brimmed black felt hat to my head. The cool Canadian northwest wind has already whisked it away more than once. Today, on this, the loftiest of New England pulpits, I am Whitman. I'm dressed in full Whitman clothes of the time—high-collared ruffled shirt under a corduroy vest, thick pants under a heavy peacoat.

    Just two days ago, I found myself on the upper floor of a creaky old former warehouse in Manchester being measured by master seamstress Mary Selvoski. The warehouse used to be a dry goods outlet called the Varick Building. Among other things, John Varick Co. would ship guns, fishing tackle, tires, watches, and linseed oil around New England via a railroad line that pulled straight into the warehouse. Those tracks still exist, and if you followed the old route, about three blocks from where Mary was measuring my inseams, you'd run into the old train shed that used to house Manchester Locomotive Works. From that engine manufacturing firm sprung some of the very first of Mount Washington's Cog Railway engines. And one of the engines built at the locomotive works in 1849 and used to haul goods from John Varick's goods empire was a Mogul locomotive named "Mount Washington."

    Mary, in her forty years of creating costumes for every community theater outfit in the state, has seen it all and was unimpressed, or perhaps just amused, that I had grown out my beard—not to Whitman's later 1880s long scraggly length, but certainly to his thick, full 1860s length. Mary poked and prodded me, whipped up a vest that fit in about thirty seconds, and told me to go scrounge around in the hat area of her costume collection. I came back with a dead ringer for Walt's black jaunty hat.

Up on the mountain, my copy of *Leaves of Grass* on this journey is, of course, the 1855 version, the original.

I am here today because it is Alton Weagle Day, a day of setting records on the highest mountain in New England, and I am attempting to become the first person to hike up the Mount Washington Auto Road while reading poetry.

I'm so lost in the words that I don't even hear the ultra-runner behind me until he overtakes me and says, "Did you lose your way looking for the subway?"

"What?" I ask, watching him pass, sporting a black headband, sleeveless jersey, and yellow tights as he huffs his way up the mountain.

"The subway," he calls back over his shoulder. "You look like you belong in the city."

This thrills me. I think it would have pleased Whitman as well, and maybe even Weagle.

It has been a long road of discovery to get me nearly to the summit of this mountain dressed like a nineteenth century poet, on a day meant to celebrate a twentieth century mountain man. My goal was to bridge the gap between the two men, to bring their souls of exploration together on this climb—and in the process, I hoped, shine a little more light on the man who used to be known as Mr. Mount Washington—Alton Weagle, the hike-guiding, drum-playing, square dance-calling, horseshoe-throwing baker, and mountain watchtower guard who holds the most records for Mount Washington ascents.

Yeah, that guy, the one you've never heard of. The one who raced a Cog Railway car to the top and won. The guy who climbed the mountain via trail, road, and rail all in one day. The guy who once walked up the mountain blindfolded, another time barefoot and another time backward.

Most famously, Alton Weagle, the guy who once pushed a wheelbarrow full of sugar all the way up the Auto Road without ever putting it down to rest.

My own road, the one that led me here chasing my own ridiculous record in memory of Alton in the persona of Walt, began in Stark, New Hampshire, in a small nondescript cemetery overlooking a famous covered bridge.

"I celebrate myself, and sing myself
And what I assume you shall assume,
For every atom belonging to me as good belongs to you."

If you pay too close attention to the glorious cliffs of Devil's Slide State Forest that shoot straight up from the Upper Ammonoosuc River, you might miss Stark, New Hampshire, as you drive along Route 110 in the North Country. To the south of the cliffs, about half of Stark is within the boundaries of the White Mountain National Forest. Follow the Mill Brook from Stark as it branches off the river, and you'll begin to climb the Pilot Range. Early hunters and scouts journeying up into the upper Connecticut River Valley used this range as a waymark and called it the Land Pilot Hills. And the 1803 land plan of Percy, New Hampshire (Stark's original name) refers to the Land of Pilot Mountain.

The range meanders up to Mount Cabot, one of New Hampshire's 4,000-footers, a mountain named after the Italian explorer Sebastian Cabot, who famously sailed his way up the North American coast—getting close to Hudson Bay—in 1508–09. On a map drawn by Cabot in 1544, Mount Washington and the White Mountains are simply referred to as "Montagnas."

This was young Alton's backyard, and he formed a deep connection with those mountains and hills, even as his family connections wore thin.

Alton Oscar Weagle was born in Stark on April 18, 1911, nineteen years after Walter Whitman died in Camden, New Jersey. Alton's father, Jason Henry Weagle, a laborer, abandoned the family soon thereafter, leaving Alton's mother, Nina Elizabeth Montgomery, to fend for herself. In leaving the family, Jason shadowed the actions of Alton's grandfather, James Montgomery, who disappeared in 1902.

(It's interesting to mention that Alton's great-great-great-grandfather, Clefford Cole Sr., was one of the original settlers of Percy [Stark], moving up from Massachusetts in 1787.)

Alton was sent to live with his grandmother Manettie while Alton's mother raised Alton's younger brother, also named James. This was a curious family situation in the early part of the twentieth century, even more unusual for a tiny rural town far from the convenient economies of a large population base.

But there appears to have been no ill effect on Alton, primarily because the two main women in his life, his grandmother and mother, were deeply self-reliant women, each a force to be reckoned with. Manettie had to deal with raising Alton of course, a young rascally child who spent more time in the river or woods than indoors. But Manettie also had three other children of her own besides Nina, three teenage uncles and aunts who became Alton's de facto siblings.

And Nina? Her legacy—besides Alton—can be seen in the thousands of images every year that artists and photographers around the world take of Stark's famous Paddleford truss covered bridge. In fact, from a rise at the very back row of Stark Cemetery, Alton and Nina's family plot sits with a grand view of the 151-foot white wooden bridge as it delicately makes its way across the river.

Built around 1860, the bridge was washed away in a flood in 1890, but men with oxen pulled it back upriver and added extra arches and refastened the old girl to her pilings. The bridge failed again, and in the mid-1950s the people of Stark voted to tear it down and replace it with a steel trestle. But Nina was having none of that.

By that time, Alton's mother had earned her place as a village elder. For years she served as the Stark Station agent, ticketmaster, and postmistress, and that bridge had become her view every day as she managed the passengers and railmen who worked the Atlantic and St. Lawrence Railway—a line that passed through Stark between Montreal, Canada, and Portland, Maine.

When her fellow villagers voted to take down the bridge, it must have felt like a stab in the back. Nina got to work, sending notices to covered bridge aficionados, artists and friends. Soon, the outcry from near and far was loud enough that village selectmen took notice. The movement peaked the day that Nina, already in her late sixties, declared she would drag her kitchen stove under the bridge and set up residence there to prevent the bridge's destruction.

That was too much for the village elders. The vote was rescinded and a new motion carried to renovate the bridge instead. A new concrete pier was added, along with steel stringers for support. Nina died in 1960 without ever having to move under her beloved bridge.

I sit up there on that hilly cemetery rise, between the granite rectangles that mark Nina and Alton's graves, and watch the sunset cast its hue down over the Devil's Slide cliffs, lower and lower, until the white siding of one of the oldest bridges in New England turns fiery orange.

In Nina, I discovered my first clue into the character of her son, the man who would make Mount Washington the palette of his life: a relentless pursuit of the nobility of the aesthetic.

At a talk he gave at the Brooklyn Art Union in 1851, four years before the first edition of *Leaves of Grass* was published, Walt Whitman laid out his grand vision on the character of heroics. He insisted that all heroic action and impulses that serve to improve life—empathy, love, joy—are strictly derived from the artistic impulse.

"He who does great deeds," Whitman said, "does them from his sensitiveness to moral beauty."

What could be more moral and beautiful than the preservation of a crucial structure that literally spans a waterway and figuratively spans the history of a small New England village? To Nina, that bridge wasn't wood and concrete. That bridge was—is—the moral fiber of her home.

Alton's moral beauty would be a little grander and a little taller.

"Stout as a horse, affectionate, haughty, electrical,
I and this mystery here we stand."

Late in his life, long after the records and the stunts, Alton Weagle became a sort of environmentalist, speaking out against the construction of Interstate 93 through the White Mountain National Forest and becoming the go-to expert for newspapers whenever a hiker went missing.

But as I wait near the beginning of the Auto Road for the annual Alton Weagle Day to begin, trying to settle into my role as Walt Whitman, my thoughts drift more toward what sort of man would decide to run up the mountain backward. Or blindfolded. How did he even come up with the idea of pushing a wheelbarrow full of sugar?

The answer, as it turns out, is nobody knows. And as I scan the Alton Weagle Day Class of 2017, that answer becomes less important. We gather early on the morning of the climb, near the entrance to the Auto Road, nineteen souls eager to try our hand at making it into the silly record books. There is a Cat in the Hat along with two young ones, Thing One and Thing Two. There are two unicorns, one fairy and one Hawaiian princess. There is Superman and Superwoman, and there is a unicyclist who plans on juggling as he rides.

There's a fellow getting ready to drive his remote control car up the mountain and a woman who is going to carry a giant dream catcher.

And there is one brave soul intent on pushing a wheelchair with an eight-foot stuffed rabbit for a patient. I feel Alton would have been particularly proud to have inspired this last one.

The Mount Washington Auto Road, a privately owned entity, launched Alton Weagle Day to celebrate its sesquicentennial in 2011. Only six participants attempted records that year. The road's general manager, Howie Wemyss, a legend in his own right in White Mountain hiking circles, tells me that the road enthralled record-breakers from the very moment construction began on America's oldest man-made attraction back in 1854.

"The road has always attracted people who have wanted to challenge it in some way," he says. "Consequently, we have quite a history of accepting and even encouraging folks to find their personal challenge here on Mount Washington."

Howie himself this day is dressed as a Scottish gentleman, in full kilt. He plans on "pursuing" his wife up the mountain. She's dressed in a Toy Hobby Horse Nessie costume.

"Alton was the most prolific of these challengers with all his various means of taking on the mountain," Howie says. "So, this way, we're just continuing the tradition and having fun along the way!"

I wander over to one fellow in a white jumpsuit covered in ribbons of differing colors. His name is Herb Fox, and he's participating in what he calls Walking for Many. Each ribbon represents a person he knew or knows who fought or is fighting cancer. There are hundreds pinned to his suit. This will be his third year in a row walking with his pins.

Herb is a gentle man, focused and determined.

"Maybe this will just give some folks awareness, you know," he says. "I don't know. It means something to me."

Herb shuffles off, his pins ruffling in the breeze, and it makes me think about my own decision to participate as Walt, which was born out of a thirty-six second wax cylinder recording of Walt Whitman reading from his poem "America."

In mid-1951, an NBC Radio program called "Yesterday, Today, and Tomorrow" played the recording. There's no reference in anything Whitman or his own colleagues wrote about making this recording, but there is a letter from Thomas Edison himself expressing interest in making the cylinder, which apparently was put to wax around 1890, when Whitman was an old hermit living in Camden, New Jersey. Voice analysts and sound engineers have happily debated whether it's actually Whitman or not ever since.

I don't know whether Weagle heard this back in 1951—or whether he read Whitman. I do know that he was a poet. Over the years he struck up a friendship with William Loeb, the powerful and controversial publisher of *The Union Leader* newspaper. In turn, Loeb published many of Alton's poems, most of which involve praising his home state.

In "New Hampshire," an eleven-verse ode to the Granite State that the state tourist board would be proud to publish, Alton doesn't shy away from the heavy-handed rhyme:

If you like to swim, hike: camp or ski
There are plenty each for you and me.
From Mount Washington, with its beautiful view
To the deep virgin forests where song birds coo.

Like nearly everything else Alton did, he wrote poetry with a childlike earnestness, oblivious to anything but celebration and joy.

Alton had that in common with Walt. And that thirty-six seconds, back in the summer of 2016 just as I had begun to track down the ghost of Alton, was what convinced me that my own record attempt would be in the persona of Whitman.

Sitting on my bed late one night, I played that recording on my smartphone: from wax to microchip with 125 years between us. And behind the haunting crackle and fuzz of that early marvel of sound engineering, there he was, that old man with the long, thick beard, the elder statesman of American letters. I listened again and again until I memorized each skip and pop, Whitman's voice—the slight affectation to his words, like a Long Island lisp—emerging from another century, giving me chills. I hope Weagle heard it, or knew of him. I will choose to believe that he did.

How else to explain Alton's wanderlust, his connection to the mountains, his almost transcendental desire to use his flesh and bone to forge a bond between himself and the landscape, much as Whitman did in New York City?

How else to explain this? I was so lost in the sound of Whitman's voice, it was my wife who brought my attention to the words.

"Love," she said. "Listen to what he says about America":

Centre of equal daughters, equal sons,
All, all alike endear'd, grown, ungrown, young or old,
Strong, ample, fair, enduring, capable, rich,
Perennial with the Earth, with Freedom, Law and Love.

Freedom, law and love. From the man who thought of America as the ultimate poem, to the man who loved the New England landscape so much that he launched a decades-long celebration of a mountain. And now to me.

I decided that night that I would try to meld Whitman's words with Weagle's actions on Alton Weagle Day.

Whitman's haunting voice plays over in my mind as the group of us gathers in front of the Auto Road sign for photos. The weather is warm down below, but up above it's foggy and cloudy. I'm worried that I'll freeze above tree line; I don't know how wool and corduroy will make me feel up high.

There is no stress, no feeling of competitive angst. In a newspaper interview, Alton was asked why he decided to set such curious records. "I like to do things that no one has ever done before," he said. That seems about right.

One of the participants, Hans Bern Bauer, first ascended the mountain as a five-year-old in 1974 with his father. Since then, he's become something of an Alton Weagle acolyte, an apostle to the Weagle tradition. He holds the current records for hiking up the mountain on stilted skis and snowshoes, on a pogo stick, barefoot backwards, and while crawling. On this day, he is attempting to hike the road while holding a forty-foot high international flagpole onto which are clipped the flags of fifty nations.

Bauer's raw enthusiasm and love for this day is infectious.

"We should never lose our inner child and innocence," he tells me. "In this day, many of the thrills and joys of childhood can be easily relived!"

And with that, Bauer has one last duty to perform before we all head up; he's the one lighting the mini-cannon to signal the beginning of the climb. With a BOOM we are all off, but as the sound from the shot echoes through the valley, no one runs, no one hurries. Instead we all wish each other well, pat each other on the back and slowly make our way down to the gate house.

As the road begins to slant up, we walk, ride, navigate, run, and push—some slowly, some quickly, all of us laughing at how wonderfully absurd such a thing is.

I enter the forest, open *Leaves of Grass*, and began to read to Mount Washington.

> "All goes onward and outward . . . and nothing collapses
> And to die is different from what anyone supposed, and luckier.
> Has anyone supposed it lucky to be born?"

There's not enough snow on this raw January day to allow Groveton's snowmobilers unfettered access to the town's sidewalks without having to roll over some pavement. But the day is young, the skies are thick and gray, and the half dozen men on their sleds rumbling down the slush-filled road look like a pack of metal wolves hunting for breakfast.

They find it at the same place I have, the North Country Restaurant. I'm sipping steaming burnt coffee, cheerfully given to me by a thin waitress with sunburned cheeks and platinum hair, when the wolf pack stomps in and takes over a long table at the far wall. The North Country is everything a lunch joint in these parts should be, from the thick drab carpet to the perpetual clink of Buffalo china. It's the sort of place where they don't ask you what kind of coffee you want—there's only one—and the mugs all have advertisements on them from plumbers, welders and funeral homes.

The special today is fish and chips with a side of Mississippi mud pie. The walls are covered with plaques in the shape of animals, each sharing a message. There's a pig that says "Dinner Time" and a cow that says "Chocolate Milk."

In a corner, two men with identical beards and identical wrinkles around their eyes—one wearing a baseball cap that proclaims his Navy service—talk politics, and the talk in Groveton, like always, is jobs, or rather the lack of them.

When the Wausau Papers mill shut down for good in 2008, the trains stopped coming and then the people stopped coming. And now tourists driving along Route 3 from the mountain notches to the south of town or from Canada to the north look out their windows at Groveton and see nothing but piles of red brick bones and brown shuttered windows, and they shake their heads and drive a little faster.

As of 2010, there were just over 1,100 souls still living in Groveton, and nearly 15 percent were living below the poverty line.

The person I'm here to meet wants all that to change. I slide a few bucks' tip under my coffee mug and make my way down the puddle-filled sidewalk to meet Jim Weagle, the great-nephew of Alton. Jim's a selectman in Groveton. Technically, according to the bureaucrats who care about such things, Groveton is merely a "census-designated place" within the town of Northumberland, but to Jim, Groveton is home, and he's never left.

I meet Jim at an intersection across from Town Hall. His wife, Wendy, is a crossing guard there, bright yellow jacket, moving in and out of the intersection as a couple of lonely cars roll by. He's leaning against a street sign as I approach, jean jacket over a hoodie, salt and pepper hair and beard.

Over the course of our afternoon, here's what I learn. Jim is a selectman, a fire precinct commissioner, Groveton Elementary's PTO chair, and a member of the Northern New Hampshire Chamber of Commerce, the Lancaster Renaissance Committee, the town's Planning Board, and the school board.

"I keep very busy," he says. "Come on, let's walk, I'm getting my son from school."

We head south down the main street, dodging mud and puddles. Jim points out a large empty building—brown shingles, scuffed windows. "Local boy owns that," he says. "Developer. Going to turn that into a gym!"

Jim walks with a pronounced limp, and I try to be casual as I ask him about it, not knowing if he's willing to talk about it. But he's fine. He worked on a sanitation truck when he was twenty. One day, he lost his grip, fell off and was run over by the truck's back wheels.

"They told me they'd never seen a crush injury like that," Jim says. "Told me I'd never walk again. That was twenty years ago, and here I am." He smiles.

"Are you still in pain?" I ask him stupidly.

"Every day," he says. "Every moment."

I remember a single line from an old article I dug up about Alton, that Mr. Mount Washington had a glass eye. He lost the real one while playing with a dynamite cap when he was fourteen years old. That injury kept Alton out of the military during World War II. I nearly mention Alton's glass eye, but resist the urge to make conversation by comparing injuries. Instead, I ask, "How did that injury affect your head? How did you manage to be able to come back and work so hard?"

Jim shrugs. "I been back to work a little bit here and there," he says.

"After the injury I felt sorry for myself for a time, but I remember some teachers I had back in school that got me interested in politics, so that's what I did. I can't really work, but I want to contribute."

Having one eye certainly didn't stop Alton.

"Do you remember much about Alton?" I ask.

Jim doesn't hesitate. "Nope. I was too young, and he lived down south, so he'd come up to visit every so often. I do remember my mom saying that he always had some new thing he was doing."

I press Jim a bit, asking if he has an opinion on Alton's odd string of records.

"He wanted to be known, I think," he says. "My guess is that a lot of times, people told him he couldn't do this or that and he wanted to show them otherwise."

Jim's son Davey comes running up, and they greet with a fist bump, then all three of us begin the walk back to the intersection.

We chat a little more. Jim points out some of the former mill property and mentions some ideas he has for getting Groveton back on its feet. Even broken as it is, Groveton has a sort of lost-world charm—the sort of place where old, bald men make weekly trips to the local barbershop and Pink Floyd is played through warbling speakers at the tiny grocery store.

I begin to understand that the connection, ultimately, between Jim and his mom's uncle may not be about family. I came to Groveton looking for family ties, but, as it turns out, the great wandering soul of Alton may have been forged in geography, in the mill where Alton worked, in the nearby hills where he cut his teeth as a mountain guide.

Alton's great-nephew is just a dad trying to make his community a better place. Jim's strength is his tether to his home community, his love of the ground under his feet, in good times and bad.

But Alton felt that connection differently, through constant movement. Alton's connection to the hills drove him to obsessively achieve, even if that achievement seemed insane to some.

Given all that, Whitman's obsession with standing out doesn't feel shoehorned into Alton's story at all. On a trip to Boston right before

Leaves of Grass was published, Whitman sarcastically wrote about how wonderful his experience in the city was, because he felt Boston was conformist in culture, manners, and dress, "cramped by responsibility."

"Everybody here is so like everybody else," he gleefully told a friend. "And I am Walt Whitman!"

I thought I'd find ancestry here, but Groveton was moving me in a different direction. I needed more. I needed to discover the source of Alton's obsessive, wandering spirit. And little did I know that my first real insight into the heart of what drove Alton Weagle was waiting for me just a few blocks away, in a nondescript, white clapboard apartment building with two faded cardboard pink flamingos pinned to the front door.

"She owns the fine house by the rise of the bank,
She hides handsome and richly drest aft the blinds of the windows."

The first thing I notice as I step into Barbara Weagle's home is the sound of a thousand toy sun dancers clicking in unison. They line every inch of space along every window. There are holiday-related figurines, Santas and reindeer and pumpkins and bunnies. There are astronauts, cowboys, dogs, cats, horses and clowns. The eastern sun beats down through the windows and lights them up. They plink and rock, so many small noises forming a trinkety heartbeat. Barbara's home is a living metronome.

"Watch where you step," Alton's niece says as I enter the doorway where the pink flamingos are pinned. "I haven't had the chance to clean up."

Her home, where she has lived since 1977, is astounding, packed floor to ceiling with amazing collections of tchotchkes and artifacts from around the world. Commemorative plates, primarily of churches, line the walls. Wind chimes dangle from every corner of the ceiling, beautiful multi-colored glass and paper and wood and plastic—some tinkle from the breeze of the closing door. There are magnets, pictures of family and places, thousands of VHS tapes and DVDs, homages to Elvis, the Beatles and Star Trek, and, lining a sofa covered with a thick colorful afghan, dozens of stuffed animals.

"Wow," I say out loud, unable to conceal my wonder. "Look at the spoons."

But there is no need to feign nonchalance. "Oh yes," Barbara says. "Would you like to see them? Come on!"

Two walls in her living room are almost completely lined with decorative, commemorative and antique spoons. Barbara says her collection tops four thousand. They shimmer like oversized raindrops against the sunbeams slanting through the blinds. The spoons are all on display, in beautiful, delicate wood cases fastened to the walls. She shows me her presidential spoon collection, the tiny head of each president smiling up from the handle. She does not yet have an Obama or a Trump spoon. There are spoons that were brought here by family members who took trips around the world, Disney princesses, California, national parks.

"Those cases were built by my father," she says. "They mean so much to me!"

That would be James Weagle, Alton's younger brother.

Barbara is comfortable, calm and happy in her little museum home, curator of the joy and contentment that comes with being surrounded by the spinning colors of her life. She sits on the long sofa, nearly the only surface unoccupied by a collection, and smiles there under her spoons, queen of collections, archivist of Groveton.

At her writing desk, under a ceramic white cat with a red ribbon around its neck, are notebooks, folders, and binders full of history—family, Groveton, the mill, cuttings of things she likes. There are hundreds of notebooks, some piles stacked two or three feet high.

"My mother used to say that my grandmother was a hoarder," Barbara says cheerfully. This is Nina she's talking about, Alton's mom. "But that's not it. It's collecting. Just about anything you give me, I'll collect."

There is an innocent exuberance in Barbara that draws me in, fills me with wonder. Just the colors alone of her home dare you to write her off as a North Country rube. I like her from the moment I walk in. Later, I do add to her collection, giving Barbara a couple commemorative plates of Manchester churches, which she cheerfully accepts and I hope she adds to her walls.

Born in 1948, after Alton had set most of his endurance records and had already moved away, from Stark to Walpole, but before he became half of the first couple to get married on the Cog railroad and before he founded one of the longest-running horseshoe clubs in America, Barbara remembers her uncle mainly through her father, Alton's brother James.

Barbara and James worked in the mill, of course. In fact, if I peer between the sun catchers lining the east-facing window of her home, the great open space where the mill used to sit is a constant reminder of her past and, perhaps, her future.

On Sept. 4, 1999, Wausau Papers set a mill record by churning out 295 tons of 80# Wausau Bright White Cover stock. Nine years later the mill was shuttered, hundreds of jobs lost, and the slow decline of the paper mill trade that began in the 1930s had reached its peak and ground the North Country to a halt. A few years later, the enormous mill, nearly across the street from Barbara, began to come down.

It must have been like a record wall of her life, right outside her window, brick by brick, coming down until all that remained was open, empty space. To some, the removal of that mill might signal rebirth. But to the Weagles, that open plot might as well be a giant grave.

In March 2016, Northumberland voters took a tremendous leap of faith and voted to borrow up to $400,000 to put in water and sewage lines to the 137-acre former mill site. The town got a partial funding grant from the feds, but the whole project was dependent on Phase Two of the grant that would bring water and sewer down to the river. Groveton is still waiting.

Barbara worked at the mill as a checker, and that was exactly what it sounds like. As the paper inventory came off the line and before it went out the door, Barbara's job was to inspect and tag the items on their way out.

It was solid North Country work, something to be proud to be part of. And every day she'd come home to her family, her notebooks, and her spoons.

Studs Terkel, in his classic 1974 book *Working*, wrote about the sustenance of work, how even menial labor has dignity and can ground a person to their community and help them discover emotional truths in life.

"Work is about a search for daily meaning as well as daily bread, for recognition as well as cash, for astonishment rather than torpor," Terkel wrote, "in short, for a sort of life rather than a Monday through Friday sort of dying."

Also just outside Barbara's window is the dead and rotting Groveton train depot. The building's deep red brick facade is beginning to sag, the white frames and doors exposed to the weather. The depot was a beautiful building once, and perhaps, as it collapses into a metaphor for Groveton itself, it becomes more beautiful. I say this because that train depot was built on the spot where once stood a vast grove of birch trees—the grove that the town was named after. Perhaps once the depot has turned to dust, the earth will once again spring to life.

I search in my memory for some Whitman parallel but can't find it. But as Barbara begins to talk about her uncle, so much more becomes clear and I finally realize the truth about Alton's Mount Washington obsession was right there in front of me all along. I just didn't see it.

"The times I saw him, he was already not living here, so when he did come up, he was always bragging about the stuff he was doing," Barbara says. "My father would always say, 'Here comes the old bullshitter!'"

We both have a good laugh at this, but when I ask her about those records—the blindfold, the Cog race, the wheelbarrow full of sugar—she shrugs. "I don't know."

"Do you have any pictures of him chasing these records?"

She shakes her head. "He did them alone."

Wait a minute. Over the course of the next few days, I ask Howie from the Auto Road. I ask Jim Weagle, the selectman. I consult the town archives, the history books. We go through photos.

Those records that for years have been reported in newspapers and whispered in hiking circles. Those records that spurred Alton Weagle Day, that created a White Mountain industry of Mount Washington challenges.

Those records that gave me so much depth and pleasure and joy as I donned my own Walt Whitman outfit to walk in the footsteps of Alton.

The only person, it appeared, who ever recorded those records was Alton Weagle.

"Barbara," I begin, almost not wanting to ask the obvious question, "did Alton actually set those records?"

She smiles, and her eyes shine. "He said he did."

On my way out of Groveton that afternoon, I stop at the little park along Route 3 just on the outskirts of town. The paper mill's old coal-fueled Switch Steam Engine is on display there, hooked to a big red caboose. The Switcher would have been used to move other engines and cars around inside the mill grounds and in tighter track areas.

I unpack a little late lunch and lean against the engine to eat my peanut butter and jelly. The train smells like old iron. The day is clear and bright; even though it's April, a summer breeze wafts down from the distant mountains and warms my bones.

The mill is gone. Groveton as it existed for a century is gone. Alton is gone. All that remains is this black hunk of steel, sitting on tracks that go nowhere, overlooking an empty lot.

Was Alton Weagle an invention? What was it that Mark Twain said? "Never let the truth get in the way of a good story."

"What did you do, Alton?" I ask the air.

Was I chasing a character instead of an actual man? A myth? The answer would be found halfway up Mount Washington's west slope, at a place called Jacob's Ladder, where the most documented and famous of Alton's records took place.

> "Come closer to me,
>   Push close my lovers and take the best I possess,
>   Yield closer and closer and give me the best you possess."

With only about a mile to go, I am sweating and freezing in turns there near the summit. The heavy peacoat had to come off down below, but now it's on again as a deep, foggy wind kicks up, whips along the relatively even cow pasture and sneaks under my damp shirt. I have to put away my Whitman hat and pull a stocking cap over my ears to keep my head warm. I justify this breach of costume—along with my modern hiking boots—by thinking that had Walt had such outdoor-appropriate wear when he was walking, he'd have worn it.

The two Things, Buddy the Elf, and Herb Fox all touched the summit long ago and have returned to the base. But reading and walking, as it turns out, takes some concentration!

I'm distracted by the views, as the mist swings in and out of the surrounding mountains. I'm distracted by the cars and motorcycles streaming up the road. The Auto Road opened to traffic at 9:00 a.m., and they have all caught up to me. And I am distracted by thoughts of my own relationship to this mountain.

I first climbed Mount Washington in 1999, with no previous hiking or climbing experience. My mentor, the great Everest summiter Jim Gagne, had to use all the tricks in his magic hiking bag to get me up there, in early spring with ice and snow on the summit. It was May. We headed up in the dark. We got back down in the dark. I could not get out of bed the next morning.

But the day was clear and blue, and I remember sitting on the ice near the summit, looking south, the Lakes of the Clouds Hut a tiny, shimmering dot under the vast expanse of the southern Presidentials. It was the first time I laid eyes on that view, and it took away my breath. I recall poking my ax into the ice at my cramponed feet and marveling at how deep blue the ice below was. I touched that Mount Washington summit sign for the first time as the sun began to set behind me. I was so tired, shoulders slumped, the mild breeze chilling me, ruffling my hair. There was nowhere else I wanted to be at that moment, and fifteen years and a new summit sign later, there is still no place I'd rather be.

Since that first summit, I've made it here by various means—hiking, the Cog Railway, driving, shuttle—perhaps twenty times, or about once a year since I arrived in New Hampshire. Alton, on the other hand, by the time he was forty-four years old, had claimed to have climbed Mount

Washington 531 times. That would be once a month, every month, since he was one month old.

And all this, the records day, the path through Groveton and Stark, the covered bridge and the mill—indeed the very words you read right now—might have been lost to history; Alton Oscar Weagle might have quietly slipped into obscurity were it not for a stunt he pulled on September 10, 1955. For all of his (mostly) self-proclaimed accomplishments on Mount Washington, the one record that brought Alton into the public eye, that received media attention all through New England and that landed him his nickname, Mr. Mount Washington, took place on the mountain's west side at about 4,800 feet at a place called Jacob's Ladder.

Named by famed early settler Ethan Allen Crawford because of the area's steep grades, that section of the Cog's ascent up the mountain has a steepest grade of about 37 percent. It was at the very top of this trestle, on a cool but clear September morning, that Alton and his new bride, Cora Carter, became the first couple to get married on the Cog Railway.

The railway smelled a PR bonanza and cooperated completely with Alton in designing the event, not to mention publicizing it heavily. So heavily, in fact, that it was this event that propelled Alton into the national limelight. Dozens of newspapers covered it, and most of Alton's records prior to the wedding were first reported in the context of this story.

He was well known in climbing and hiking circles and was a registered guide for the state of New Hampshire, but he was known for other things too. In fact, Alton's own local newspaper, the *Keene Sentinel*, opened its story on the wedding with the following less-than-epic opening line: "Alton O. Weagle, well-known Keene square dance caller, will be married Saturday." And while I was thrilled to learn that among all his other talents he was also a square dance caller, the facts of his climbing records mostly took a back seat.

But Alton and the Cog aimed to change that and went all in for this event. Alton was interviewed again and again, and over and over he repeated his records to eager newspaper reporters. The Cog named the car used for the wedding "The Honeymoon Special" and affixed a banner to its side for photographers. So eager was railway management to capitalize on Alton's wedding that they had the engine stop in the middle of the trestle and turned off the steam to add to the solemnity of the event.

The Cog reserved an entire forty-four-seat car for the wedding and in the end thirty-eight of those seats ended up being the wedding party. Everyone wanted a piece of the publicity. Keene Mayor Laurence Pickett was part of the party, along with two councilmen. Former New Hampshire Governor Hugh Gregg sent a congratulatory note, which was read aloud. Cog Railway manager Arthur Teague himself made the trip.

And not missing a beat, Alton invited as guests of honor Mr. and Mrs. James Main of Groveton, who in 1941 had become the first couple to get married at the summit of Mount Washington.

Practically lost in all the hoopla was Alton's bride, a widow whom Alton met while working as a driver for the Cheshire Beef Company. Cora Carter is quoted only once in all the writing about the wedding, saying that she was "very much excited" about the event. She did bake her own wedding cake, however—a three-tiered fruit cake that was served at the summit of Mount Washington at a reception after the Cog ride.

The wedding cemented Alton's role in Mount Washington history, gave regional reporters a name to put into their Rolodexes for every time they needed a quote from a "Mountain Man," and appears to have satisfied Alton's desire to set records on his favorite mountain.

In this final act on Mount Washington—to literally create himself, to sing his own song—Alton finally purged the mountain from his soul. To Whitman, passion and obsession about art or a place were the means by which impulse or instinct were unchained from servitude. For Whitman, that impulse took the form of *Leaves of Grass*, which he rewrote and worked on for nearly forty years until his death.

And even though Alton's final big Mount Washington act appeared to have been his last, he wasn't finished setting records. The final chapters in his life had little to do with Mount Washington and everything to do with Alton's endless desire to turn the mundane into the truly unforgettable.

"Great is life . . . and real and mystical . . . wherever and whoever.
Great is death . . . Sure as life holds all parts together, death holds all parts together;
Sure as the stars return again after they merge in the light, death is great as life."

On a warm, clear, early summer morning, I slowly navigate my car into a tight parking space in a far corner of Wheelock Park in Keene, New Hampshire. My windows are rolled down, and I can hear my destination long before I see it—the sharp clink of steel on steel, forty-eight tiny hammers striking forty-eight tiny anvils.

The Lawrence Croteau Courts and Clubhouse are located in the farthest corner of this city park and campground, and I have to walk through a gorgeous grove of red pine to get there. There are bleachers, hot and roasting in the sun, facing the courts, which are behind a chain-link fence.

A sign on the fence reads: "Warning, Beware of Flying Objects."

This is the place where Alton made his final stand, or throw, depending on how you consider his legacy. In 1957 Alton became one of the founders of the Keene Horseshoe Club, and now I am here to meet a champion pitcher.

As a matter of course, pitted against the guiding, records, marriage, and all Alton's other accomplishments, founding a horseshoe club doesn't seem to carry the same weight. After all, among Alton's hobbies in his later years, he became a mountain guard atop Mount Monadnock, where he learned to bake something he called appleberry pies, using apples he carried up and blueberries he found on the mountain. He founded his own orchestra called The Canadians, in which he played drums. He was the founder of the Keene Drum and Bugle Corps. He dreamed up the idea of holding the world's largest square dance on a city main street. And even in his later years, when his muscle began to fail, he donated more than fifty pints of blood to various Red Cross organizations.

But the Keene Horseshoe Club was his final contribution to New Hampshire, and, as it turns out, the world.

And once again, Alton and Walt's paths intersect. I had to look hard for it, but it turns out even America's greatest poet, in his later years, had reason to take up horseshoes. Bill Duckett, the poet's young and controversial companion in the 1880s, wrote that Whitman moved in only three houses down from where he had been living. Duckett and some of his friends had formed a quoit club, an earlier version of horseshoes, and Whitman endeared himself to the lads by buying them all a "handsome set of quoits for pitching." Soon, Bill had moved in with Walt, and the two lived together for five years.

My exploration of the Keene Horseshoe Club is more innocent. And once he's pointed out to me, it's easy to see why forty-five-year-old Rick Howe from Gardner, Massachusetts, is easily the best player on the courts that afternoon. I watch him pitch a game. He's dressed all in blue with a St. Louis Blues baseball hat covering a mop of salt and pepper hair. He has a knee brace. And like a professional baseball player, he has a swing ritual at the beginning of a toss that he repeats with each turn. He throws ringer after ringer, and at the end of a match where he annihilates his opponent, he's gracious, pats him on the back and tells him how much he enjoyed the game.

This is horseshoes and easy to dismiss, but it dawns on me that I'm watching the pitcher equivalent of Wayne Gretzky or Tom Brady. This is not a playground horseshoe club. It is a professional club, twenty-four courts, world league play, certified by the National Horseshoe Pitching Association. In 1965, 1968 and 1974, the club hosted the World Horseshoe Tournaments. And speaking of records, Alton was present at the 1965 tournament when the greatest horseshoe game in the history of the sport took place on Court 10 in a match between Glen Henton of Iowa and Ray Martin of Illinois. The two men tossed an incredible 349 ringers in that one game. All four shoes were on the stake sixty-three times during the game. Glen squeaked out the win, 52-49, after nearly 390 horseshoes had been pitched.

Alton's Keene Horseshoe Club wasn't a passing fancy. The club is one of the best in the world. Inside the clubhouse, in a dusty folder in a corner under some rules manuals, I find a typed club history written by *Keene Sentinel* reporter Tom Blake. Alton was the one who got the ball rolling, finding a few interested pitchers, looking up the rules, writing to the national organization and pressuring the city government to cough up enough space for the courts to be built. As it turned out, Alton was a terrible pitcher. In the history, Blake deadpans, "He pitched only about 15 percent ringers playing horseshoes, but he was a pretty good candlepin bowler."

But despite the credentials and all-or-nothing determination that helped Alton build the Keene club into a horseshoe powerhouse, I'm reminded of what all this is about by Rick Howe. We chat between games—he's competing in a regional tourney—and he sips Coors Light out of a can and shows me his shoes (Deadeye brand, ten pounds), explains his style of throw (turn and a quarter) and reminisces about his father teaching him the sport, which he's played since he was eleven.

But then he gets to the heart of the matter.

"There's a special aspect to all this," he says. "The people are friendly. These are all salt of the earth types, and I just love being with them."

Alton would be proud. So would Walt. As am I.

"I know I have the best of time and space—
  and that I was never measured, and never will be measured.
  I tramp a perpetual journey,
  My signs are a rain-proof coat and good shoes and a staff cut from the woods."

A corner of the long, sweeping summit visitor center juts out beyond the tourist entrance. It's here that state park employees, observatory staff, and volunteers use an open storage space to carry in goods and supplies during the winter months. In the summer, it's rarely used. But outside, just under the pile of summit rocks, the area serves as a nice shelter from the wind and a perch to watch the summit madness, full of hikers, runners and families milling about the highest place in New England.

The weather up here is less than ideal. A foggy mist rolls up over the Tip-Top House and seems to cascade down onto the summit cone, a swirling gray blob of air. I am sweat-soaked through and through, and clearly a bit dehydrated and dry-mouthed from reading aloud to the mountain.

I'm only about ten vertical feet from the actual summit, but I hesitate to make that last walk.

I think about how many times Alton was up here, how when he was taking tourists to the top via the Cog he put them on the train and would pocket his ride share and run alongside all the way up in order to make a little extra cash. This place, this holy place, gave Alton life, energized him, tested him. Mount Washington gave him a reason to be Alton Weagle.

And all that despite the tourism, the hot dogs at the concession stand, the cars and shuttles and motorcycles. All that despite the "damn fools" Alton recalled helping to rescue.

I bunch up my collar and smile pleasantly at the few people who look sideways at me. I stick out up here, of course, but perhaps not as much as the tourists who are wandering around at 6,288 feet, freezing in shorts and T-shirts because it was 70°F at the base when they started up.

Alton's love affair with this mountain was identical to Whitman's love affair with New York. The poet took long constitutionals—he called them saunters—aimlessly seeking out signs of the lifeblood of his city, much as Alton sought personal epiphany from the rocks, trails, and elevation of this mountain.

Whitman would sit for hours in one place, watching and writing about the hectic lifestyle of those who passed him by, people who "run after steam boats, with hats flying off and skirts streaming behind!"

That was just like what I was doing now, watching tourists rushing to the museum to buy a refrigerator magnet, shivering in line to get their picture taken next to the summit sign or dropping their quarters into a tower viewer to try to find some distant landmark.

And then it occurred to me: Weagle and Whitman didn't find revelation in spite of the rushing of people; they found it because they were surrounded by them. Walt loved standing out, proclaiming his witness to the heartbeat of America, not just in New York but among all living things. And Alton loved showing off, not to be boastful but because he wanted others to feel about this place like he did—and he didn't care if those people were his family, hikers, or tourists.

Both men created their own passion and then lived it unapologetically.

I take a long, deep breath there in the swirling mist, the mountain air tinged with the fumes of the nearby shuttle exhaust. I stand and begin to read:

My left hand hooks you round the waist,
My right hand points to landscapes of continents, and a plain public road.
Not I, nor anyone can travel that road for you,
You must travel it for yourself.
It is not far . . . it is within reach.

The tourists seem to move aside as I climb those final few feet, parting like a madman is passing. My voice grows stronger as I attain the summit; the two souls of Alton and Walt feel comfortable in my breath, like the three of us are sharing the same lofty air here above New England.

I run my fingers over the damp summit sign, the deep groove that forms the W in Washington. I look around. There is no view, and perhaps that's as it should be. People are waiting, watching me.

"All done," I say to the spirits as I shut *Leaves of Grass* and head off to find a shuttle down.

— CHAPTER FOUR —

Voyage of Life

Life Lessons on the Passion of Grief
from a Ninety-Seven-Year-Old Runner

At the starting line of the annual Mount Washington Road Race, I stare at the back of the head of ninety-seven-year-old George Etzweiler, but I'm thinking about my father, Joseph, who passed away thirteen days ago.

My sister, Andrea, was at my dad's side when he went. For years, she and her family had been his caretaker, bringing him in to live with my nephews, making the arrangements of his care taking, and finally, rightfully, being with him as he passed. He was eighty-nine.

So now, mid-way through my study of this mountain, I'm struggling to focus. I don't want to be here. My heart feels heavy and raw; my legs can't possibly be up to the challenge of today. I feel guilty and lost at being without either parent for the first time in my life.

And there he is in front of me, this incredible little man—his shock of white hair standing nearly straight up on his head—ready to run up this mountain once again. I was thrilled a couple months earlier when George and his family enthusiastically gave me permission to run with them, to be part of his team this morning, a team that consisted of Berta DeDonato, George's trainer; Bob Etzweiler, George's grandson; and Kirk Horton, a film student from New York making a documentary on George. With me, the team came to five.

But now, as the huge running crowd gathers and I try to regulate my breathing, I just look at George and see only my dad. I don't know if I'll be any use to them. I begin to question this whole year, the point of this whole project, the end result of which my father won't see. In my bones, I can feel my confidence wavering, feeling as fleeting as the wispy clouds moving over the summit above us. I just don't know if I can do this.

The starting cannon snaps me out of my daze. "Let's go!" George says, more to himself than anyone around him. I can feel the familiar gravity and heat of being surrounded by hundreds of people as they begin to move as one. The race begins. I try to shake off the doldrums and move with the crowd. The mountain waits for us.

It is the winter of 2014. Meena is eight months pregnant with Uma. And I'm sitting in my dad's hospital room, trying to talk to him, but thinking about his stroke.

I froze when I got the simple text from Andrea, my sister: "Dad had stroke, on way to hospital." As a reporter, you're taught to distill information, to base your coverage decisions on what's important, what's real, and how fast the information is coming. That text message gave me so little to go on, yet generated so much fear; I just sat there on my bed, late at night, nearly five hundred miles away from him, unable to move.

"It doesn't matter," my wife said. "If it's nothing or serious, you're going home, soon, in the morning. Just focus on that."

So that's what I did.

I spend most of my days here with him, or down the street at a cafe when he's asleep, and I'm able to begin to get to know his nurses a bit. They are polite and engaging. At one point, a nurse asks him what he used to do for a living, and she seems taken aback as he launches into a story about working in the steel mills for most of his life. From the window in his room, we can look west toward Lake Erie, over the dome of the grand Our Lady of Victory Basilica and to the Buffalo waterfront where the mills sat, where my dad worked, where now a row of wind turbines cast shadows on the brownfield sites that remain where the great power that drove this city used to reside.

He never took me to work when I was a boy. He never took me because he said that a steel mill wasn't where I should work, isn't the place where I should end up. He was afraid I'd like it, so he never took me.

Nurses call him sweetie and hon. A very young nurse in a beautiful light blue hajib says, "It's been a real pleasure taking care of you today, buddy!" I watch my father take in this attention from all these young woman. As she tests his eye movements, one nurse compliments him on his shining blue eyes and he actually appears to flirt with her. He tells her they hadn't always been blue.

What? I think. "What?" she says. But he can't get it out. "Oh, you know . . ." and he trails off, the connection between whatever clever explanation was in his head and his ability to bring it to words, cut off.

The stroke did that to him, of course, sliding between his brain and his mouth and throwing up roadblocks. He was always a man of few words, and now even fewer.

Still, despite the challenges, if I close my eyes tightly I can imagine him using this charm on my mother, in another lifetime. It worked back then, apparently, as my mother's diary entry for the day the two met is simple and direct: "I met the man I'm going to marry." I make a mental note to ask him what he said to her that day at a bowling alley.

During the days I'm there, we spend idle time chatting about family, his two grandsons (my nephews), and of course the granddaughter who's on her way. We both avoid the obvious disclaimer—whether or not he'll be able to hold on long enough to meet her.

My dad was an older parent like me, in his early forties when I was born. And I beat him up pretty good, doing somersaults on his belly, canoe trips, backyard camping, messing around with him in his basement tool room. It never actually occurred to me that he was old; he was just my dad. Later, when I got to high school and college and was sometimes told how nice it was that my grandfather came with me, it started to sink in.

He just seems tired now, done with the running. Done with being an older dad, just wanting to be old instead. But there are still hints when he talks about the coming baby.

He gives me advice about his coming granddaughter, little nuggets like, "You're in for a world of trouble changing a girl's diaper; boys aren't as messy." Those moments make me feel like he's still engaged, still interested and looking forward to maybe having one more little one on his belly, or at least his knee.

If nothing else I know he's a flirt, and I'm sure my daughter will bring out those blue eyes one more time. If only he can last that long.

In past years, I've covered the Mount Washington Road Race for *Competitor Magazine* and served as a cheerleader for friends, but I have never made the cut to run, as my wife did, twice. Elite runners, the ones from Colorado and California, have the option to run year after year. Invitations also go out to some of the running clubs around the country.

George has been welcomed back year after year, as often as he could, and as long as his health held. This year, his number is ninety-seven, same as his age.

The rest of us put our names in a lottery in March, and then wait to see if we're selected. I don't know what it feels like to win that lottery, but I can tell you there is a little bit of relief in not winning.

One of those runners who did win the lottery, twice, was my old friend and longtime hiking partner Neil Lovett, of Gilford, New Hampshire. Back in my days as an arts and entertainment reporter in Manchester, Neil was my photographer; a startling shot Neil took of Willie Nelson still hangs in my office. We hiked Mount Katahdin in Maine and nearly died together during a grueling and ridiculous winter hike of Mount Carrigain in below-zero weather.

That first time, when Neil got in and I didn't, that was the hardest part. I wanted to run with him.

"Lining up at the start of that race was one of the most intimidating experiences of my life," he recalled. "They ask you to line up where you think you're going to finish, so naturally, I headed toward the back."

Intimidating. That's the word used by nearly every Mount Washington runner I've ever talked to. Here's why: A runner must gain 4,650 feet of elevation in the 7.6 miles to the finish line. The average grade on the way up is 12 percent, with a heart-exploding grade of 22 percent at the end of the race. And once the runners are out into the open, above treeline, there's no telling what weather awaits them. Runners, even some of the most elite in the world, simply accept that they will walk part of this race, make it part of their strategy for tackling the mountain.

Neil, for example, attempted to run the whole race, but that lasted only 3.5 miles before he realized that the time and energy being expended trying to "run" was actually slower than if he simply walked.

Many runners adopt what's called a philosophy of incrementalism on the mountain. You start running high and walking low and end up running low and walking high. In other words, you might run five hundred paces and walk one hundred, but by the end of the race you're running one hundred and walking five hundred. Or just plain walking. The race gives you three hours to get up there to have your time count, but there are dozens of official, registered runners each year who don't make it in that time, but finish anyway. Partly because in order to get a ride down, you need to get to the summit.

But there's something else that happens to you, a hook that the mountain sinks into your skin. I have felt that connection many times on this mountain—from the trails, the SnowCoach, and the observatory. But today, feeling the most depressed and out of touch with the mountains as I ever have, I was being called upon to help a near centenarian get to the top. But I'd soon learn that as much as I was part of his team, as much as my job was to somehow help George, it soon became clear that it would be this inspirational man from Pennsylvania who'd be helping me.

In February of 2015, my daughter is two months old, it's the middle of winter, we have our own health issues to tend to and can't yet get to

Buffalo to visit my father. My sister calls me and says, "Dad is dying, you need to talk to him."

My father has suffered some sort of episode. He's drifting in and out of consciousness, mumbling. My sister calls a priest who performs Catholic Last Rites while I listen on the phone. My father-in-law is with us that week, and I move to the kitchen to sit among family; I can't bear to be alone while this is happening.

There is a surreal fog about all of this. After waiting so long, after the plans to see my dad soon, after everything we all had forged through to make sure Dad met the baby at least once, for this to happen now, out of nowhere, is a cruel turn. Death is not so terrible as dying itself, as being part of the dying. Were I to have been told that my father had passed, the sadness would be deep but contained, like an empty bucket. But paying witness in this way—by phone—was like watching the bucket empty out and not being able to at least let the water flow through my fingers.

"I'm putting the phone to his ear now," my sister says. "Say what you need to."

I want to shout at him to not dare leave yet. How can you be so inconsiderate, I want to yell, why do you not wish to meet your only granddaughter? Don't go!

"Dad, I love you, Dad," I say instead, crumbling, the words, I'm sure, not making any sense. Meena stands by the side of the chair. My house is so quiet. "I love you." I say this again. Later, I think of all sorts of things I could have said. That I'd make him proud. That I'll be a good dad. Heck, to say hello to Mom. But I don't.

There's a commotion on the other side of the line, voices, movement. I hear my sister saying something but can't make it out. After a few minutes of this, she comes back on the phone.

"He's back."

"What?"

"He's just back." Her voice is trembling as well. "He just sort of opened his eyes and sat up and said he was hungry. I don't know. I just—he seems okay. Let me call you back."

Not this time. Not yet. He decided to stay. We still had time.

Moments before the starting cannon goes off, I ask George what his running strategy will be for today's race.

"Slow," he deadpans.

This attitude—mischievous, self-mocking, humble—as it turns out, is not some affectation in response to all the attention a nearly hundred year old man running marathons is bound to receive. As I came to know George over the year, it became clear that this is who he is. And maybe those traits are part of the reason he's made it this long.

This is the twelfth time George is running up Mount Washington. The first time was at the age of sixty-nine in 1989. He has won his age group seven out of the eleven years he's run the race. The fact that in recent years his age category has been a field of one doesn't matter a bit to him. He currently holds three all-time Mount Washington Road Race records: 85–89, 2005, 2:33:20; 90–94, 2011, 2:48:25 and 95–99, 2015, 3:28:41.

It seems unlikely that those records will be beat, and in 2020, race officials will have to create a new category—100+—just so he can set that record.

In an interview for some local media a couple years ago, George said that he hoped the Auto Road would have a hearse waiting for him at the top of the mountain for his one hundred-year-old race because he planned on dropping dead after crossing the finish line. But he's changed his tune as that goal begins to become a possibility.

"Yeah, I think I could go past that maybe," he tells me. "Still, I always tell anybody who's up there with me to just make sure I'm dead before you call 911!"

The pack of runners moves, first down a slight incline—the only one of the entire race. The road then makes a hard left, jags upward and stays that way for the remaining haul. When I was running seriously, there used to come a moment in many long races where I'd switch to what I jokingly called "old man shuffling" where I wasn't quite walking but wasn't quite running either. It was a kind of in-between movement that let me rest a bit, but kept me sort of running.

Now, as George begins the long turn upward, he steps himself into a kind of old man shuffle pace—a not quite a walk, not quite a running stride—that he'll basically hold for the entire run. It's fast enough that I'm not exactly walking and can pretty immediately feel a tingle in my thighs as the grade comes up to greet us.

I keep step pace behind him, giving him a solid few feet, watching how he approaches his breathing and steps. Rhythm comes fast with him, an obviously practiced breathing routine and stance. He is clearly and immediately aware of his pacing; it's pretty awesome and intimidating to watch. This is what a nearly one hundred-year-old ultra-athlete looks like. After the first half mile, despite his old man shuffle, I become aware that I may not be able to keep up with him.

Before long, we more or less have the road to ourselves. The leaders are nearing the top, the main pack is scrimmaging a half mile ahead. But George's pace is his own, and the team is here to support that. Bob, Berta, and Kirk catch up, each having their own role to play, and the five of us fall into a sort of collective pace. When Bob reaches George, he touches his grandfather's shoulder. "Doing good?"

"We there yet?" George asks.

Bob wears a baseball hat, the back of which has the inscription "Just One Hill." A hunter and outdoorsman from northern Vermont, Bob's big black beard just touches the top of his t-shirt. He and his dad, George's son, have been the driving force behind what's becoming an annual family tradition.

George and most of his family are from the State College, Pennsylvania area. Each year the family will rent a couple cabins in Lincoln, New Hampshire, spend a couple days hiking, and then help George tackle the mountain. His son and daughter, along with some other family, are waiting at the top for him.

We all chat as we walk. George focuses on his breathing. Down here, the day is warm; the breeze is above treeline so we slowly peel off layers to keep him from overheating. I'm the only one carrying a day pack, so George's windbreaker and gloves get put in there, and I'm thrilled to be able to help.

Kirk lines up a couple shots of George walking past. He's wearing a big camera contraption, like a harness, that allows him to swing and move the camera without the shot being shaky. That thing looks heavy, but Kirk's young. I learn that this will be both Kirk's and Berta's first time to the top of Mount Washington.

George uses humor and self-deprecation to stem the tide of well wishes as we move up. Folks at the water stations cheer. Spectators along the road take pictures. By the end of the race, I'd estimate that George will show up in the iPhone of several hundred strangers.

I mostly try to keep out of his and Bob's way. They have a system: George needs focus, and Berta works hard to keep a dialogue going with George about his breathing, how his muscles are feeling, and hydration.

At a quiet point, somewhere around the four-mile mark and near the spot Ernie dropped me off for my trek down four months ago, I notice George is looking quiet and focused, so I ask him what he generally thinks about while on a run like this.

"Well, for the first half, I try to get to the second half," he says, between long pulls of air. "Then, in the last half I'm usually thinking, 'why in the hell would I be doing this again?'"

George grins and takes a deep breath, but below that humor there's something more lurking, a determination that keeps him moving. I wouldn't understand George's deeper motivations until many months later, when I traveled down to Pennsylvania and he took me up his other mountain.

In May of 2015, only a couple months after my father's episode, we pack his five-month-old granddaughter in the car and drive nearly five hundred miles to visit him for the first time. Even at such an early age, Uma has a fierce spirit, unafraid, curious.

My sister meets us in her driveway and sweeps the baby into her arms, auntie and niece together for the first time. Uma squeals in delight through the kisses. My two nephews, Ben and Max, run out to greet their new cousin. It takes us all a while to get into the house. The collective past few months of unknowns, my sister's rock-like character in the face of taking care of our father, all seems to waver and soften. The baby is here. We are here. We made it.

Later, at my dad's assisted living home, I'm trembling as I lift Uma out of her car seat and carry her to my dad's room. She's bubbly, straining to understand her surroundings. Every single person who sees her—residents, nurses, visitors—smile, laugh, want to touch her, speak to her. Just walking with her the one hundred yards or so to his room becomes a little overwhelming.

This is a place of finality. I don't recognize that as a bad thing, but to be here is to be in a place where the light will extinguish. To bring a six-month-old here is like holding a brilliant, burning lantern up to those who have little glow left. To some, Uma is a reminder of mortality. To others, she is hope and strength. It occurs to me that this has nothing to do with Uma. This is life.

My dad is waiting for us, sitting in his wheelchair near his bed in a bathrobe over a sweatshirt and sweatpants. He's in his socks. With his round face, stringy silver hair and oversized glasses, I'm reminded of a Muppet. He's seen Uma through pictures and Facetime, talked to her.

"Hi, Dad," I say. "This is Uma." I sit next to him on the bed. The room smells like cough drops and tea. There's a newspaper scattered on his reading tray. "Uma, this is your grandfather. This is my daddy."

She squirms a bit. This is an unfamiliar place. I can't put her on my dad's lap; he'd be unable to hold her. So, I move her to my knee so she's within reach, and she puts her tiny hand on his. There are eighty-seven years separating them.

"Well, aren't you just a doll," he says. "You're a little dolly."

And for the briefest of moments, everything comes together. I understand that we're just stardust, that the odds of this meeting even happening are too astronomical to even calculate. I understand the connection between time, realize that history isn't linear, that the circumstances that brought me (us) here—the geography of location, schools, jobs, our marriage, all of it—retreats into the pin prick of this second, in this place, with these humans.

I am changed. We are changed. My father's weathered hand, his knuckles twisted at angles from factory work, his nails thick, palms wrinkled, and my baby's pink, unlined fingers, thin and untested—their skin touches, and somewhere an old man dies and a new baby comes alive and another star is born amid a rupture that creates a new galaxy and we all spin again and again.

And then it's gone. Their hands move away. Uma retreats to her mother's lap, and I put my arm around my dad's shoulders, and he just smiles and shakes his head.

"Such a doll," he says again. "Such a doll."

After nearly four hours, George is powering through. The elites crossed the finish line three hours ago and already are back down, under the big tent, feet up, getting back rubs. Most of the secondary crowd has finished. Some are down already, some hanging out at the top watching finishers, some eating pizza at the summit concession. The news crews and photographers are mostly gone. The auto road is open to traffic.

But George Etzweiler continues, head down, huffing deeply, with the help of his family, to run his own race. A century of heart beating to the rhythm of the stone; deep, long pulls of air against the warm wind at his back. Every so often he'll wobble and Bob will touch his shoulder or back. Or if a sideways wind hits him, he'll tip back and I'll touch his back. These moments don't lend any equilibrium to George; the human touch is just a reminder to refocus and regain energy. He'll feel a finger at his elbow and straighten and keep putting one foot in front of the other.

I don't use this word often, but his effort is remarkable. With about a half mile to go, we are alone, perhaps the last ones left in the

race. Organizers give runners three hours to get to the top to attain an official time. They waive that requirement for older runners, and for George.
He'll get an official time no matter how long it takes him to get there. The
weather is cool but clear, and there are drivers, runners, hikers all around
us, coming and going. And something amazing begins to happen.

As runners heading down pass our little team, they fall silent, or in
some cases gently touch George's shoulder or hand, touching the man like
he was a patron or a prophet, like you would pay respects to a holy man.

The first people here in New Hampshire named the mountain
Agiocochook because there on top was the home of the Great Spirit.

There's precedent for this, of course, going back not just to the
Paleo-Indians of what is now Northern New England, but across the
globe. In Japan, mountain worship is referred to as Sangaku Shinko,
and is common among Shintoists. In Nepal, the Sherpa name for
Everest is Chomolungma, or Mother of the World, and the high
Himalayan peaks are thought to be the homes of the gods. Some
American Christians practice a new form of prayer called Worship
Evangelism, based on the Old Testament, where they come together
at a summit to celebrate.

Watching George, I think of the passage from scripture, Micheas 4:1.

And it shall come to pass in the last days, that the mountain of the
house of the Lord shall be prepared in the top of the mountains,
and high above the hills, and people shall flow to it.

Mount Olympus. Mount Etna. Mount Sinai. Mount Fuji. The list
goes on and on, holy heights, sacred rocks; mountains as cultural plat-
forms, literally, for the gods, and we have been flowing to the top since
we could walk.

And like many of the holy men from those legends, George is a
reluctant prophet, simply trying to connect a century of flesh and blood
to the ancient rock, while cars full of young runners, teenagers, and
ultra-athletes stop, backing up traffic, to take him in. People roll down

their windows and take pictures and shout over and over again to George, "Thank you!" and "You're beautiful!" and "God bless you!"

Many simply yell out, "Inspiration!"

Sometimes, George lifts a hand or smiles, but at this stage of the race, every ounce of energy needs to be conserved. And besides, this day isn't about God, it's about muscle and guts, and about George doing it his way.

It is one year earlier, and my father is being stubborn. Again.

His laundry sits bunched in a corner. He hasn't left his room all day, and the frustrated nurses at his assisted living facility tell us he rarely ever asks them for help, even if something is wrong.

"I just don't want to bother anyone," he says. "They have better things to do."

I'm not surprised. This is the man my sister and I have come to know. Since leaving his home of forty years, he's become more insular, less likely to reach out. My father has never been an open, emotional man—part and parcel of that generations' modesty.

After growing up during the Depression on the East Side of Buffalo, he spent his life in the steel mill and knew nothing but work and being a provider. And now, here he was, forced to have people do things for him, and he didn't like it one bit. In fact, he openly resisted, just letting little things (or what he thought was little things) slide so other people wouldn't be bothered by him.

"That's why they're here, Dad," my sister says. "That's why you're here."

My sister is a caregiver, and up until he became too much of a handful, my dad lived with my sister and her family. My father's strong will was passed down to my sister; she is our (my) rock, my touchstone of level-headedness and strength. Over the years, I've spent sleepless nights mulling over the fact that I don't believe I could take care of anyone like she is able to do. It pains me to admit so.

She heads out to talk to one of his nurses, and we're given some time alone.

These past couple years have been difficult for him, and us. He seemed to be burning through his nine lives with each passing episode after the stroke—bouts of delirium, falling—worse than the last. But, he just kept bouncing back. Now though, he's tired, like he's beginning the process of giving up.

"Your sister is always mad at me for something," he says, but he's smiling when he says it. "It's like being in the Army again."

He brings up his Army days quite a bit. My father was drafted, right at the end of World War II, and spent a couple years in occupied Japan. He was a supply sergeant and what he calls a "fixer upper," keeping equipment functioning and the men geared up.

"Was somebody always mad at you then?" I ask. Dad's short term memory is shot. Ask him what he had for breakfast, and he'll just shrug. Ask him about his time in the war, and it pours out. I've heard a lot of Army days stories, but I am willing to hear one again if it means getting our minds off his stubbornness. But instead, he opens up, and for one rare moment in time, I begin to finally understand the man he became.

"Not the ones you'd think," he says. And then he tells me a story I'd not heard before, a story that begins about four hours away from Osaka, where he was stationed, on the tallest mountain in Japan.

"We had gotten it into our heads to drive up Mount Fuji," my father begins. "Of course you can't actually drive all the way up, and the roads were terrible back then. But me and a couple buddies 'borrowed' a Jeep and we took off. We didn't know what we were doing, but we were bored and we thought we could get up there.

"Remember, we were occupiers. Those people . . ." He drifts off for a moment, searching for words. "They should have hated us. Maybe they did, I don't know. But there we were on our way up this mountain, three American Army guys, off base, thinking we owned the place.

"And then of course, the Jeep broke down halfway up. Well, I couldn't get the damn thing fixed. We didn't know what was happening. But every one of those people who walked passed us, do you know what they did?"

I shake my head.

"They asked if they could help. They didn't care that we were in their country. Or if they did, it wasn't their way to ask. So, they just wanted to help us." Another long pause and a laugh. "Maybe they just wanted us off their mountain!"

And as my dad tells me this story that took place sixty-five years ago, I realize suddenly, he's telling me who he is, how he became the man I have always known as my father.

"So, we just put that thing in neutral, opened it up and coasted all the way back down that mountain, flying down who knows how fast!

"We get to the bottom, and this tiny old man comes up to us. None of us can understand a word he's saying, but he sticks his head under the hood, does something, and just like that the Jeep starts up. Can you imagine our surprise! We're all shaking his hand and patting him on the back, but he's embarrassed, waving us off."

"So what happened to him?" I ask breathlessly.

"He just walked away." My dad leans back in his wheelchair, story finished, lost in a time in his past when he wasn't quite a boy, but wasn't yet a man, wearing the uniform that defined his identity up until that moment. "What he wanted, which I guess was for us to not be there, didn't matter. He wasn't angry, or sad. He was quiet. He helped us and he left. That's it."

Could this one small moment while my father was a young soldier representing his country in a far away and hostile land have served as the foundation of the man he became? This reluctance to complain, to seek help, to simply bury his own needs under the recognition that most folks are in a far worse place. Why bother troubling someone over clean laundry? This little old man had just lived through war and despite that, stopped to fix the engine of his occupier's Jeep.

My sister comes back in and the connection between us breaks. She tells him that the nurses are going to be fine with checking in on him more often, but if he needs anything he'll have to speak up.

He and I share a knowing glance, before he sighs, and says. "All right, show me again how to operate that help button."

George is talking about inspiration. More specifically, he's attempting to put into words how he feels about being an inspiration for runners, or anyone really. In the time that I have known him, I've never known him to have difficulty expressing himself.

"I keep being told that, but I don't think I feel that way," he says, running his hand through his mat of white hair, which, as always, is standing straight up on his head. "I've never felt terribly competitive. I don't try to run races to get medals."

It is six months since we ran together in the Mount Washington race. We sit in his daughter Shirley's home, where George now lives, in State College, Pennsylvania. George looks sharp in gray slacks and a dark cardigan. Around his neck, he wears what is essentially an amplifier, a plastic box about twice the size of a matchbook designed to turn up his hearing aids.

Shirley's home is a low, one-floor Prairie-style ranch on a surprisingly quiet residential street, considering it sits just up the road from Beaver Stadium, home of the Penn State Nittany Lions and the third largest stadium in the world.

For thirty-seven years, George was a professor of electrical engineering at Penn State. He retired in 1990.

"I'm costing the retirement system an awful lot of money," he says.

The walls of the living room are covered with paintings and photographs of the White Mountains and Mount Washington. Above the fireplace mantel is his 2016 Mount Washington Hall of Fame plaque. Shirley brings me a cup of steaming coffee in a white ceramic mug with an image of snow-covered Mount Washington on it. I lean back, sip coffee there in the home of one of the greatest athletes to ever set foot on Mount Washington, and let George tell me the story of his life.

He feels a bit anxious this day. He recently strained the glutes in his left leg and was taking most of the month off, and he was eager to get back into training because as much as his leg might hurt now when he runs, "lying in bed would be a lot worse."

My first thought is how a nearly one hundred-year-old man could get back to training after an injury, any injury, but my curiosity is quickly dispelled. He's already had cartilage damage to his knee repaired, bypass surgery when he was eighty, and he broke an ankle on a flight of stairs when he was ninety. He has a pacemaker.

It seems that physical damage can't stop the man. But he is slowing down.

"I'm seeing signs of my physical limitations because I seem to have hit a wall in 2017," he says. "As the years go by I'm getting slower and more tired quickly."

His time six months ago was a full half hour slower than his time in 2016.

"How are you handling that?" I ask.

"I have to get more naps." George doesn't miss a beat.

We both laugh, but he knows what question I'm really asking.

"I've never been afraid to talk about death," he says and trails off before mentioning his wife, Mary. "I guess I just never wanted to die before her and leave her with any sort of trouble."

She was born Mary Ada Richards. A friend of George's was organizing a class reunion and asked George if he wouldn't mind taking her. In Kirk's film, called "For the Love of Mary," George explains his love in the simplest possible way.

"I guess she brought out the urge to protect and dedicate my life to her," he says.

They married in May 1942. Mary died of pulmonary fibrosis in December 2010, two days before Christmas.

When George started running at the age of forty-nine, he had not run one full mile at once before that. He was overweight and says he couldn't stay awake in the afternoons. Mary supported his new hobby, running occasionally with him, encouraging him to go longer, harder. Back in those early days of running, Mary bought George a green knee-length pair of shorts—he continues to use those shorts fifty years later for every Mount Washington race.

"Her dying was hard," George says. "Emotionally, I had to just go and keep running. I felt like I wanted to go out and keep running and not stop."

And he hasn't.

Grief is not a pinprick, not a sliver. Grief is a hole blown into your heart, a gaping wound that begins sucking you down, burning out your life from the inside. It can't be repaired permanently, but you can fight it, patch it with passion and memories. But you have to get to it fast, recognize the danger, immediately begin working on living with that hole in your heart. Work on living.

I am not a fan of running, though I do run. It has never brought me the sort of euphoric pleasure that, say, hiking or writing has. I *do* like finishing, though. This is called intrinsic value running—I need to be healthy because of some greater purpose, therefore I endure the creaky knees.

But ultra-runners like George aim for a higher level of experience, sometimes called a Sartean Phase, named after the French philosopher Jean Paul Sartre. In this phase, reason has no authority over you, motivation plays no role. If there was a pill that gave you all the same benefits of running, you still would run because of the purity of the act itself. Further, Sartre would tie this relationship of a pure act to anguish. Running, for example, is not easy and it can hurt, but that pain, despite the odds and the challenge, is a sort of freedom.

And that anguish can come in many forms. Survivor guilt. Uncertainty. Anxiety.

Grief.

There's a pause in our conversation, a moment perhaps where our mutual heartbreak bubbles to the surface, but it doesn't last long. George takes a deep breath and says, "Would you like to see where I train?"

"Your gym?"

"No," he says. George turns, looks outside the large living room window and points to a ridge in the distance. "The mountain!"

Shirley drives, and they give me the passenger seat. George sits in back, between us, talkative and excited like a teenager, like a man returning to a place that allows him to be free.

Tussey Mountain in nearby Boalsburg is a 1,819-foot ski area mountain with a hard-pack road to the top. This is George's mountain, where he trains for Washington, where he tests his muscle, heart, and head three times a week.

George chatters on as we drive out to the mountain: about his running group, where the other men live, their strategy for running up Tunney, and what draws him to this little peak.

"I don't feel like I train very hard," George says, once again wildly understating the extent of the work he does, fifteen to twenty miles a week. He says he's run up Tunney "maybe five hundred" times.

"I just want to go out there and do that mountain," he says. "When we're out there, it's just silence and peace and we can't find anything to argue about."

The average grade on Tussey is about six percent, child's play compared to Mount Washington, but it doesn't take me long to realize that it's this place—not the Rock Pile—that generates George's light and strength.

"See that switchback here? You have to be careful coming around," he says as we drive up, like a sports announcer doing a play-by-play of a mountain road. "This is the halfway point, and right here is the steepest slope."

In 1842, Thomas Cole painted a four-part series of landscapes titled *The Voyage of Life*. Each painting depicts a different season in the life of man: Childhood, Youth, Manhood and Old Age. Each stage is represented by the four seasons, and by a river travelling through a mountainous landscape. While painted as a Christian allegory of man's faith journey, I'm reminded of the series as I listen to George talk about Tussey.

"With winter coming, we don't go up here as often," George says. "When the weather is bad, we run on the side streets near the ski area down below. There's a good loop down there."

On any other trip through this area, I would barely even recognize the tiny, nondescript mountain as anything other than a bump in the landscape. But a person's connection to geography is personal and intimate, and to George it's everything,

Shirley pulls over near a rise in the road. There's a small beaten path that leads up a little higher. Some swirling, nearly imperceptible snow has begun to fall.

"This is it," George says, enthusiastically launching himself out of Shirley's truck, eager to show me around. "This the top of the road and our turnaround point when we run."

There are no views, no memorials or flowers, only a patchwork of leafless poplar and beech, many with tiny rings of lichen growing in intricate circles on their trunks.

"This is a beautiful tree," George says. He scrambles up a rise near the road and leans against the largest tree in the area, just him and his little mountain.

I step up there with him, put away my pencil and pad, cinch up the collar on my fleece and say, "Tell me about your mountain, George."

He does, and for a little while, this bump in the middle of Pennsylvania is the fountain of George's power, his mountain of youth. This is his landscape, the place where he runs to live, he runs to remember, and he runs for Mary.

Three weeks before stepping onto Mount Washington with George, and six months before George took me to Tussey Mountain, I have my final conversation with my father. He's lucid, aware—a rare time. We sit together in a sunlit room just off the dining area of his center, just before dinner. The room is packed with other residents waiting to be let in. It's noisy and chaotic, but I'm glad to see activity and movement.

He has one week to live.

We navigate through our standard small talk. He used to like food a lot more than he does now. One of my favorite memories with him is when I was a kid, maybe seven or eight, he'd announce that it was "man time," and he and I would sit at the kitchen table and make the stinkiest, most preposterous sandwiches. Limburger cheese. Onions. Mustard. Rye bread. It was man time because the smells would chase my mother and sister out of the room.

Sometime in my teen years, I discovered a box of old Army mess tins from his time in Japan. He just shrugged and said, "Well, let's see." We opened those forty-year-old memories and discovered that, somehow, the crackers were still fresh. We ate them all.

After mom passed, he would cook up catch-all casseroles filled with cheese and hamburger. I never fooled myself into believing he was a healthy eater, but my better memories with him, nonetheless, revolved around eating together.

Today, he doesn't remember what he ate for breakfast and has no idea what's on the menu for dinner.

We move to other subjects—the weather in New England, the batteries in his hearing aids, my work—I show him some pictures of Uma, and he nods.

And then I mention something about how busy my schedule is while I'm in town. In two days, I'd be heading to Toronto for a book signing. He perks up at that, as this is an excellent opportunity for him to let me know that certainly if I had better things to do, that I should be doing those things instead of visiting poor old him.

When I was a younger man, that sort of eye-rolling martyr complex would frustrate me. But not now, we've moved far beyond that, him and I, and I understand him better. This is just him. At his core, someplace deep in his DNA, a need to not be in the way, to not cause trouble, to not be a burden motivates him, even to the end. Like that little man in Japan.

So now, I just laugh. "You're not, Dad, and I don't have a thing that's better than this."

He grunts. "Must be a pretty boring life then."

We both laugh at that and there's a flash of the past, then it's gone behind the clatter of dining room dishes and the squeak of wheelchairs heading for parking spots at meal tables. The room begins to clear out, and we wait until nearly everyone is gone.

"Let me wheel you in there so you can have dinner," I say.

He shakes his head. "I'm just going to sit here for a bit," he says. "You go. The nurse will take me in."

I hesitate but relent. I hug him and stand. "Okay, I'll see you soon. I love you."

"Yeah," he says.

And I leave. And we're done, my father and I.

A week later, at a red light, on my way home from the grocery store, I get a call from my wife telling me to come right home. Come home and call your sister.

The final stretch of auto road to the finish line is brutal. Just awful. It makes you want to die and question your very existence.

After the heat, wind, blacktop, and sweat, the final one hundred yards or so of the road swings west and blasts runners up a 22 percent grade before a final straightaway jaunt to the finish. If the Marquis de Sade designed a race, this would be it.

The upside is that the summit is mayhem. The Cog has just arrived and loads of tourists line the road to watch the final few stranglers making their way to the finish. Many runners remain up top, waiting for exactly this moment. George's reputation precedes him, and people want to see him finish.

Along the lower heights, the sun and breeze were a little rough at times, but up here, the weather is perfect: light, fluffy clouds billowing at the edges, nearly no wind, expansive views.

As we round the final corner and come into view of that final steep climb, the announcer at the finish line starts cheerleading George, saying his name and records. The crowd responds, and people surge forward to the sides of the road. It's been about four hours since the starting gun went off.

We make our way up that 22 percent, crawling up there at six thousand feet, and people cheer wildly. My legs burn; I can't imagine what it feels like to George. Kirk is filming this from some other location up ahead. The three of us walk close at his sides and back at this stage, willing ourselves to be an organic force field to get to the end.

I feel overwhelmed, struggling to keep my focus on this place, this accomplishment.

The team makes it up to the straightway, and I tell Bob I'm going ahead so I can take pictures of George crossing the finish line. I jog the remaining thirty feet and cross the finish line without even realizing that I made it as well. My time won't be registered.

The organizers set up a separate yellow finish line tape for George, and many family members join him in that final few feet. It feels delirious, like barely controlled chaos: the roaring of the crowds, a Cog whistle sounds, the announcer in a frenzy. A nearly one hundred-year-old man has run up this mountain in just over four hours.

Bob and Berta are consummate professionals, keeping their focus on George, staying away from the frenzy, making sure the path is clear. Even to the very end, they monitor his movement.

I watch George, but his head is down, trying to put a final push into the race, willing his white legs to shave another few, final seconds off his time. I wonder what could be inside a man to be able to do this? Is he thinking of Mary?

George hits the yellow tape unceremoniously, simply pushing it aside. His finish lets all the pent-up air out of the people on the summit. The tension of the race gone, people climb up off the rocks and go back inside or on the train or begin the walk down to their cars. The mountain returns to its resting state.

A milk crate is brought out of the signal house, and George collapses onto it. He's given a warm lime green fleece, a gift to all finishers, and someone has put the finisher medal around his neck. Bob stands close, ever the protector.

I give them all space; now is not the time to pepper George with questions. From past races and treks, I'm all too familiar with the post-race low that sinks into your brain once you've finished with such a lofty performance. George looks annihilated, just pale and beat down.

He stares into the middle distance for a while, not responding to anyone's inquires. This is a gaze I'd see over and over again in folks I'd meet through the course of my time around Mount Washington; deeply set, intimate, yet alone. A moment of going inward.

Someone hands George a cup of water, and he comes back out, seems to look around for the first time to see his family surrounding him, and his eyes smile. Bob puts a hand on his shoulder, and George puts his hand over Bob's.

The clouds swirl. The Cog leaves the station. The mountain was kind today. A small white-haired man rests on a milk crate. Soon, everyone will leave that place, and the mica and the wind will return to their own peace again.

The next morning, I'd discover how George really felt. I'd finally understand the depth of what this mountain meant to him. And I'd feel my own guilt and grief finally begin to lift as well.

My father's wake and funeral are as I'd expect. The funeral home has been in the family for years. My mother's wake and funeral took place here in 1982. Family comes, cousins, friends. If you knew my father, you loved him, but he's the last of his generation, so turn out for his wake is light.

The day after he died, I woke up that morning realizing it was the first morning in my half century on Earth that I no longer had a mother or father.

It is the first wake Uma attends, and she doesn't understand. I carry her to dad's coffin and she says, "Wake up, Grandpa."

In the back of my head, in a fog thick enough to be at the summit of Mount Washington, I realize I need to run that race with George in a few days. It's all too much.

But as we stumble through the familiar funeral rites and burial routines, as the hours turn to days, something starts to happen. I begin to learn.

I learn that my dad was far more than just a steel worker or a machine tinkerer, that he was a teacher as well. From all the young (now older) men who worked with him in the mills and machine shops—one after another over the week came to me with stories about my dad as a teacher, how he'd build with them, mentor them as they learned their craft. One man tells me that he enjoyed going to work every day because he was certain that dad would teach him something new. I didn't know that.

I learn that as a scoutmaster, my dad was beloved—that he earned respect not through authority and order, but through compassion and a listening ear. Scout after scout tells me stories of how he changed each of their lives through tiny acts of kindness—helping fix a car, listening to girl problems, always having their backs. One tells me that the respect for my father ran so deep that any show of disloyalty to him would be frowned upon by the troop and a scout's status would diminish. I didn't know that.

I learn that he loved to dress in outrageous Halloween costumes, and I learn that he kept a small notebook of crib notes of jokes in his pocket he liked to tell when he was looking for an icebreaker. He did these things because he loved to be loved, and even though he was a man of few words, those words were often weighted with meaning. A friend called him the Mark Twain of Buffalo. And to meet that goal, to be loved, he would love you first. In his own way to be sure, sometimes quietly, sometimes telling dirty jokes, sometimes just listening to the sob story of a confused teenage Boy Scout.

The formality of the rituals melt into a big banquet at a gin joint named Ray's Lounge that's been a staple of Buffalo's now-Polish Kaisertown neighborhood since the early 1960s. It's the kind of place that still has a piano lounge alongside a bar made of thick glass blocks. Ray's is where you go to spend $15 on lazy pierogi and sweet and sour cabbage, and to drown your sorrow when the family's patriarch dies.

And by the time the second helping of mashed potatoes arrives from the old, well-used kitchen, the mood has lightened and I'm beginning to feel human again. Uma and her mother play with the daughter of one of the cooks, and all the cousins and friends take part in an old Shaker tradition of telling stories about Dad—tales from the Boy Scouts, fishing trips to Canada, Halloween parties.

Once the fruit salad and coffee gets there, Uma and my sister's kids, Max and Ben, are let loose. There they are, at the head of this banquet hall—the boys in dark suits, Uma in a black dress and saddle shoes—and they begin to play. They run. The boys' jackets, and then ties, disappear. The kids are loud, and we let them be. They wrestle, and we let them. They laugh, and everyone needs to hear.

The days of mourning end with the thump of kids' feet on linoleum, my daughter laughing like a lion as the boys circle and tease. This is as it should be, literally the circle of life performed in front of our eyes.

Were dad made aware of this display, he'd shake his head and tell me that I had better things to do, that we all die, that the past is the past and the important stuff is right in front of me. He'd tell me to go get it, go get that.

I see my wife, my sister. I can hear the joy from my daughter and my nephews. My mountain reclines, ever passive. My home is calling me back. Time to move on.

On the morning after the race, with my thighs buzzing pleasantly and the bottom of my feet feeling like a ball-peen hammer had been tapping my toes all day, I swing down to Lincoln where George and his family are holed up inside a cabin compound they rent each year. We're on the other side of the White Mountains here, just south of Franconia Notch and only a couple hundred yards away from the famous Clark's Trading Post, a roadside attraction that dates back to 1928 that used to be called Ed Clark's Sled Dog Ranch. But around 1949 Ed's sons, Murray and Edward, began training bears, and today visitors come from all around the world to watch those bears ride bicycles and jump through hoops.

And though they may not be interested in performing bears, George, Bob, Shirley and the rest of the family—the race behind them—are settling into their yearly role as tourists.

George greets me at the door, lively and spry, his hair still standing straight up, reaching for the sky.

"How do you feel?" I ask.

"I could have pushed myself more," he says, then shrugs. "A little bit sore, but not as much as I should be."

I want to interview him about his cool down rituals, regrets, plan for next year, how it felt up there. My list is long. But none of that is going to happen. The race is over, the heat and the tar and the rocks are behind him. He has other things on his mind this morning.

The little bulldozer, that professor with the mischievous grin and quick joke, does something I don't expect but perhaps should. He walks me around the cabin and then outside and introduces me to his family. All of them. I can't remember all their names, but there are cousins, and grandkids, a daughter-in-law and great-daughter-in-law, if that's the proper term.

Mary's brother came up here in the 1960s, and the tradition grew. It occurs to me that what George is telling me and showing me is really what defines him. The running is a means to last longer, to be able to experience what he actually loves. This place, tiny cabins stacked next to each other like Lincoln Logs, children and family running from porch to porch, fires at the pit in the evening when the sun sinks below the ridge and the air is cool and the fireflies begin to buzz.

George had been coming here with Mary before that first run in 1969. The running was not an end, it was a means to another end. George and I look out the old, bent screen of that cabin that has welcomed his family for decades and watch some grandchildren playing in the packed rock driveway between the cabins. We're alone for a moment between visits from some other campers. And I finally get it. Jean Paul Sarte was wrong. There's another way to achieve freedom from anguish, a purer way to deal with that hole in your heart. George doesn't have to say it, but he does anyway.

"Everybody thinks I come up here each year to run up a mountain," he whispers, as though telling me a secret. "But really, it's for this . . ." He waves his sunburned hand at the family around him.

Then, with a wink, he says, "Though next year, I'm hoping for a better time."

CHAPTER FIVE

Taking a Breather at the Halfway Point

Of Ducks, Minis, Christie Brinkley, and the
Transient Beauty of a Passing Sunset

Quick, what does Mount Washington, Mini Coopers, and 1980s super-model Christie Brinkley have in common?

Give up?

Well, hang on, I'll tell you in a minute. Right now, my goal is to secure as many bathtub rubber duckies for my daughter, Uma, as I can. That goal is fulfilled quickly and easily. Here at the base of Mount Washington on a warm summer evening, I am swimming in rubber duckies. They are literally tossed out into the crowd, handed out to eager collectors. I secure a pirate ducky, a policeman ducky and a clown ducky.

Through the course of the year, the Mount Washington Auto Road opens its gates for a variety of club days—motorcycles, ATVs, veterans, and today, about two hundred Mini Coopers rev and growl, their owners eager to drive to the summit for a sunset.

Today is the annual Minis on Top, a fund-raiser and community event organized by New Hampshire Mini owners. They gather, eat, share their collections of rubber duckies, drive up, watch the sunset, come back down, eat some more, hand out prizes, and generally cause a ruckus. And today, after a half year of hiking, running, walking, talking, and recording, I am merely a passenger, riding shotgun at the invite of my dear friend and hiker Stephen Crossman.

I first met Stephen during a memorable hike up Mount Major. It was my daughter's first big mountain, and we were part of a large group. It was also the first time I climbed something that high with her on my back, so I was slow. But Stephen stayed with us, entertained the baby, told stories. He is also a regular observatory volunteer and gave me all manner of tips as I was getting ready for my own service a couple months ago. His heart is as big as he is and as I climb into his red convertible Mini, I'm eager to sit back and enjoy some views.

Oh, and Christie Brinkley? Turns out the tradition of Minis and rubber duckies began in Flanders, New York, on Long Island. Down in Flanders sits The Big Duck, a roadside attraction built in the 1930s: a building in the shape of a duck to serve as a kind of billboard for what once was a nearby duck farm. Today it's a souvenir shop.

Ed "MAXIMINI" Smith was a friendly man who frequented many Mini events throughout the North East and drove a 2003 electric blue Mini Cooper with white wheels. Ed bought a rubber ducky at The Big Duck, stuck it on his Mini's antenna and then proceeded to hand out rubber ducks to pretty much anyone he met.

The duck love took off, and now Mini owners around the world proudly display their rubber ducky collections in their vehicles. In the mid-eighties, the voice of The Big Duck, played on speakers inside the buildings and out on the grounds, soothingly beckoning the curious to stop by for some "duck-abilia," was none other than Christie Brinkley, who was married at the time to Long Island native Billy Joel.

Meanwhile, the auto road attendants have given the Mini gang the go-ahead and we're off. There's something worth mentioning at this point about Minis. They are low to the ground and have big engines. Combine that with the fact that the auto road is closed, and let's just say this Mini group takes great pleasure to testing the outer limits of what their cars can do.

Stephen waits until the cars ahead of him are out of sight and then lead-foots his 2012 S Mini up that auto road like he's trying to outrun a bear. The top is down, I'm wearing only a fleece and Stephen is blaring classical music; life is good. And when we hit that Cragway dirt and the thick, darkening Presidentials come into view, I marvel at the curious happenstance of a Mini day, how Mount Washington's pull extends deeply into subsets I wouldn't otherwise think would give the mountain a glance. But they come. They all come.

"There's nothing like this," Stephen says at one point, and he says it in a way that makes me think he'd say it even if I wasn't there.

At the top, he heads off to take some pictures. I trot up to the summit to touch the sign out of habit, but I then crawl over behind the Tip-Top House to watch the summer sun set, another first for me.

The fire sky cuts the cotton clouds, leaving violent, jagged tears in them. We're here for a long while, until the summit is nearly empty, and I understand that I am nothing here against the flaming sky. That gives me strength. I take a long, hard breath. Let it out into the sun.

Against this sky, the events of the past few weeks—my dad, my aching body, my troubled mind—seem laughably small. This feels like a place to cry, to recognize my impermanence and mourn what's lost.

Instead, I find comfort in suddenly understanding that beauty is transient, that nothing lasts. That makes it all perfect. The orange sky. The red Minis.

I reach into my jacket pocket and clutch the rubber duckies.

Perfect. It is all perfect.

Photo Album

A MOUNT WASHINGTON AUTO ROAD SNOWCOACH ROARS
THROUGH A FEBRUARY NOR'EASTER AT ABOUT 4,000 FEET.

SNOWCOACH DRIVER AND PHOTOGRAPHER ERNIE MILLS AND I GET
OUT TO STRETCH OUR LEGS IN THE MIDDLE OF A STORM.

THE MAIN TOWER OF THE MOUNT WASHINGTON OBSERVATORY STANDS TALL ABOVE
THE CLOUDS DURING A CHILLY APRIL AFTERNOON AS THE UNDERCAST ROLLS IN.

MARTY THE OBSERVATORY MASCOT LOUNGES ON HIS FAVORITE SHELF
IN THE WEATHER ROOM. KITTY MASCOTS HAVE BEEN CONTINUOUS
RESIDENTS OF THE OBSERVATORY SINCE ITS FOUNDING IN 1932.

MEMBERS OF THE OBSERVATORY CREW CATCH A BRILLIANT SUNRISE ON
THE FIRST MORNING OF MY VOLUNTEER WEEK AT THE SUMMIT.

METEOROLOGIST CALEB
MUETE IN THE OBSERVATORY'S
WEATHER ROOM KEEPS
HIS EYE ON THE RADAR.

AFTER A STORM, RIME ICE HAS NEARLY COVERED THE SUMMIT'S
TIP TOP HOUSE. RIME ICE FORMS WHEN WATER DROPLETS IN FOG
OR MIST FREEZE TO THE OUTER SURFACES OF OBJECTS.

FELLOW VOLUNTEER JOHN DONOVAN AND I FOLLOWING AN
EXCURSION OUT ONTO THE OBSERVATION DECK IN 85 MPH WINDS.
THAT'S RIME ICE THAT HAS FORMED ON OUR JACKETS.

MASTER SEAMSTRESS
MARY SELVOSKI PUTS THE
FINISHING TOUCHES ON MY
WALT WHITMAN COSTUME.
MARY HAS BEEN SEWING
COSTUMES FOR GRANITE
STATE COMMUNITY THEATERS
FOR FORTY YEARS.

DRESSED AS WALT WHITMAN AND READING FROM
LEAVES OF GRASS AT ABOUT 5,000 FEET

TO TAKE PART IN ALTON WEAGLE DAY, I BECAME WALT WHITMAN, COMPLETE WITH BEARD AND FLOPPY HAT. (THE HIKING BOOTS WERE MY OWN ADDITION.)

THE ALTON WEAGLE DAY CLASS OF 2017 LINEUP NEAR THE START OF THE MOUNT WASHINGTON AUTO ROAD. AMONG THOSE TRYING TO SET RECORDS IS BUDDY THE ELF, SUPERMAN AND SUPERGIRL, AND A DOCTOR PUSHING A GIANT BUNNY IN A WHEELCHAIR.

NEAR THE SUMMIT OF TUSSEY MOUNTAIN IN BOALSBURG,
PENNSYLVANIA WITH ULTRA-RUNNER GEORGE ETZWEILER

NINETY-SEVEN-YEAR-OLD GEORGE ETZWEILER, CENTER, GETS HELPING
HANDS FROM HIS GRANDSON BOB ETZWEILER, LEFT, AND TRAINER,
BERTA DEDONATO. THE TEAM IS APPROACHING THE SUMMIT OF
MOUNT WASHINGTON DURING THE ANNUAL ROAD RACE.

GEORGE ETZWEILER, LEFT, AND HIS GRANDSON BOB ETZWEILER AT THE SUMMIT AFTER FINISHING THE RACE. GEORGE FINISHED IN JUST OVER FOUR HOURS.

MINI-AFICIONADO STEPHEN CROSSMAN AND I AT THE START OF THE MINIS ON TOP SUNSET DRIVE UP MOUNT WASHINGTON.

A LONG STRING OF MINI COOPERS MAKE THEIR WAY UP TO THE SUMMIT DURING
THE CLUB'S SUNSET RIDE. ABOUT TWO HUNDRED MINIS MADE THE DRIVE.

DURING THE MOUNT WASHINGTON OBSERVATORY'S ANNUAL SEEK THE
PEAK HIKING DAY, THE LINE TO THE SUMMIT SIGN GROWS LONG!

HIKING JUSTICE OF THE PEACE CHRISTIE GIROUARD PREPARES
TO MARRY AMY KOSKI AND MARK LAQUERRE AT THE SUMMIT.
PROPOSALS AND WEDDINGS ARE COMMON HERE.

POWERHOUSE ULTRA-HIKER
ALLMUTH "CURLY" PERZEL
SHOWS OFF SOME OF HER
HIKING PATCHES AT HER HOME
IN PORTER, MAINE. CURLY
RECENTLY BECAME ONE OF A
HANDFUL OF HIKERS OVER THE
AGE OF SEVENTY-FIVE TO SUMMIT
ALL OF NEW HAMPSHIRE'S
4,000-FOOT MOUNTAINS.

ONE OF THE ORIGINAL AMC HUT GIRLS, BARBARA HULL RICHARDSON BROKE THE
HIKING COMMUNITY GLASS CEILING BY GETTING A JOB IN PINKHAM NOTCH IN 1943.

VOLUNTEERS SPEND A COUPLE DAYS EACH YEAR PICKING DANDELIONS FROM
THE FLANKS OF MOUNT WASHINGTON. THE PROGRAM IS A STATE-SPONSORED
EVENT DESIGNED TO HELP FLORA INDIGENOUS TO THE MOUNTAIN FLOURISH.

EVERY YEAR, THE COG RAILWAY HOLDS A STEAMPUNK FESTIVAL TO
CELEBRATE THE RAILWAY'S PECULIAR ROOTS IN THE INDUSTRIAL
REVOLUTION. HERE, ATTENDEES GATHER AROUND OLD PEPPERSASS, THE
RAILWAY'S FIRST ENGINE, FOR A PARADE AND COSTUME CONTEST.

THE COG RAILWAY ENGINE AMONOOSUC GETS READY TO PUSH A
CAR FULL OF STEAMPUNK FESTIVAL ATTENDEES TO THE TOP.

LARRY MRUK OF EXPLORE BUFFALO PREPARES TO LEAD A GROUP INTO SILO CITY, A CAMPUS OF OLD GRAIN ELEVATORS ALONG BUFFALO'S WATERFRONT.

DURING HIS EARLY YEARS IN BUFFALO AND CHICAGO, COG RAILWAY FOUNDER SYLVESTER MARSH INVENTED, AMONG OTHER THINGS, A GRAIN ELEVATOR DRYER THAT MADE HIM WEALTHY. TODAY, CONCRETE GRAIN ELEVATORS FROM THE TURN OF THE NINETEENTH CENTURY PROVIDE HISTORY AND RECREATION FOR TOURISTS IN BUFFALO.

LANDSCAPE ARTIST BYRON CARR SETS UP CREEKSIDE TO PLY HIS ART.

ARTIST BYRON CARR AND I TAKE A BREAK WHILE PAINTING MOUNT WASHINGTON.

MY PAINTING NEXT TO
THE MASTER'S, SET
UP IN A PARKING AREA
ACROSS THE ROAD FROM
MOUNT WASHINGTON.

MY DAUGHTER GETS READY FOR HER FIRST DIP IN A MOUNTAIN STREAM.

MY DAUGHTER ALONE
FOR A FEW MINUTES ON
THE MOUNT WASHINGTON
OBSERVATORY DECK

SHARING A TRIUMPHANT MOMENT AT THE SUMMIT

MY JOURNEY ENDED IN MOUNT WASHINGTON, MASSACHUSETTS,
ONE OF ONLY TWO TOWNS IN THE UNITED STATES SO NAMED.

BASH BISH FALLS IN MOUNT WASHINGTON, MASSACHUSETTS
IS ONE OF THE TALLEST IN THE STATE.

CHAPTER SIX

Where the Heavens and Earth Intertwine

Every Year, for One Glorious Day, the Mountain is Owned by Those on Foot

I wait.

The observatory visitor center is quiet now, before 9:00 a.m., but this is, as the observers will say, the calm before the storm. They are coming. If there was a way to measure the vibration of boots on rock, soil, and road that is happening on the flanks of Mount Washington right now, the result would be like an earthquake.

There are hikers up here nearly every day of the year, sometimes a few, sometimes hundreds. But nothing like there will be today. Today, the mountain is owned by those on foot. They are coming up the road and up Huntington, Ammonoosuc, and Tuckerman ravines, and up the Great Gulf. Some are coming up alongside the Cog Railway tracks.

Some are eating breakfast at Lakes of the Clouds, Madison, or Mizpah huts before stretching their legs, filling their water bottles, and heading to the summit.

They are coming here via the Gulfside Trail or the Crawford Path. They are coming up past Lion Head or cutting over the Bigelow Lawn. Some will tag other peaks, like Monroe or Jefferson, before coming here to celebrate.

Some hardy souls are attempting what's called a Presidential Traverse, hiking the full nineteen-plus mile length of the Presidential Range, tagging the Mount Washington summit for a midday snack or water refill.

Some are coming up in vast teams of five or ten or fifteen, whole brother and sisterhoods of hikers with team names like The Valley Crushers, The Weather Geeks, White Mountain Bling, and Slow N Steady. Others go inward and come up alone, preferring community only upon reaching the top.

In all, the Mount Washington Observatory estimates that over 400 teams or individuals will have officially registered for this year's annual Seek the Peak hiker challenge. Many, many more hikers will come up on their own today, using the annual event to bask in the connections and community of other hikers.

Seek the Peak is the observatory's largest fund-raiser. For eighteen years, the observatory has registered teams and individuals to take the challenge of summiting Mount Washington as a day of communal hiking. They open the doors to the observatory for tours, have booths set up outside the museum and give participants a big dinner afterward at the base.

By the end of today, hikers who love the observatory and are passionate about weather and the outdoors will have raised nearly $175,000 for the institution.

The auto road and Cog is open for the tourist trade today as well. The weather is cloudy but not cold. In a few hours, the visitor center will be so packed, the concession line will extend to the door. Not a table seat will be unoccupied. And hikers will share the long line outside with drivers and Cog riders to touch the summit sign.

But for now, the doors to the visitor center open, and in strides a man with a full, bushy beard and a kilt. They are coming. I pull out my notebook and get to work.

The first to arrive is Jason Dubrow, from Dunbarton, New Hampshire, a member of the Kilted Hikers, a group that John Donovan had been associated with and one of the strongest and highest fund-raising groups to hike for the observatory. This is Jason's third year taking part in Seek the Peak, and he looks relieved to be at the summit after a 4:00 a.m. start up the mountain.

"It's nice being the first one up here," he says. "But when I got here, the building wasn't even open yet, so I froze a little bit!"

Meanwhile, out at the summit, teams are beginning to arrive. Rob Harrity from Somerset, Pennsylvania, came up Tuckerman Ravine with a group of friends, carrying an enormous American flag all the way. He stands up at the summit sign for a bit, waving the banner in the brisk wind.

"Listen, I'm a proud American," he says when I ask him why he carried the flag. "I'm proud of the stars and stripes."

Waiting in line to get a tour of the observatory, I encounter two-year-old Nola Thibeault from Lebanon, New Hampshire. She wears pink hiking shoes and a light blue stocking cap with moose antlers. She rode up here in her dad's backpack. Parents Faithanne and Jeremy tell me it's the first time Nola has been to the top of Mount Washington, but not her first time hiking.

"It's what we do for family time," her mom says. "We want to teach her the joy of being up high!"

Relaxing under the watchful eye of Mountain Mike, I find Jocelyn Gould and Eric Carlson from Boston. This is their third Seek the Peak together. They are also working on their 4,000 footer list.

"Mount Washington has the best views," Jocelyn says. "But today she's being mean, can't see a thing."

They shrug and smile and dig back into their muffins and juice.

My friend John will tag the summit today as well, though sadly our paths won't cross.

The hikers up here share a fellowship of community that the observatory actively works to inspire and encourage. Today is about more than just fund-raising, says Mount Washington Observatory president Sharon Shilling. This day is about stewardship as well.

"All types of communities come together on this day, from the hiker who loves the trail system of the Whites to the naturalist who loves nature," she says. "This day is also about the conservationist who wants to make sure that for generations to come the mountain is available for all to enjoy and also the thrill seeker who likes the challenge of something they have never done."

The observatory's new president is up top on this day as well, her first Seek the Peak in that role. Outgoing and gregarious, Sharon and her husband Kirk are all in, having moved up to New Hampshire from Virginia for the job and are currently hard at work building a home in the valley, one with a view of Mount Washington from the living room.

She's brought a dedication to detail and near boundless energy to the job, stemming no doubt from her twenty-two years with the Coast Guard, where she retired in 2006 with the rank of commander. In 1984, she was in one of the first classes of women to graduate from the U.S. Coast Guard Academy.

And of all the fellowship from a wide variety of hikers from around the globe that this day represents, Sharon, along with the observer team up here, understand that it always comes down to weather.

Outside the mezzanine windows, the summit is cloaked in a thick fog. That brings everyone inside, into close quarters.

There are two older women standing by the windows and talking about the summit. "They were right," one says. "It is a totally different climate up here!"

A family of Amish take up an entire table, chatting happily about their ride up on the Cog. One man has his binoculars around his neck.

I chat for a while with two women who spent the night at Lakes of the Clouds hut, about a mile below the summit, before making their way up here this morning. The highest and largest in the AMC eight-hut system, Lakes of the Clouds was originally a shelter, built in 1901. It was rebuilt as a hut in 1915, then rebuilt and expanded several more times over the years. It now sits at 5,030 feet and can hold up to ninety hikers.

In many ways, it's been the hiking class that propelled the whole industry surrounding Mount Washington and the White Mountains.

The hikers are the original tourists, the reason for the observatory, road, Cog, and huts to begin with.

To better understand the generational appeal of the hiking community that flocks to Mount Washington every day of the year, I sought out three women collectively representing a century of powering up this mountain, at times in a climate that wasn't terribly fond of women hikers.

And I would begin with one who could not be up top today, one of the originals, the one that shattered the glass hut system ceiling and has been forging her own trail for nearly a century.

Since the 1888 founding of AMC's first hut in the White Mountains of New Hampshire, staff members (a.k.a "croo") have had the reputation of being tough and resourceful—perhaps none more so than the croo who reported to Joe Dodge in interwar- and World War II-era twentieth century. Working Greenleaf Hut or Porky's Gulch under the watchful eye of the AMC's legendary hutmaster thickened one's skin pretty quick.

And if you were a woman on croo, well, that was nearly unheard of.

"The guys didn't like that at all," says Barbara Hull Richardson, her eyes twinkling. "They felt I was invading their territory."

Now ninety-five and living in a retirement community in Keene, New Hampshire, Barbara is only five years younger than the White Mountain National Forest, which received its federal designation in 1918. She is slight in stature but as high-energy as she must have been in 1943, when she became one of AMC's first "hut girls." With the men off to war, Joe was struggling to fill AMC positions. Pinkham Notch—the lodge and visitor center at the base of Mount Washington, later renamed in his honor—needed somebody to run the front desk.

When Joe picked Barbara, a petite twenty-year-old on summer break from Bryn Mawr College, to do the job, she unwittingly became one of the first women to crack the male-dominated hut system. And once again, Joe proved how well he could read people.

The youngest croo member of the season took her experience and the lessons learned in the notch and went on to become a lifelong children's advocate, a social worker, and eventually a decorated New Hampshire state representative.

As for toughness? It was only a little more than a year after her AMC experience that Barbara had the accident that changed her life. But getting shot will do that to you.

For her twenty-second birthday, Barbara had gone home to visit family in her hometown of Waverly, Pennsylvania, a rural farm community north of Scranton. Back in the 1940s, Waverly had about five hundred residents. (By 2010, the number had increased to six hundred.)

She was celebrating with a pregnant friend and the two of them decided to take a long walk around a nearby lake. Coming off Barbara's recent stint at Pinkham Notch, a few miles of flat hiking would barely cause her to break a sweat, but she was concerned about her friend's stamina.

The two women had stopped along an open section of trail and sat down on a log to rest when they noticed a couple of town boys on the other side of the pond, shooting tin cans floating in the water.

Next thing Barbara knew, she was lying on the ground.

"A bullet had ricocheted and hit me and knocked me off that log," she recalls. "Well, I just got right back up. I didn't really think it was too serious."

Her friend raced back into town to get a doctor, something Waverly hadn't had until two weeks earlier.

"I just watched his face turn white," Barbara says. "He put me back in his car and we raced to Scranton Hospital at sixty miles per hour, which was pretty fast back then!"

Barbara was surprised to discover a Catholic priest waiting for them; he began giving her last rites. She laughs now at the memory. "I told him, 'But I'm not Catholic!'"

Turns out the bullet had missed her heart by a mere quarter-inch—so close that the doctors weren't able to remove all of the shrapnel.

"I had a recent X-ray that showed there's still some pieces of that bullet in me," she says and smiles. She has been carrying that life-changing day in her chest for seventy-five years.

Looking back now, Barbara credits those experiences—first, breaking glass ceilings within the AMC and then a near-death close call—with directing the path of service her life would take.

"I realized I was so lucky that I had to do something with my life," she says. "I decided that would be to help people."

She takes a deep breath and gets quiet for moment, then says, "We should all be doing that."

Since 2012, Barbara has lived in a cozy, book-lined apartment at Bentley Commons, a sprawling retirement community in Keene that used to be a pail-manufacturing mill.

"Best place to kick the bucket," she quips.

In her sitting room, over her reading chair, hangs a portrait of Robert Frost. Books from Sinclair Lewis, Diane Ackerman, and Grace Paley peek out from under piles of paperwork, newspapers, and notebooks. On her walls are dozens of citations and awards of appreciation, including a commendation Barbara received from Governor John Lynch when she retired in 2010 from serving as a New Hampshire state representative.

Above her bed and along her walls are paintings of horses and meadows, created by an artist friend. Down a long hall between the living room and bedroom are photos of Barbara and her family through the years.

Everything in her apartment speaks to motion and movement—fitting for a woman whose whole life, from her days of making sandwiches for hikers in Pinkham Notch to her current hobby of writing political essays for the local newspaper, was about helping those around her.

Not too long after her incident at the pond, Barbara married Elmer, a World War II B-17 pilot who flew twenty-five missions. Barbara's brother had helped Elmer study for his Air Force exams.

"Elmer was going with this girl, but she fell in love with my brother,"

Barbara recalls. "But Elmer was still invited to their engagement party, and after, I had to get a ride back to Boston, and he tried to impress me by making some phone calls and getting me on a flight. It didn't work."

They ended up driving, and the long ride was enough for Elmer to ask if he could call on Barbara again. She said yes.

The two moved around New England quite a bit following Elmer's career as a sales manager for a ball bearing company before finally settling in the Richmond and Fitzwilliam area of New Hampshire.

Although married to a conventional man of the time, Barbara was looking for a way to keep the promise she had made to herself years earlier, of pursuing a life of service.

"I remember having to get my courage up to ask my husband if I could take a job," she says. "Back then, with all my friends, it was the men that worked."

Elmer came around, and Barbara began a career in social work.

She wrote grants for nonprofits; founded Project Share, a donation-based organization that collected furniture for low-income families; and worked as a longtime councilor for Court Appointed Special Advocates of New Hampshire.

In 2012 Barbara received a letter from a former foster child who had been in the New Hampshire state foster care system while Barbara worked there as a social worker. The woman explained that, after her experience with Barbara, she chose to become a social worker herself, had married, had children, and was now earning a master's degree. Barbara ended up speaking at the woman's graduation.

"It hadn't just made my day or my year," Barbara says. "It made my lifetime. Nothing that we do is inconsequential, even if it's just doing laundry for hikers!"

Barbara's job at Pinkham Notch wasn't terribly specific. Although Joe hired her to work the front desk, like most croo then and now, she became something of a jill-of-all-trades.

"I did some office management and bookings," she says. "I made lunches, assigned rooms, cleaned rooms, and washed the toilets. Of course, everybody had to work hard!"

Barbara remembers overloading a washing machine, being called away, and returning to face a flooded laundry room. She also recalls a particularly uptight male visitor who arrived late in the day, looking for a bed. Barbara accidentally booked him into a bunkroom already occupied by three young women.

"We fixed it, of course, but that didn't go over well with him," she says. "He left very early the next morning without a word."

During her free time, she'd hike. Barbara surmises she must have hiked to all of the then-seven huts and made several trips to the summit of Mount Washington.

She was aware of the bias against women working in the mountains but tried to keep her head down and work hard to prove she could do it.

Her tenure was made easier, in part, because Joe didn't care what your gender was as long as you did the job you were hired to do. "Everyone liked him," Barbara says. "He was very friendly and approachable."

The summer in the notch was the first time Barbara had spent any substantial time in the White Mountains though she had come up for an occasional weekend to ski. But after that summer, she decided to come back that winter to ski Tuckerman Ravine.

"I spent a week back there, skiing the ravine," she says. "I don't recall if I climbed all the way or not, but there weren't too many other women doing that. I think I had become quite a tomboy."

She also had a grandfather who insisted girls and boys should be equals in opportunity and in treatment.

"He's the one who encouraged me to look for work where women usually didn't work," she says. "That's how I got the hut job to begin with, just by believing I could."

In later years, Barbara kept hiking, though her work and family life demanded she keep her outdoor activities closer to home. In her case that was southern New Hampshire, and she quickly became a fan of Mount Monadnock and the Jaffrey region.

"I always had it in my mind that I would someday hike the Appalachian Trail," she says. "But I ran out of time!"

She did manage, however, to pass along her love of the outdoors and service to others to her children. One daughter became a competitive equestrian, one managed a day care and currently lives off the grid in a hillside cabin in Vermont, and her third daughter lives in Washington state where she is the Director of the Friends of San Juan Marine Protection Program, where her work focuses on safe shipping and oil spill prevention.

"I wanted them all to find their own passion," Barbara says. "As a parent, I tried to facilitate their individuality."

That sense of service to others—jump started in Pinkham Notch—served her well years later when she set off on another trailblazing campaign: to become a New Hampshire state representative.

Like many episodes in Barbara's life, her decision to enter the world of politics grew out of a sense that, in order to get things done, she'd have to do them herself.

In 1991 she had reached out to her New Hampshire state representative.

"I don't even remember the issue, but when I talked to him, he acted like he agreed and was on my side," she says. "But when the vote happened, it turned out he wasn't. So, I decided to run myself."

At age sixty-eight, Barbara got a map, put on comfortable shoes, and began knocking on doors—every door in her district.

"As soon as they found out I wasn't proselytizing or selling something, people were nice," she says. "I learned a lot."

She won, of course, and kept on winning, serving nine terms until deciding to retire at age eighty-seven. During her time at the state house, she attached her name to a wide swath of progressive bills. She was an early proponent of environmental protections policy, activism that stemmed from her love of animals and natural places. She's been a vegetarian for half her life. She also worked to repeal the death penalty in New Hampshire, the only New England state to still have it on the books.

Though she never found legislative success in either of those areas, her proudest moment came right at the end of her career, as Barbara appeared as a co-sponsor on the bill that passed allowing same-sex couples to marry in 2010.

"That was a big deal to me and to our state," she says. "That meant a lot."

Despite officially retiring from public life, Barbara has continued to be an active voice in her community. Since 2011, she has written op-eds for the *Keene Sentinel* on a variety of topics, from congressional greed to deregulation.

And she's kept a close eye on the new generation of women coming up through the #MeToo movement.

"I think it's wonderful to see people are finally coming out and fighting," she says. "Back then, we dealt with harassment, and worse, all the time, but just didn't give it any thought, it was just how it was."

To Barbara, her generation had to keep a lower profile, but her advice to women today is just the opposite.

"This has to come out now, voicing your opinion, do what you want to do in life because it's all much healthier that way," she says. "As it turns out, Anita Hill was right all along!"

From teenage hut girl in a world of men to social activist and progressive politician, Barbara Hull Barbara has been scaling heights since she first set foot behind the Pinkham Notch desk.

Through it all, one lesson has been the most important.

"Honor yourself," she says. "If you don't love yourself, how can you love anyone else?"

One of those women benefiting from Barbara's early activism walks into the visitor center on Seek the Peak day, and there can be no missing her. Allmuth "Curly" Perzel struts in wearing a Hawaiian shirt complete with lei like she owns the place, like she is the red, curly-haired queen of the trails. Curly walks into a room and takes all the oxygen with her. The triple-crown hiking, red-line completing, one hundred-highest summiting rock star of the New England hiking community is seventy-seven years old.

She's just completed her third Seek the Peak, coming up Tuckerman Ravine, and her eyes are on fire, blazing from the morning on the rock and the feel of the mountain in her muscles. I have no idea I'm talking to New England hiking royalty as I ask her about her hike, but about twenty seconds into our conversation she says, in a thick German accent, "Why don't you come out to our cottage in Maine and we'll have lunch and go for a swim and then we can talk all day about hiking?"

And that's how, a month later, I find myself steering through the tiny lake town of Porter, Maine, searching for the cabin of a red-haired powerhouse whose exploits deserve a book of their own. There are certain parts of Northern New England that Google has still not found, that need stovepipe directions—in other words, where to turn based on landscape, not street names. I roll past the old Porter Country Store, its white shingles peeling, roof sagging, and before long I come upon the sign tree, a tall poplar at a cross in the road upon which is fastened dozens of family names with arrows pointing left or right, directions to the cabins sprinkled along the sides of Colcord Pond.

Before long, I'm at the end of a long hard-packed drive. I turn left and there they are, George and Curly, waiting for me in front of their brown-shingled home. A sign in the front yard garden, surrounded by plastic pink flamingos, reads "Wasserhaus," the couple's water house. This is their summer home. When they are up from Florida and have hiking in their bones, this is their base camp.

"Welcome, welcome," Curly says. "How do you take your coffee?"

She's wearing a green t-shirt and hiking pants. A beaded necklace is around her neck, at the end of which dangles a wooden lizard. At her waist is a multi-colored belt full of jangling medallions. Today, her hair has only hints of red, more yellow, but still curly.

She shows me around their home, tight and cozy, decorated with art and photos of family and of the mountains. She's an award winner; just this year she was given the Brad Bradstreet Award, honoring her for her fund-raising efforts and volunteerism at the observatory. There are murals painted directly onto her walls and doors by friend and artist Patti Carter. One of the paintings is of Mount Chocorua, the first mountain Curly climbed back in 1970 and the one that set her on her fifty-year love affair with hiking. Other paintings are of Colcord Pond and are by her son, Peter Martin Perzel, an award-winning landscape artist.

The cottage, built in stages by her husband, is everything you'd expect it to be—comfortable and quaint at the end of a dirt road along a mountain pond, including little touches that speak to the couples' mischievous humor, like a little man in a pink hat on a unicycle rolling along with the toilet paper roll.

We go out onto their second-story porch for lunch, a simple feast of grilled burgers, salad, cantaloupe and homemade blueberry pie that I can still taste in my mind. They talk about their life, how they met in American Samoa, about their children, about this lake. In 2020, they will celebrate their fiftieth wedding anniversary. They tease each other, George's wide grin betraying his pride every time he gently jabs his wife about her passion for the trail. Time drifts by here like the slight breeze on the pond, and it occurs to me that I have barely asked a single question.

"Tell me about your hiking, Curly," I finally say.

She smiles. "Where shall I start?"

I shrug. "At the beginning, of course."

And so, there on a quiet mountain pond in Maine, with the sound of water lapping up against the rocks, one of the world's premier hikers tells me her story.

She was born in Bremen, Germany, and came to Rhode Island, sponsored by her uncle, and studied English and United States history.

The first time she hiked Mount Chocorua, she says she had no expectations.

"My husband was a hiker, I wasn't," she says. "I got to those bare rocks and thought, 'I can't do this,' but when I got over them and saw those glorious views, I was hooked!"

But her duties as a mom of two boys and her work teaching high school health and physical education kept her away from the mountains for four years. Chocorua never left her mind though, and a trip four years later to the Green Mountains in Vermont inspired her to take her boys back up Chocorua on her own.

At around the same time, she saw an article about the Appalachian Trail.

"I was so out of shape—well, what I would call out of shape," she says. "I have high standards."

She started section hiking parts of the AT in New Hampshire, coordinating with George to pick her up at trail heads. But that wasn't enough, of course.

So, in 1992, she solo hiked the whole thing, all 2,200 or so miles of it. Her trail name was Bag Lady, as she carried so much of her gear in plastic bags. For some, such an adventure might satiate their restless spirit. For Curly, it inspired a decades-long hiking tear—the Pacific Crest Trail, the Continental Divide Trail, the New England Hundred Highest—that culminated in 2016 when, after forty-six years of pursuit, she became only the thirty-second hiker to finish red lining the White Mountain National Forest. A Red Liner is someone who hikes every trail listed in a particular edition of the White Mountain Guide. There are only forty-three hikers registered as officially completing that list.

But Curly wasn't finished. In September 2017 she stepped onto the summit of Mount Moosilauke to complete her quest of becoming one of only a handful of hikers over the age of seventy-five to finish the New Hampshire forty-eight 4,000 footer list.

Along the way, Curly's trekked to Annapurna Base Camp in Nepal and stood at the summit of Mount Kilimanjaro in Tanzania.

"When you get close to your goal, it doesn't matter what it is, you become obsessed," she says. "Sooner or later the day is going to come when I can't do this anymore, then I'll stop and just sit here."

She has never broken a bone hiking, though her hip is a replacement, and she can't run or jump anymore. She still hits the gym, working primarily on yoga and stretching, though she's been known to lift a dumbbell or two.

I wonder if George Etzweiler could give this young pup a tip or two.

And though her goals are still high, her obsession is tempered by realism. She's becoming more pragmatic about her passion.

"I still feel wonderful but am aware I have to prevent falling," she says. "I don't have the same agility or quickness. It's all slower, but I have the experience and that makes all the difference."

For now, her attention is focused on Mount Washington. Curly has hiked the Rock Pile a couple dozen times, but the last three years going up on Seek the Peak day has been particularly satisfying for her.

"The draw to go up there is always to get spectacular views, of course," she says, "but lately, my draw up there has been the observatory. They are so kind to me, it's a special place."

For nearly all of Curly's life, Mount Washington and the White Mountains have served as her nerve center, the place that has defined her life and her character. Her advice to the new generation of hikers hitting those trails? "Get in shape and do your homework."

Curly wraps up some pie for me to take home, and as I slowly make my way back into New Hampshire and turn my back on my mountain to head home, I can't help thinking about who may be the next Curly, not in distance necessarily, but in heart.

Back on the mountain, I may have found her under a wedding veil and wearing a bright white tutu.

The bride wears an aqua long sleeve Techwick shirt over a white leotard, complete with a white tutu, knit fingerless gloves and a matching cap and veil ringed in flowers. She has shoulder length blue hair done up in tight pigtails.

The groom wears a black knit hat and a t-shirt with the image of a tuxedo on the front.

They have many tattoos. They both wear boots because they both hiked up here like that. And they both are silly, and happy, and nervous. The mountain is their altar.

On this day of wind and blue sky and elbow to elbow hikers crowding the observatory visitor center, Amy Koski and Mark Laquerre are going to be married. A whole wedding party of friends—that includes a baby, parents, and a justice of the peace—took the Cog up to join them, and the whole posse makes their way out to the observatory deck, weaving around tourists and kids and couples.

Earlier, Sharon Shilling herself had stopped by their table to wish them well. As they move to what will become their chapel, people take pictures and whisper congrats. Amy has given me permission to tag along—to crash their wedding, as it were—and as I fall into step behind the party, it's impossible to not think about my own wedding, across the valley, atop Mount Lafayette, nearly seven years ago to the day.

Nineteen friends and family had joined us for that hike, and many more strangers took part there at the top. Our justice of the peace, a dear bearded friend we all call Farmer Bob, turned to me to recite some words I had prepared, but I reached into my pocket only to realize I had left them down below. I winged it, there at the top of the first mountain Meenakshi and I had climbed years earlier, shouting to be heard over the wind.

Now, I think of those words I wanted to read by Anne Morrow Lindbergh as Amy and Mark's party heads out onto the observatory deck to begin their own journey:

> The only real security is not in owning or possessing, not in demanding or expecting, not in hoping, even. Security in a relationship lies neither in looking back to what was in nostalgia, nor forward to what it might be in dread or anticipation, but living in the present relationship and accepting it as it is now. Relationships must be like islands, one must accept them for what they are here and now, within their limits—islands, surrounded and interrupted by the sea, and continually visited and abandoned by the tides.

Much like a mountain wedding. Make too many demands of the mountain, and the mountain will crush your dream of the perfect wedding. But accept it for what it is, how it is, roll with the wind and the air, learn to accept the tides, and there is nothing like professing love at 6,288 feet.

"We expected at best no one would be able to see us through the fog and be frozen, and at worst have to take the Cog in both directions because of dangerous hiking conditions caused by rain," Amy tells me after. "But we were blessed with an amazing view of the Presidential Range and a wide-open observation deck. It was a little breezy and a wee bit frigid, but beautiful! We know we were lucky."

Amy's veil blows up above her head like a moth wing, the stiff breeze forcing the wedding party to tuck in closer, come together there at the rail in a tight half circle around the couple. In the center, between Amy and Mark, presiding over the wonderful madness is Christie Girouard. Around these parts, she's what's called a hiking justice.

The New Hampshire State Parks service estimates that about ten couples a season get married atop Mount Washington, with many more engagements. And that's just the folks who call ahead and tell the department they are coming. Amy and Mark just went ahead on their own and did it. So many couples get married in the mountains and wilderness around northern New Hampshire, in fact, that Christie does a brisk business helping folks tie the knot in atypical situations.

Christie has lived in Northern New Hampshire for nearly forty years, built her home on land that has been in the family since 1959. Her dad skied Tuckerman Ravine. Her love of the Mount Washington Valley has existed in her DNA since before she was born, and for the past fifteen years she has been working to bring some of that passion to the ceremonies she helps plan.

She has hiked with a head lamp at 3:00 a.m. to officiate a sunrise wedding atop Mount Kearsarge North. She's driven an ATV into the Sandwich Wilderness to a ceremony. She has skied, hiked and climbed to a mountain chapel. And she has waited at the top of Mount Willard in February with a couple's four children as the bride and groom ice-climbed their way to their altar.

She's lost track of how many couples she's married at the top of Mount Washington.

"This mountain is not an intimate setting, obviously. Mount Washington is the most accessible place out here a couple can get married," she says. "But at the same time, those who choose a mountain setting have some kind of connection to the mountains, it's personal and intimate to them. They want it to be theirs!"

Christie zips up her fleece and waves the attendees together toward the couple. She's wearing flip-flops. The wind howls. "Are we ready?" she asks, and one more commitment begins at the top of New England.

The universe conspired to bring Amy and Mark to this place of wind.

They both grew up in East Springfield, Massachusetts, in the same neighborhood. They went to the same church, made their First Communion together. There's even an old video of the two of them standing next to each other at a church play as little kids. Mark worked at a video store when Amy was a teenager, and she had a crush on him then.

But of all those opportunities, the two didn't know each other until, as adults, they both signed up for an online dating service that brought them together, and they discovered they had known each other all along.

Amy is a personal care assistant. Mark bakes donuts for a local family bakery and comes home smelling like sugar.

Mark was a Boy Scout, Amy was a Girl Scout. The outdoors it seems had always been part of their lives. They started dating out of a love for hiking.

"The first time up Mount Washington for both of us, there was a bit of fog blocking most of the Rock Pile, we were completely engulfed," she says. "It seemed like a never-ending stretch of hopping and climbing, we could just barely make out the cairns. We had never been on anything like that before, and it was quite a surprise."

But their decision to get married atop Mount Washington came out of service to another. When one of Amy's favorite uncles, Mike Koski, passed away, the family began Hike for Mike during the annual Seek the Peak day to keep his memory alive, and give back to their favorite place.

"We thought it'd be a blast doing a grueling hike up the tallest peak around before having a ceremony, and it was," she says.

The mountain inspires art and energy, it inspires people to test their limits, it inspires grace. And it inspires weirdness.

"I thought it would be hilarious to make a tutu that I could pull up over my hiking pants," Amy says. "So I didn't hike up in my gown, but I managed to squish that thing into a one gallon Ziploc bag and barely even noticed its weight!"

Don't be fooled by the concession stands and Cog whistle. This mountain creates connection. Even up there, surrounded by strangers, Mount Washington can be yours alone, as it is for Amy and Mark.

"When you climb them, it feels like you are touching the sky and standing among ancient gods," Amy says. "There is no room left for worries, only contentment. How wonderful it is to join lives together where the heavens and earth intertwine."

How wonderful indeed.

Two humans pledge their love for each other there in an ancient place. Two lives come full circle, witnessed and celebrated by family and strangers. They kiss, the mountain watches. The party heads down, amid shivers and smiles.

Tomorrow or the next day or in ten minutes, two others will kiss there in that spot. Before Amy, Curly found her destiny tied to the mountain and to the mountains. And before her, Barbara put her head down and worked to earn her spot among the mountain men, and in so doing opened the door to all the women who came after. And today, Sharon, the woman in charge of the top of that mountain is a United States Coast Guard commander who is building her home in view of the observatory she runs.

This mountain does things to people. She can make a timid man brave, she can break a strong man and make him weep. She's not high. Look close enough, and you'll see her steel and wood, you'll see sandals and stuffed animals and pizza. But she still calls you.

At night, sometimes, behind my eyelids, she whispers. That voice is the great Canadian wind that shears up from the Great Gulf and smells like pine and scrub, that brushes the back of my neck.

Her voice is the sound of a boot on ice, that sound when your sole takes hold, sure and deep, and you're certain that the mountain is holding you.

Her voice is like the changing air, how it feels against your face at the trailhead, murky and humid, and then how it feels at the door to the observatory, alarming and raw.

Her intentions can sometimes be cruel, her justice apathetic, and she'll strike you down in a second and leave you drowned in a water bar or frozen in the ice. Other times, she'll give you a day or an hour or a moment that will make you feel like you're the only person on earth, and you'll slip back into your car dirty, wet, and bruised feeling as close to God as you ever have.

She is all of that simply because she is. Because for hundreds of years she has humored our aspirations.

We've littered on her, landed planes on her, driven stakes into her earth and into her rocks. We've changed the very way she looks. But this mountain does not care. She can shrug us off her anytime she pleases, and she does often—just shrugs her wide shoulders and if you're not paying attention, if you think for one single solitary instant that you have beaten her, she will humble you. She has humbled many, violently and mercilessly.

But they still come, these grand hikers. They come in sneakers and boots, they come on skis and on snowshoes. Sometimes, they come barefoot.

They carry small children on their backs, children who will never remember this view, the hot chocolate, the air, but maybe someplace in their bones the mountain will leave a mark. They come up slowly, their joints aching, just shadows of the hikers they were twenty, thirty, forty years ago.

They come in kilts and tie-dyes. They fly flags off their backpacks. They come because they have beaten cancer or are fighting it. They come because a loved one lost that fight.

They come to profess love. And kiss.

Hike this mountain once, just one time, and you will leave with her soil in your hair and under your fingernails and in your heart. There are some who come up here only once; it's too crowded, they say, too commercial. But they come. And then they come again, maybe in the winter, maybe at night.

They always will come.

After Amy and Mark have left, I tuck myself into a corner, on the floor, Lizzie Bourne right over my shoulder. It is a madhouse, elbow to elbow in the same place where only a couple months earlier I could hear my boots echo. It all has its place.

Soon, they will get on their shuttles and on the last trains down. The hikers will fill their water bottles, stuff their pockets full of snacks from the concession, put on new undershirts and disperse back into a dozen paths and routes and down the road and into the ravines. Some will stop down below for a dinner and award ceremony in their honor. Others will find a favorite rock, or a favorite gas station, and eat their trail mix while their sore feet rest.

And every single one of them, myself included, when they go to bed this evening, before they drift off to sleep, they will feel the mountain air on the back of their necks and they will think about the next time.

CHAPTER SEVEN

In the Teeth of the Lion

Few Living Things Create More Trouble
for the Mountain than the Meek Dandelion

I am back on top, and despite it being the middle of summer, Mount Washington is unhinged this morning. The mountain can't decide what it wants to do: wind, mist, clear sky, or sunshine. The old girl is having a fit at the summit. I'm up on the observation deck with some time on my hands, so I just watch the chilly mist roll up from the valley, pour over the summit like a gossamer river and within minutes the summit is clear again, the sun beating down on the rocks. Then it all starts up again.

I never tire of this.

Still, if I could communicate with the mountain this morning, I would tell her to lay off a little bit. After all, I'm here to help her today, to partake in a battle to prevent an ongoing invasion of her summit that has been taking place for hundreds of years. In the last couple decades, though, Mount Washington has been losing this particular fight. So the state of New Hampshire has decided to step in.

That battle, being waged literally right under the noses of tourists and hikers, is the fight to eradicate the lowly dandelion from the highest point in the Northeast.

The most well-known weed on the planet, the ubiquitous dandelion plant—the scourge of lawn maintenance gardeners everywhere—is up here too. But that war is going poorly. The dandelions are winning hands down.

In a place like Mount Washington, the plant has had to adapt, change its form slightly, be sneakier about propagation and location. The dandelion we know from our backyards down at sea level—that bright yellow flower head, long hollow tube shooting up toward the light, and of course the gray and white seed head, blown by children for centuries—is not quite the creature that grows up here.

Here, where the wind howls, temperatures fluctuate wildly, and grand lawns are nowhere to be seen, *Taraxacum officinale* has to be more clever. At the summit of Mount Washington, dandelions sneak into the crevasses between the rocks and gravel near the parking areas. They thrive where tourists and hikers congregate, near the front of the observatory observation deck and near the doors and entrances. And they love the main popular trails, the Crawford Path in particular, where the paths are wide and hikers come up from the valley and down from the summit.

They are hardier up here—small flower heads, roots that spread out under the thin soil, and they peek out from behind the rocks to absorb the sun when it's out and use the rocks for protection when the weather is bad. They are more green up here than yellow.

But once I start looking for them, it's all I can see.

And today, I'm here at the invitation of New Hampshire Natural Heritage Bureau (NHB) to be part of a program that, in typical bureaucratic fashion, the state calls "Invasive Dandelion Removal in the Alpine Zone, White Mountain National Forest."

In other words, I'm going to spend most of the day at the top of Mount Washington pulling weeds.

I meet my team leaders in the main parking area, just below the stairs that climb up to the summit. They are Amy Lamb, an Ecological

Information Specialist at NHB, and Eric Feldbaum, a Community Recreation Specialist at the New Hampshire Division of Parks and Recreation (DPR).

The chain of command for this program reads like a walk-through of virtually every agency in the state that has something to do with Mount Washington. The NHB is the umbrella agency of the state Division of Forests and Land, which controls the Department of Natural and Cultural Resources. And beside the DPR, the program has sponsorship from the White Mountain National Forest, which is under the U.S. National Forest Service. The Appalachian Mountain Club, observatory, Cog Railway and auto road all have their fingers in this program as well, which is in its third year.

So for three years now, all those agencies, businesses and institutions have been trying to push the poor dandelion off the summit of Mount Washington. They have not succeeded, and likely never will entirely. But that's not the point.

No agency, governmental or otherwise, will ever eradicate the dandelion completely from Mount Washington, not so long as hikers hike and the tourists come. This battle is being waged on many fronts, all around the world. Denali and Rocky Mountain National Parks have their own programs, and their own measurements for success.

A 2016 study by the U.S. Forest Service found infestations not just in the area surrounding the summit of Mount Washington, but along the auto road and the Cog's Marshfield Station as well. Further dandelion growth was discovered near most of the alpine huts, near and around many trailhead parking areas and even high up at some ski resorts.

But the program on the mountain has made some strides in keeping the little weed contained, and most importantly, from strangling out the flora that's supposed to be here. The decision was made to nip this problem in the bud—or the tap root, as the case may be—by aggressively tackling some of the major problem areas by using a tried and true method of getting rid of weeds that dates back generations.

Amy hands me a shiny new green-handled weed digger and says, "Let's go find some dandelions."

Dandelions are not from around here, and by "here" I mean the Northern Hemisphere. The little yellow plant run amok is Eurasian in origin.

Back in the seventeenth century, when early settlers were trying to gain a foothold on the East Coast of the Americas, there were actually two invaders in those waves coming to the New World. One of those waves—the human settlers—nearly didn't make it, suffering extreme hardships, starvation, and a whole host of other ailments as they struggled to get by in the area of the Massachusetts Bay Colony.

The other invader—the dandelion—had no problem at all gaining a foothold, spreading, and proliferating. Rocks and sand were often used for ballast for ships to the New World, and that dirt contained seeds. The ballast was usually just dumped dockside. Other seeds infiltrated the New World in boot soles or pant cuffs.

A botanical survey by John Josselyn of Boston in 1672 called *New England Rarities Discovered* reported them as well-established plants. It was also around this time that the Spaniards were bringing them to California and Mexico, and the French were hauling them up to Canada.

But according to Anita Sanchez, a New York State environmental educator who has written books about dandelions and poison ivy, those early settlers brought the dandelion to the New World on purpose as well, in the form of seeds.

"Early settlers planted seeds for the same reason that modern day travelers take refuge at a McDonald's or Holiday Inn," she says. "When you're far from home, the greatest comfort lies in the familiar."

But unlike McDonald's, back then dandelions weren't brought over for food—the Pilgrims were big on meat and potatoes and didn't much care for wine, even if it was dandelion wine. Instead, dandelions were herbal medicine. In doing this, the early settlers were just following in a millennium of herbal traditions so old, in fact, it's impossible to say exactly when humans began using dandelions for this purpose.

A Neanderthal burial site in Iraq, discovered in 1960, was found to have fossilized pollen scattered around the bones. And since pollen is only present in blooming plants, archeologists have suggested that our ancient cousin had been surrounded by flowers. Further, of the six species scientists were able to identify, three of them were close relatives of the dandelion, and all of them—yarrow, yellow groundsel, hollyhock, ephedra, and St. Barnaby's thistle are used to this day in herbal medicinal concoctions. In other words, it would appear that the old fellow in the cave was being given medicine.

"They're found worldwide, spread across the planet on every continent except Antarctica," says Sanchez. "They are below sea level and above tree line, growing in fertile fields and desert canyons, lining the clay soil of riverbanks and basking in the sun on sand dunes."

So, for forty thousand years (give or take a century) dandelions basically have ruled the environment.

No one in our little team of ten there at the gusty summit of Mount Washington believes we have a chance against one of the strongest, most versatile and resistant organisms on the planet, but we get to work anyway.

There are, after all, indigenous alpine flora to save. Mountain cranberry, Diapensia lapponica, and Lapland rosebay all grow up here, and dandelions have a way of crowding them out.

And then there's the Robbins cinquefoil, sometimes known as the Dwarf cinquefoil.

Discovered along the Crawford Path back in 1824 by famed Harvard botanist Thomas Nuttall on an expedition up Mount Washington, the tiny yellow flowering perennial (named after fellow botanist James Robbins) grows only in the alpine zone of Mount Washington and along Franconia Ridge. By the time the plant was put on the endangered list in 1980, only about three thousand were thought to exist. The forest service, working with the Appalachian Mountain Club, rerouted part of the Appalachian Trail, and the petite member of the rose family was taken off the list in 2002. And off the list is where the state wants to keep it.

We break into two teams and I follow Amy down to the secondary parking lot, which is fairly empty on this misty, cold day. Eric and his team work the service road and median near the Cog platform and deck. We all gather around Amy as she shows us the proper way to dig in and scoop out the dandelions. On a lawn, this is an easy, if somewhat monotonous task. But here, in between the slick rocks, getting down into some of the crevasses in order to pull out the full tap root, is a chore. The dandelion has smaller roots that spread out near the surface, but if you want to make sure the plant doesn't come back, you have to bring up the tap root. According to author Sanchez, tap roots can penetrate as deeply as fifteen feet! Given Mount Washington's gravelly hardpack and boulder piles, it's unlikely a dandelion can get down anywhere near that far, but it does take some wiggling and fancy positioning to pull each individual out.

There's another benefit to this project as well. Each of us is given two garbage bags. One for the dandelions, but also one for regular garbage. From a distance, like when you are a tourist walking from the parking lot up the staircase to the observation deck or the visitor center, Mount Washington State Park appears tidy and clean. But as I pick my way, sometimes on hands and knees, through the rock fields surrounding the parking lots, I'm shocked to see so much trash: plastics, soda cans, and even pieces of hiking gear. We begin to fill up both bags.

Katherine McNeil, in her book *Long Days of Small Things,* writes about finding spiritual meaning in everyday, mundane tasks, in her case the everyday job of house cleaning. And though McNeil approaches the philosophy of meaningful work through the lens of her Christian faith, she's not the first to look at the topic of finding growth and power in everyday work.

The United Society of Believers in Christ's Second Appearing, otherwise known as Shakers, believed that it wasn't just the routine of everyday tasks that led to spiritual growth, but to become an expert at those tasks—whether it be furniture making, gardening, or cooking—was a means of praise and ultimately salvation. Their leader, Mother Ann Lee, is quoted as saying, "Do your work as though you had a thousand years to live and as if you were to die tomorrow." At the height of the movement, there were a dozen Shaker communities in New England.

Even the great Vietnamese Buddhist monk and activist Thích Nhất

Hạnh had something to say about menial tasks, in particular about washing the dishes. He said, "I enjoy taking my time with each dish, being fully aware of the dish, the water, and each movement of my hands. I know that if I hurry in order to eat dessert sooner, the time of washing dishes will be unpleasant and not worth living. That would be a pity, for each minute, each second of life is a miracle. The dishes themselves and that fact that I am here washing them are miracles!"

So here I am, my bare hands against the wind-scoured rocks, the northern wind cloaking the summit in cool mist. Perhaps it is a miracle that I'm here, that the weeds give me focus and head space. I remember McNeil's three suggestions for meditative task work.

Don't rush. I take my time with the tool and feel the hard, cool handle against my palm. I use my right hand to dig, my left to trace the dandelion down to the earth or gravel and direct the forked point of the tool into the ground. I try to remember what that surge of muscle in my forearm and shoulder feels like as I push the tool down, seeking the tap root. I scrap around the secondary roots, in no hurry.

Keep your mind on the task. Even in mist, even on a weekday, there is much to distract me at the summit of Mount Washington: the Cog whistle, the cough of a motorcycle, the swirling wind that reveals blue sky. Children playing in the parking area. But I try to be mindful. This is why I'm here, to connect with this beautiful, ancient plant as old as humans.

See the value. We are all here today to prevent the dandelions from choking out indigenous alpine flora, that's clear. But there's something else at work here, a cycle of cleansing, like doing the dishes or washing the floor, or indeed of weeding your garden. These rotations of clean to dirty to clean again need not be discouraging, but a source of grace in routine.

Step, find, dig, bag. Repeat, repeat, repeat. The tinny sound of metal on rock. The mountain sings a song of renewal, the dandelions loosen their grip and fall away. For now.

In ancient symbolism, dandelions have stood for power. This is somewhat owed to their common name, which comes from Medieval Latin, dens leonis, meaning "tooth of the lion." But while the leaves of the dandelion do appear serrated, why a lion?

The etymology of the word is puzzling, until you consider just how powerful a dandelion actually is—sort of the king of the plant kingdom. To the ancients and the New World settlers, the dandelion was a sort of catchall for whatever happened to be ailing you, sort of like an aspirin or chicken soup. Loose teeth? Stiff joints? Sores, fevers, poor sleep, can't wake up? There was and is a dandelion concoction for you.

As it turns out, mostly, they were right. Dandelions are a vitamin powerhouse. Pound for pound, dandelions contain more vitamin C than tomatoes and more vitamin A than oranges. Toss some protein, iron, calcium and potassium into the mix, and nutrient-wise dandelions are as powerful as lions.

But how do they taste? Only one way to find out.

On the mountain, we're not allowed to take the dandelions home as the state collects the bags to sort through, weigh and dispose of properly to prevent seeding. I do sneak a bite of one of the dandelion leaves, but it tastes as one might expect—tough and bitter.

A basic internet search reveals hundreds of dandelion recipes ranging from fritters to pancakes, and even more recipes for tea, coffee and wine.

But I'm looking for something more basic and I find it, along with a story, in Claremont, New Hampshire.

At seventy-two, Halford Jones is still quite the man about Claremont. Slim and well dressed with deep, thoughtful eyes, Halford will talk your ear off about his hometown, where he records mini documentaries on the city for local community TV. In the sixties, Halford spent some time in the Philippines learning and teaching arnis, that country's traditional national sport, a form of martial arts that emphasizes weapon-based fighting techniques.

Halford has never been to the top of Mount Washington. "I think I can excuse myself from ever setting foot on it by invoking the old Native American belief in not going to the top," he says.

But he has eaten dandelions the old-fashioned way.

By 1912, about thirty Polish immigrant families lived in Claremont, and they formed an organization for men called the Thaddeus Kosciusko Society, after the Polish-Lithuanian military engineer who played an important role in the American Revolution by, among other things, designing the fortifications at West Point.

The society decided it was time for the burgeoning mill town to have its own Polish church. In 1920 they purchased an empty plot of land on Elm Street and got busy building a parish. Halford's grandfather, Frank Jones, worked for one of the original construction companies building the church. This was back in a time when the men would march down to the church from all points of the area, bringing everything they needed for a full day of outside work. One of the easiest and most filling types of food was a loaf of bread. And the men had plenty to put on that bread to make sandwiches. All they had to do was pick dandelions from that empty, weedy lot.

"The Polish workers dug dandelions and ate them raw on bread they brought and put salt on them to eat at lunch time," Halford says. "Dandelions have long been a staple food for some, especially those close to the land or farms and in rural recipes and foods."

While it's understandable that salt could take some of the bitter taste out of dandelion greens, it's also true that warm, homemade bread would likely taste good with nearly anything on it. I also have some fuzzy memories of my own grandfather bringing in baskets of greens from his backyard when I was a toddler.

Halford's story was in my head later that day on a trip to the supermarket where I decided to try the ancient weed for myself. It had never occurred to me that one could buy raw dandelion greens in the produce section of the supermarket, but there they were. I took his advice about the salt, but decided to fry them in oil to soften the leaves somewhat. I also added a pad of butter to set off the bitterness. About ten minutes on medium heat and they were done. They tasted nearly as one would expect: salty, soft dandelion greens with a hint of butter. My daughter wouldn't touch them. My wife, who eats kale and quinoa by the handfuls for snacks, wrinkled her nose. "Could have waited till spring and got these free in our backyard," she opined. Indeed.

At the summit, tourists and hikers are beginning to notice. Our efforts could be attracting attention due to the mist that seems to have locked down the top of the mountain. Without views, folks on their way to and from their cars notice us instead. Most have no clue what we're doing. Like myself, the idea of picking weeds at the summit of Mount Washington is not something that really occurs to anyone.

An older gentleman wearing nothing but a light windbreaker, his white hair tousled by the wind, approaches. He's surrounded by what looks like some grandkids and his wife.

"Trash collecting?" he asks. "Do you work for the park?"

"No sir," I say. "This is a volunteer program, we're weeding dandelions."

There's a long pause where no one says anything, and I watch him furrow his brow.

"Well, how do you like that," he finally says, turning to the kids. "Even up here they have to weed!"

Amy comes over and chats with the family a bit, explaining the program. The kids don't appear as interested as the adults; weeding gets a bad rap generally. What's curious, though, is how deeply ingrained the legends and mythology of dandelions are in the human experience. And most of those stories have to do with children.

I can't imagine there's anyone reading these words who has not, as a child or recently, picked the seedling head of a dandelion and blown the seeds into the wind.

In his book and last manuscript before he died, *The Dispersion of Seeds,* Henry David Thoreau was well aware of the magic of that seed bundle and wrote that "boys blow to see if their mothers want them." In New England, the belief is that if you didn't blow all the seeds off the stalk in one puff, that meant it was time to head home to do your chores.

Other legends involving the seed ball include wish making (get your wish if you blow off all the seeds), romance (if any seeds remains, your love interest has no interest in you), and reproduction (the number of seeds that remain after one blow is how many children you'll have). A variation of that last myth is that the number of seeds that remain are how many years you have to live.

When woven into a wedding bouquet, dandelions provide good luck to the newly married couple. If you dream about a dandelion, a happy union is in your future.

One legend says that the tallest stalk a child can find in early spring will show how much taller that child will grow in the coming year.

In his book *Encyclopedia of Magical Herbs*, Scott Cunningham, the author of more than thirty books on herbs and Wicca, suggests that eating dandelions as tea can help increase psychic abilities. A tea of the roots left steaming and placed beside the bed will call spirits, and dandelions buried in the northwest corner of the house will bring favorable winds.

Here on the summit, the wind has picked up and as the afternoon begins to fade into evening, our day of dandelion picking winds down. The teams reassembles at the truck to hand in our tools and sort the bags. There are at least twelve bags of dandelions and about half a dozen filled with trash. Eric and Amy sort the piles, and then Eric hands us all a Mount Washington State Park patch as a reward for our day of service.

We chat and shake hands. Amy and Eric assure us that more volunteer days like this will take place again next year, and everyone disperses.

Back at my car, before heading back down the mountain, I change my boots into sneakers and strip off my damp windbreaker, fold it and lay it gently on the passenger seat. In the pocket of the jacket, I've smuggled a little something off the mountain and want to get home quickly before it gets too dry.

By the time I pull into my Manchester driveway, it's dark and a perfectly clear city summer evening. We're fortunate to have a little square of open lawn behind our home; an area that my wife rings with a vegetable garden. In the glow of the dim alley light, a row of tomatoes gleam in splashes of red and green color, and tangled in the vines along a fence are a few not-quite-ready-to-pick cucumbers. Like the early settlers, she's planted herbs and asparagus. And towering over it all, mid-summer sunflowers droop and lilt, their fiery yellow heads casting evening shadows over the tiny patch of lawn we call our own.

What my wife has not planted is the most popular and sturdy plant of them all, the lowly dandelion. But she doesn't need to because even in our small city patch of lawn, the dandelions come. They get cut and they come back. The children play in the sprinklers, making a muddy mess, and the dandelions come back. Through dog poop and car exhaust and crabgrass, they come back.

There is a not terribly old saying that goes, "If it's God who invented grass, it's the devil who invented lawns."

But maybe we're just looking at it the wrong way. Maybe it's the lawns that need to be weeded out, and the dandelions tended.

I reach into my jacket pocket and gingerly remove the full dandelion plant I've smuggled from the top of Mount Washington. The tap root is intact, a decent six inches or so. The poor plant is tight and folded, its leaves bent like it's been avoiding summit wind its whole life. The yellow head is barely open.

So there in my backyard, in a splotch of grass surrounded by an old neighborhood in a place once called Amoskeag by the Pennecook to describe the area as a "good fishing place," I get down on my hands and knees in the dark and dig a little hole. This is my splotch of grass, in a place where my daughter plays and my wife grows food, so I push my fingers into the lawn and soil and slowly scoop out a few inches of dirt.

Then, satisfied that I've given my dandelion a fighting chance to take, I tuck the tap root into the hole, cover the plant with dirt and wipe my hands. Tomorrow I'll show my daughter the new, ragged-looking dandelion that has popped up in our backyard. We'll water it together, to honor the mountain and to take our place in a line of growth and sustenance that has existed before humans were human and will continue long after we've all drifted off into the wind, like so many seeds from a dandelion.

CHAPTER EIGHT

The Gears and Pipes, and the Steam

The Mountain's Living Anachronism
Continues to Shoot for the Moon

A middle-aged man with a round face and smiling eyes sweeps into the festival grounds as though he's royalty, like a prince, or perhaps a duke.

His ankle-length overcoat is finely embroidered in silver paisley. His velvet collar is high and turned up, reaching nearly to his ears. Across his chest, his lapels are fastened with glimmering silver buttons. His French cuffs are thick and black and extend halfway down his hands.

He wears Ray-Bans. And on his head is a tall, black top hat; instead of a hat band though, he sports a glimmering, light gray pair of welder's goggles. They are his tell, a cosplay signature that alludes to his steam-punk intents.

He says his name is Jim, but he calls himself the Baron. He doesn't shake my hand, he tips his hat and says, "Good morning to you, Sir."

I am deep in the White Mountains, on the west side of the mountain, at the iconic Marshfield Station, home of the Cog Railway. The day is crisp and clean; slivers of clouds move lazily over Mount Washington in no hurry to leave the sky. This is the sort of day you can feel on your skin, where the air is perfect and the mountain calls for exploration and celebration; the sort of day hikers and tourists pray for and will tell their grandchildren about years later.

And here where the whistle blows and the cinders fly, where the air smells like hot iron, the annual Railway to the Moon Steampunk Festival is raging, and the Baron is in his element. If there is a better place in the whole wide world to delight in the Victorian styling of the Industrial Revolution, well, I certainly can't think of one.

The attendees strut and preen, displaying their handmade costumes and sharing stories from their various steampunk chapter groups. Later, they all plan on filling up one of the Cog passenger cars and clinking and clanging their way to the top.

For now, the Baron is greeted by a party of fellow attendees, all awash in velour hoop skirts and trousers, colorful headwear and more brass, copper, and silver buttons and buckles than a tailor could use in a year.

The ladies curtsy to me and the men bow and the group sashes off to browse among the steam-powered metal sculptures, the wire jewelry and ornaments, the mechanical arms and Wild West pistols and all the other accoutrements of a time that never was.

And through it all, a nearly 150-year-old marvel of engineering growls and howls to the mountain that made it famous.

By any measurement, even one applied to current engineering standards, the Cog Railway seems impossible. Like a Hollywood movie contrivance, the Cog feels like an incredible background for an action hero to save the day and jump on in the nick of time, or drop to the roof from a dirigible.

Imagine how utterly far-fetched the concept of the Cog must have seemed to most people in 1858. We don't actually have to imagine; it's on record. When Cog Railway inventor Sylvester Marsh applied for a state charter in June of that year, he brought a small model of his proposed engine to show New Hampshire state legislators how the train would conquer the steep slope. Marsh—a wealthy, accomplished native son who owned nearly half a dozen patents—was laughed at. He said later that he was shocked how the room burst into spontaneous laughter at his proposal. One lawmaker remarked that the state may as well "let him build a railway to the moon."

So dismissive were legislators—so skeptical and unable to conceive that anyone, even someone with a track record like Marsh—could accomplish what was deemed impossible, that they handed him a five-year charter. At the end of it, they extended that charter another five years. Go ahead, crazy man, they said, we dare you to do this, and they turned their backs on him, surely figuring they'd either never hear from him again or they'd be able to say *we told you so* at his funeral.

Instead, in 1868, that same body watched incredulously as a steam-powered engine that resembled a pepper sauce bottle powered its way to the summit of Mount Washington. The *Boston Transcript* called the railway "one of the great wonders of the time."

Even the *New York Times* gushed that "Hitherto there has been but two ways of conquering the inequalities of the earth's surface—by going around or through them. Mr. Marsh proposes to obviate this by going over them."

Marsh fulfilled the charter contract in time, and the state sold him a ninety-nine foot corridor all the way up the mountain for $91.50. That charter remains to this day, and though some outdoor purists feel the days of such an industrial age dinosaur should be numbered, the tourists, train buffs, and steampunk aficionados could not be happier.

The site of the steampunk festival is the back of Marshfield Station, the train station where you can normally get tickets for a ride, browse a museum on the history of the Cog, and eat hot dogs and chicken tenders at a cafeteria-style commissary.

It's not easy to get to this place; it requires a six-mile drive deep into the wilderness from the west side of the mountain, toward Ammonoosuc Ravine. During this drive, due to some marvelous quirk of the landscape—and perhaps the ingenuity of road engineers—Mount Washington rises up directly in front of a traveler, enormous and menacing.

Back when Marsh was struggling to get passengers to his curious engineering wonder, the plan was to construct a connecting line from the Boston, Concord and Montreal (BC&M) Railroad's White Mountain line, which ran along Route 302 down into Crawford Notch. The problem? Marshfield Station stands more than 1,100 feet above the passing tracks near Route 302 and literally no engine of the time could get up to the Cog; the adhesion locomotives were too light and would spin their wheels at such an ascent. That meant spending an enormous amount of money to get the Cog down to the normal rail line.

But Marsh had a plan for that as well, and it involved an engineer and businessman from Manchester, New Hampshire who went by the curious name of Aretus Blood.

Blood's Manchester Locomotive Works was already churning out engines for Marsh, but in 1876, Blood did something that changed the railroad industry in New England, and he did it for the express purpose of getting passengers to Marshfield Station by rail. In the summer of that year, the first heavy locomotive chugged out of Blood's plant, a twenty-nine-ton Goliath with three pairs of driving wheels. It would become the most powerful locomotive operating in the Eastern states for many years.

Its name? Mount Washington.

Finally, as Sylvester Marsh had envisioned, the summit of his mountain via the Cog Railway was at last connected by rail to every major eastern city. And as he predicted, the people began to come.

The festival grounds are really a wide, sloping rectangle with the boarding tracks along the north end and picnic grounds along the south end. For the steampunk fair, vendors and sellers are lined up primarily along the picnic grounds, though spillover is everywhere. In the center of the rectangle, protected by an old fashioned wooden fence, is a display of past engines and equipment. And in the center of it all sits the remodeled Old Peppersass, the Cog's original little engine that could.

I take my time wandering through the festival, which is, as you'd expect from a steampunk gathering, a visual and oratory cornucopia of odd creations, stunning colors, and fantastical costumes.

There is a steam machine sculptor, a little man sporting a scratchy beard with a pork pie hat and overalls. His booth of steam-run machine art pieces crackle and pop, wiz and whir. People come up and pull the whistle on one of the bigger pieces, the sound rivaling that of the Cog trains across the way. There's a jewelry booth, with earrings and necklaces made out of what appear to be bolts and gears.

The Steampunk Society out of Springfield, Vermont, is represented, their members holding tea biscuit dunking competitions. And members of Gate City Steampunk out of Nashua, New Hampshire are selling copies of their anthology written by members and containing—you guessed it—steampunk-inspired short stories.

The most curious attraction is Kevin McNatt of Mansfield, Massachusetts, in his Victorian pantaloons bicycle pants and jaunty riding cap. He's a member of the Wheelmen, a nationwide group of antique bicycle enthusiasts. Today, Kevin is showing off his collection of penny farthings. They are one-geared, high front-wheeled nineteenth century bicycles that used bone-jarring solid rubber wheels. Riding one puts you about five feet off the ground.

Kevin had already peddled his regular racing bike coast to coast twice when he happened to wander into an antique shop a few years ago and stumbled upon a penny farthing. There was no going back.

"I thought, 'oh God, I have to have one of those,'" he says.

In 2012, Kevin spent sixty-six days riding his reproduction 1885 bike from Delaware to Oregon, 3,400 miles. Some days, he'd ride seventy miles. He's on a short list of about fifty humans who have taken that ride on a penny farthing.

The term "penny farthing" comes from the Victorian era British penny and farthing coins, one much larger than the other, like the wheels on the bike. If you look at a penny farthing from the side, it resembles a penny leading a farthing.

I badly want to try to ride one, but Kevin is rightfully skittish about anyone getting up on these monsters. He demonstrates the complicated technique of rolling the bike forward, stepping on a lower pedal and launching himself up into the seat. He takes a casual spin around the festival grounds. People stop and gaze up at him in wonder as he passes.

Watching Kevin there atop this horse-high heavy metal beast, the relationship between the Cog Railway and the aesthetic known as steampunk becomes apparent and obvious. And here's the weird thing about the movement—while it's a clear throwback to the culture and commodification of the Victorian era, it's also as wildly unauthentic as those early Hudson Valley School painters claiming stewardship over landscapes that never existed in the first place.

Back in 1885, nobody who was actually employed in a yarn or shoe factory enjoyed working there, but here, 140 years later, steampunks are dressing up as grubby engineers and factory workers. The only difference is that they now have mechanical arms with a pistol or claw at the end. I mean, even the participants wearing high-end ballroom clothes like those of wealthy aristocrats of the time are also wearing the same oily engineer glasses, as if to suggest that any of the one-percenters back then could at any moment get into the cab of the Cog and start shoveling coal.

So, what's going on here?

The writer of the popular steampunk blog Silver Goggles, Jaymee Goh, has suggested that this sort of aesthetic "cannibalism" can be a double-edged sword.

"On the one hand, it allows us to reclaim our histories through our actions in the present—whether through cultural heritage, or hands-on talent, or aesthetic quirk," she writes. "On the other hand, this sort of cultural cannibalism lends itself to cultural appropriation under the assumption that in our post-modern, post-colonial, post-racial world, anything can be abstracted, taken out of context."

In other words, most dress up cosplay—say, super heroes—has to do with appropriating fictional worlds. Even Civil War or medieval reenactments strive for strict accuracy. Not so with steampunk.

This fantastical overlay is, perhaps, exactly why the Cog Railway and Mount Washington itself is such an attraction to many, not just those who enjoy wearing top hats and spats. This place, this mountain, spans history and is current, all at once. Where else can you find a nineteenth century coal-driven locomotive to take you to one of the most modern, high-tech science observatories on the planet? And where else can you do that wearing a kimono or hoop skirt?

The local steampunkers, for the most part, simply rejoice in the look and style of the movement.

Plymouth, New Hampshire author Kyle Newton and his girlfriend, Krissy Guilfoyle, are special guests of the Cog and have a signing table right at the front of the parade grounds. Business is brisk as Kyle specializes in steampunk novels and stories.

His newest young reader book series, *The Cog Railway Mysteries: The Mystery of Mister Marsh*, features the railway's founder.

Kyle is the perfect example of the mixed genre aesthetic of steampunk, there in a deep purple, vaguely Asian-style pullover and kilt. Krissy hues more toward traditional steampunk, her fiery pink hair setting off her mostly black lacy Victorian Wild West outfit.

Kyle fell into steampunk after discovering that his interest in the Victorian age, coupled with a love for Westerns, could be combined in this alternate reality universe. And it was all brought together by the Cog Railway.

"I think the Cog Railway's creator, Sylvester Marsh, would be happy knowing people are still being inspired by his train station," Kyle says. "He did the impossible. I don't think that's a message we should forget. His enthusiasm for life matched that steampunk element of vibrantly captivating and encouraging imagination. I think he'd be entertained by mystery books about kids finding their courage at his train station; that's where he found his, isn't it?"

Good question. In all the ink spilled over the engineering wonder of the Cog, it's easy to forget that Marsh was already wealthy and sixty-five years old when Peppersass first chugged its way to the top. That's a lot of living in the mid-nineteenth century before creating his masterpiece.

And though he may have been a native son born in Campton, New

Hampshire, the foundation that lead to his drive to build a railway to the moon began far from the mountains of New Hampshire. To find the fire that ignited Marsh's burning inventor impulse, I'd have to travel west, first to Chicago and then back home.

I'd have to return to Buffalo.

I sit on a park bench, nearly on the footprint of where Sylvester Marsh made his fortune. I'm eating what the operator of the nearby food truck optimistically called a Mexican Spring Roll, in other words a spring roll with orange rice. There are two in the box, with a side of lettuce and tomato and slathered with some sort of sweet red sauce. The food truck is parked ten feet away from the main entrance of KeyBank Center, home of the Buffalo Sabres.

As I ordered my food, the three hockey players depicted in the statue of the French Connection (the greatest offensive starting lineup in Sabre history) looked over my shoulder with hard copper eyes. Their 1970s-style hair and mustaches are a giveaway to the period of time when hockey electrified this city, and also to when my cousin Joey would stuff me into his Nova muscle car and take me to hockey games to watch those very three men in that violent and beautiful ballet.

In other words, I was home. But Buffalo is nothing like when I left her. When the steel plants collapsed in the early 1980s, the Buffalo waterfront along the Niagara River collapsed with it. My uncle worked for Bethlehem Steel. In 1982 the company reported a $1.5 billion loss and began shedding workers, nearly seven thousand in the Buffalo area alone. The company never recovered and nearly took the city down with it.

But in the late 1990s, this place, Canalside, jerked up from the ashes of Buffalo's painful brownfield past and a renewal began to take place. The original terminus of the Erie Canal was dug out and renovated. A large lakefront park was established.

Along with a rejuvenated Buffalo Naval Park and Museum, this area of the city is vibrant and colorful. Children are swarming over whole row of rainbow-colored Adirondack chairs. Just over my shoulder, a group of middle-aged men and women are taking a yoga class on the grass. Outdoor sculptures dot the landscape.

When Sylvester Marsh was here making money in the 1840s, the concept of the river or lake as a place for recreation would never have occurred to him, or city leaders for that matter. Before the twentieth century steel mills moved in, Buffalo was the largest grain and flour port in the world, and this part of the city was industrial, vibrant, and rough.

It was called Central Wharf back then, and if you were a businessman in Buffalo in the mid-nineteenth century, odds are you spent a lot of time here. No one lived in Central Wharf, but it was the center of commerce for the insurance industry, one of the largest ports in the Great Lakes and the center of grain activity along the Erie Canal shipping channel. There were more bars, gin joints and houses of ill repute than anyone could count. A then-unknown hobo named Jack London was picked up for vagrancy in 1894 and came through the area on the way to Erie County Correctional Facility for a thirty-day stay.

But it was right here, along these shores, right where my spring roll was getting eaten, where Sylvester Marsh showed up, flush with wealth from Chicago, and changed the direction of the Industrial Revolution.

Marsh's path to Buffalo was indirect and reads like a Forest Gumpian romp through early nineteenth century American history. He was born into a Congregationalist family on a farm in Campton. His mother, Mehitable, died when he was nineteen and his father, John, left the farm. With the family broken up, Sylvester packed a bag and walked the 117 miles to Boston, and through a little bit of luck and no small amount of self-salesmanship, he managed to get a job in Boston's brand new Quincy Market, working the provision and meat trade with the two men who would form Sylvester's life-long ideology about progressive reform through technology.

Sylvester's first bosses in his young life, the brothers William and Francis Jackson, were early abolitionists and involved in the women's suffrage movement. The brothers' homestead, the Jackson House in Newton,

Massachusetts, still stands as the home for the Newton Historical Society. The Jackson home served as an important stop along the Underground Railroad.

Sylvester came away from these relationships with a clear liberal bent but also with a fascination with rail. William Jackson was a politician, eventually going on to become a U.S. Representative. But during his days in the market with Sylvester, William was one of the founders of the Boston & Worcester Railroad, Boston's first steam railway.

By the time Sylvester left Boston for Chicago in 1833, the thirty-year-old was a successful businessman, deeply involved in the politics of the day and already with visions of how modern technology could make both business and travel faster, easier, and safer.

When he arrived, Chicago was a frontier town with fewer residents than his hometown of Campton, but that meant land was cheap, and he knew the railroads were coming. He nearly single-handedly founded the Chicago meatpacking industry, building a steam-operated, three-story packing plant along the Chicago River only yards from Lake Michigan. Trump Tower currently stands on the approximate location of Sylvester's factory. The railroad showed up and terminated behind his plant. And along the river, corn-fed cattle and hogs were delivered directly from the prairies. In one door, out the other.

His first patent was a lard rendering device which made processing so fast and kept the beef so fresh that the *Chicago Press and Tribune* reported that his brand was "so well-known and so highly esteemed as to sell readily at the top of the market without inspection."

And where did Sylvester sell his beef? Well, Boston of course, via the Erie Canal out of Buffalo.

One other moment of note in Sylvester's Chicago life is worth mention: a lawsuit known as the Sandbar Case. A land dispute over about five acres of land between Sylvester and a local real estate developer was finally brought to District Court in 1860, long after Sylvester had already returned to New Hampshire and had begun work on the Cog Railway.

Nonetheless, he decided to hire the best Illinois lawyer he knew to represent him, a tall beardless fellow from Springfield. The lawyer won the case for Sylvester, and it turned out to be the last time the Springfield attorney appeared in a courtroom, as one month later, Abraham Lincoln was nominated for the presidency.

(Sylvester would have one more brush with the White House in September of 1869, when in a publicity coup that rippled across the country, President Ulysses S. Grant arrived with an entourage to ride the newfangled mountain railway. A cannon was fired as Grant's car reached the summit. The president then took a walk-about on the summit and the whole party posed for a now-famous photograph in front of the Tip Top House.)

By the time Sylvester got to Buffalo, he had already invented and was benefiting financially from one of the most important technological inventions of the industrial age, and one that nearly no one knows about. Once again, in the dramatic rhetoric of the time, the *Chicago Press and Tribune* wrote an article on Sylvester's newest invention saying, "We regard this as one of the most important discoveries of the age, and its enterprising ingenious inventor will live in history as one of the benefactors of his species."

Sylvester named his invention "Marsh's Caloric Grain Dryer." And I came to Buffalo to figure out exactly what that was and why it made the Cog Railway's inventor one of the richest men in the country.

In 2016, *The Telegraph*, one of Britain's largest newspapers, ranked Buffalo, New York, as one of the world's smelliest cities. This was not a slight. In fact, so thrilled was the Buffalo tourist establishment that they held a celebration at the city's convention center where they heralded recognition of the city's iconic scent. The tagline of that celebration, printed on t-shirts and bumper stickers, was My City Smells Like Cheerios.

As I cross over the grated South Michigan Avenue Bridge in Buffalo's First Ward, that distinction becomes pleasantly apparent, for on the other side of the bridge, along the Niagara River, General Mills has been producing the classic cereal for nearly eighty years. I roll down my window and take my time rolling over the bridge, in part to take in that familiar smell, but also because the view of the massive silo city along the river-front is particularly impressive from here.

The post-Revolutionary War history of wheat and grain shipping in the country is complicated, but the short version is this. Prior to 1825, in order to get wheat and grain from places like the central plains, Ohio, or even Pennsylvania to New York City, the product had to be transported down the Mississippi to New Orleans and then around to the big city markets, a costly process that could take three to six months. Then in 1825, the 363-mile Erie Canal opened, connecting Buffalo and Lake Erie to Albany and the Hudson River. That changed everything, and Buffalo went from a backwater to the most important port of call on the Great Lakes nearly overnight.

But the city needed to figure out a way to handle the wheat and grain traffic and keep it safe and stored on its journey to New York City, and figure out how to move it from lake vessels to canal boats. Enter the steam-powered grain elevator, an invention by necessity created by entrepreneur Joseph Dart and engineer Robert Dunbar.

Buffalo historian and State University of New York professor Francis Kowsky writes that Dunbar's invention improved efficiency to such an extent that he was praised as the father of the grain elevator system.

"By means of a steam-powered vertical conveyor belt made of leather or canvas and equipped with buckets, Dart could unload grain directly from the hulls of a lake vessel moored alongside his storage elevator," Kowsky writes. "Inside the ship, men who before this had carried barrels on their backs from boat to dock now shoveled grain into the conveyor belt buckets. They were the first generation of 'scoopers,' as the laborers—more often than not Irish immigrants or their descendants—who unloaded the lake vessel cargoes in this way came to be called."

By 1865, the Buffalo waterfront had at least twenty-five of the enormous grain elevators working the lake and port with a storage capacity of nearly two million barrels. The city had become the world's largest grain port, surpassing even London.

But it took one final invention—one small addition to the industry—to push the city over the top, and that's where Sylvester came in.

The grain in the lake vessels often became damp in the traverse across the lakes, and elevator operators needed to find a way to dry the product and keep it dry in storage before being sent onto the canal. Enter the Marsh Dryer, a separate structure that attached onto the side of a grain elevator. The elevator's marine leg would lift the grain onto a square, metal surface, sometimes up to eight hundred square feet around. The square was perforated with tiny holes. As the grain was raked over the square, blasts of hot air from below would dry the grain, and then a blast of cold air would cool it before being shunted into the elevator's storage bin.

The idea and application was simple and practical, and before long Marsh's Dryer was attached to dozens of grain elevators, including one of the first, the Dunbar Reed Grain Elevator. One of the largest of its kind, it sat on the water where the Buffalo Naval Park greets visitors today.

In the foyer of the Buffalo and Erie County Historical Society Museum is a wall-sized map from 1863 called *Bird's Eye Views of the City of Buffalo, NY.* The map is deeply detailed, showing a three-dimensional view of the city from Lake Erie. The detail is so specific, if you look closely you can see the windows in the buildings and even illustrations of people and horses and carriages moving along the streets. There at the waterfront is a grain elevator, taller than any building in the area. It is marked "Reed Elevator."

And butting up against the left side of the elevator, half as tall, is a square, flat-roofed building. It is marked "Marsh Caloric Grain Dryer."

Marsh was a problem solver. How do I get out of rural New Hampshire and find a good job? I walk to Boston and work for men with connections. How do I get meat packed and preserved? I build a warehouse on cheap land along a river in a city about to explode. How do I make money off of grain and wheat, the biggest economic engine of the day? I invent a machine that increases productivity and keeps the product fresh.

Over and over again, Marsh found a way to make a burgeoning industry faster, safe, easier. And he had one more trick up his sleeve. He'd come back to his home state and find a way to push the brand new tourist industry up to the summit of the North East's highest mountain.

I had one last stop to make, one final question I wanted answered. Like Alex McKenzie. Like Alton Weagle. Like Barbara Hull and George Etzweiler. What was in Sylvester's bones, in his spirit, that drove him—in the shadow of Mount Washington—to do what most thought was not possible? I found that answer, surrounded by towering white concrete storage towers, in a place called Silo City, from a tall man with a loud voice and a tattoo on his arm that read "In Rust We Trust."

Larry Mruk is a big man, six foot easy, with a long chin that ends in a bushy reddish beard and a wide grin that seems to take over his face. He gathers us all together in a gravel parking lot where we stand in a semi-circle around him. At Larry's back rises up the collection of enormous grain towers and elevators that make up Buffalo's newest tourist destination, Silo City. The brilliant white silos seem to touch the bright blue sky, each a football field long, connected by walkways and elevator belts all turned a striking deep red by rust and metal decay. And behind the collection of worn but beautiful mills, the Niagara River calmly flows. There are kayakers in the river, drifting idly by the ruins.

This place has many names: the grain belt, the grain mill corridor, concrete jungle, river of industry. Its detractors, those that would like to see them all brought down and condos or parks built in their place, call this place an eyesore. Supporters, like Larry, see potential and a link to what once made this place great, and could possibly again.

You can call Silo City a lot of things, but to Larry, don't you dare call it a wasteland.

"This place is special, this place is spiritual," he says. "I call it a campus."

There are six distinct structures out here, built between 1906 and 1930. They are all abandoned now, but the Lake and Rail Elevator building was only recently decommissioned in 2017. This hulking monster of a mill once had a grain capacity of nearly 4,500,000 bushels. The building still has running water and electricity.

To Larry, these are not crumbling abandoned buildings. They are his children, each with its own distinct personality and characteristics, each with its own history and connection to the city. In fact, Larry's flesh and blood daughter had her wedding pictures taken inside one of the silos. Larry, a design teacher and photographer, also designed her dress.

Nowadays, he works as a docent for Explore Buffalo, a historic preservation and tourist organization that takes the curious inside these structures for the sole purpose of raising awareness and working to refurbish and redesign places like Silo City into everyday destinations. The owners of this campus, for example, want to open a restaurant on site, and they already run a series of art exhibits and theatrical shows on the grounds.

One of the first things Larry does before leading us into the silos is roll up his sleeve. Near his shoulder, he has a tattoo of a view of the silos as they look as you roll over the South Michigan Street Bridge. The background is red and rust colored. The words under the image read, "In Rust We Trust."

"They call me the silo guy," he proclaims. "Other people call me crazy. But crazy is good, if crazy is good!" He winks, and we're on our way.

Our first stop is the Marine A Grain Elevator, built in 1925. There are thirty concrete silos in this monster, each 120 feet high and thirty feet around. We walk down toward the river, make a hard right through a beaten path with high weeds on either side and enter through a short door at the lowest level of the building, directly into the bottom of a silo. The reverberation down here is startling, the echo so pronounced, it's difficult to hear Larry speak. Above us is 130 feet of air, in front of us is four hundred feet of silo chambers. At the other end of the building is Silo City's performing arts center, a space for poetry readings and Shakespeare in the echoes.

There's a bit of graffiti, but nothing serious. There is a caretaker at Silo City, a fellow known as Swanee Jim who lives in an off-the-grid shack on the site, but there's a lot of doors, windows and holes in the walls around here, and kids still get in.

I poke my head into an adjoining silo and notice an interesting tag: an image of two woman wearing flowing dresses in an embrace. One has white hair, the other blue. The blue haired woman has no face. The one with the white hair has enormous eyes, curved up like a Thai Buddha might have. They have the silo to themselves and the effect, there in the shadows that play on the wall from the tiny window above, is haunting and melancholy.

But Larry isn't interested in melancholy. This holy place, to him, is one of strength.

"Here's what I all want you to do," he says, his voice booming and echoing in the concrete chamber. "When I count to three, I want you all to look up and shout 'Silo!' as loud as you can, and then let's time the reverberation. I bet we can make it last a minute!"

I scramble to get my voice recorder up on my phone and barely hit record in time for the group of a dozen adults to scream to the concrete. The sound bounces around inside that tower, the silo seeming to vibrate. Everyone gets quiet to listen as the walls themselves speak to us over and over, until the sound is just a whisper. It lasts a long time. I look down at my phone: 47 seconds.

"See," says Larry, "pretty cool, right?"

The morning rolls by in wonder and exuberance. We wander through a literal tour of twentieth century industry; the Perot Malt House and its 150-foot-tall elevator, its imposing furnaces with heavy, green iron doors still intact; the ferry *Columbia*, once a tourist boat that took riders from Buffalo up to Crystal Beach and Niagara Falls, now a splendid rusting hulk alongside the Marine A; and a broken-down stage and some props, including a Wild West carriage that is used by theater groups for show in front of the silos and tourists who come to see the laser light shows.

We conclude the tour down by the river, behind the Perot Elevator, its massive barge arm still resting along the old tracks, ready to roll back and forth extracting barley out of lake ships. Larry insists that with a little grease and a good electrician that side arm could be back in service.

The tour nearly over, I have a sudden twinge of regret. This campus was born four decades after Sylvester's dryer took the industry by storm. His invention was used primarily in the great, original wooden mills. He could never have predicted how far the industry would have come by 1906. Earlier, Larry had pointed out the modern grain mill equivalent of the Marsh Caloric Dryer. Near the top of Marine A was a bulging metal turbine, called a cyclone grain dryer or cyclone dust collector, that served nearly the same purpose at a tenth of the size of Sylvester's dryer. The cyclone uses centripetal force to separate the grain from the dust and the air, letting the grain drop down into the bin while pushing the dust and air out—almost like air sealing.

I wasn't going to see a Marsh Caloric Dyer, because one no longer existed.

But once again, my quest to understand a piece of geography 550 miles away led me to a moment of raw emotional discovery, a pure instant where the connection between Larry and this place brought the connection between Sylvester and the Cog Railway into stark focus.

There in a beautiful old entrance hall of the Perot Malt House, with a modern art piece of long, colorful pipes hanging above us and the ancient, dusty furnace as a backdrop, as Larry thanks us all for being part of the tour that morning, much to all of our shock, he begins to cry. A docent helper comes over and puts her arm around his shoulder, and he sobs for a moment. No one knows what to do.

"I'm sorry, I'm so sorry, I promised that I wouldn't do this," he says. "But my wife passed away last week . . ."

And there we are, a dozen strangers from around the world brought to this industrial alter by chance, and we all come together, each of us moving in, moving closer, closing the circle on a man who came here not to grieve but because this place—these monuments—help him heal.

They had been together thirty-eight years, Ellen and Larry, had three kids, were college sweethearts. "She was my Irish bride," Larry says. Ellen fought cancer for eight years. She and Larry had two grandchildren on the way when she passed.

After the well wishes and handshakes, as we all separate and begin to head home, I walk with Larry over to his truck where he shows me family photos. He has them in his truck, has been carrying them around with him. Some of Ellen and Larry on vacations, some of his family.

He leans back on the hood of his trunk and takes a deep breath, the tour behind him, the restraints of being a showman loosening. We're alone out there now. He doesn't want to leave. I can't say I blame him.

"That was brave of you to open up like that," I say.

He shrugs. "I didn't mean to do that, they told me to stay home, but I couldn't."

"This place is special."

Larry nods. "Want to go see the building they want to turn into a restaurant?" he asks.

"Lead the way!"

We begin a slow walk across the gravel to an old red brick building that will soon become an eatery, and the river flows like it always has, and the old concrete pillars of progress wait to rise up again. And people come, like Larry, to be reborn amid iron and metal.

I came to Buffalo looking for insight into Sylvester Marsh's inventions, but what I found was a window into his soul.

At the steampunk fairgrounds, Sylvester Marsh and his wife Cordelia are handing out awards for best costumes. In an interesting scene, where the past and present seemed to merge, the actors playing Sylvester and Cordelia stand inside the cab of Old Peppersass as the steampunk participants gather below them. There are speeches, awards, and cheering.

Earlier, as I watched the parade from the second-floor deck of Marshfield Station, I overhead two older women chatting. They had not come for the festival.

"Well," one said to the other, "that's the parade, I guess."

"I guess," her friend said. They watched Kevin squeak by on his penny farthing. "I think I'm ready for lunch now."

Cordelia is played by Rebecca Metcalf, the railway's marketing director. Sylvester is played by Wayne Boyce, also an employee of the Cog Railway and a jack of many trades it seems.

When he's not donning a top hat and sticking long, bushy sideburns to his face, Wayne works for two days a week at the top of the mountain at the summit post office. The other three days of the week he works at Marshfield Station.

He's much younger than Sylvester was during Marsh's Cog years. Sylvester was also thin as a weed and had a chin-only underbeard of all white. Wayne is none of those things. But he is an engaging performer who has owned this role the whole day, and he brings Sylvester's passion for all things mechanical to the character.

"People have always told me what a ham I was," he says. "But when you're doing a job like this, you have to tell stories, make it interesting so people can relate."

Telling stories is what he does in his spare time as well, as he's the lay pastor of a nearby church where he gives regular homilies. This is only his first year working for the Cog, but he's already developed a solid understanding of the way the trains work, as you'd think he'd have to in order to play the Cog founder.

In short, Sylvester invented a rack rail design system, using a ladder-like rack rail with open bar rungs. Those rungs are engaged by the teeth of the center cog wheel, which is the force that powers the engine up the mountain and allows it to not slip on the way down, much like a bicycle gear grabbing the chain. The open bar rungs also prevent the rack from getting clogged with snow or debris.

The passenger car is not coupled in any way with the engine, which pushes the car up. On the way down, the car rests up against the descending engine, and brake men work brake chains from inside the passenger car to keep the car from clanging against the engine. The passenger car is not coupled because should something catastrophic happen to the engine, the brake men could, in theory, halt the passenger car on the tracks without the engine.

The current Cog uses both steam and biodiesel engines. The trip is about three miles to the top. On the way up, the Cog can move at just under three miles per hour. On the way down, though, with a practiced crew, she can get up to about five miles an hour. The Cog Railway on Mount Washington has an average grade of about 25 percent, on Jacob's Ladder—where Alton Weagle was married—that grade jumps to nearly 38 percent. The Cog is the second steepest rack railway in the world. The first is the Pilatus Railway in Switzerland.

Wayne tells me these things in far more words. His technical knowledge is impressive, and his obvious passion for the Cog is a thrill to behold. But what interests me the most is that this whole operation—the railway,

Marshfield Station, the patents and inventions, the tourists, all of it—is the direct result of a case of indigestion.

Riding the Cog is not comfortable, let's be clear. The experience is jarring and the passenger car is cramped, in particular because we are full to the brim with costumed steampunk festival-goers with big hats, heavy boots, and goggles. I'm pretty sure every one of them wears goggles. Some have goggles on top of their goggles. If the wind catches the train at just the proper moment, ash and cinders from the engine will waft into the car and sting exposed skin. And it's very, very loud.

If this were a normal experience, say the auto road coach or an airplane, you'd want your money back.

But not here. Here, as the tree line opens to the magnificent west side views of Mount Jefferson and the engineer lets loose with a thirty-second blast from the iconic Cog whistle, it is—without hyperbole—a ride unlike any other on the planet. It has always been that, and that's what makes the Cog Railway such a deeply satisfying encounter. Riding in that car—especially if you're in the steam engine—is a momentary blurring of time, like space itself has folded over to give you a glimpse into the soul of the last century.

People laugh on this ride, laugh for no other reason than because of the impossibility of it all, the very fact of its continued existence. Even Sylvester, so the story goes, did not come back to New Hampshire to create a railway to the moon. He came back—accomplished and retired at fifty years old—to live out his remaining days as a gentleman of standing and leisure. But that's didn't work out.

Sylvester was unable to sit still and found not doing anything far more difficult than working. He became depressed, had a hard time eating.

He came down with a terrible case of what at the time was called dyspepsia. In other words, indigestion. The doctors told him he needed exercise, maybe some fresh air. Sylvester, typically, interpreted that to mean that he should find the most difficult outdoor pursuit that could be found and do that. In 1857, that was climbing Mount Washington, which he set out to do with Boston pastor Augustus Thompson. The two men set out on a clear, mild morning and very nearly became casualties of the mountain.

Overtaken by a storm along the Crawford Path, the men barely made it to the Tip Top House before collapsing in exhaustion. Later, Marsh wrote that his first thought upon finally crawling on his hands and knees into the safety of shelter was that there must be "some easier and safer method of ascension."

There wasn't. The carriage (auto) road was not going to be completed for four more years. So Marsh decided, like he had over and over in his life, to do it himself.

Meanwhile, my train has chugged, shimmied, rattled and whistled its way to the summit where the steampunks make a grand show of exiting their car, capes flowing, dresses billowing. Most of them put on their goggles at the summit. It's a grand display, full of due process. It occurs to me that this is another perfect moment, another instant when the summit of an oversized pile of rocks once again creates legend and memory out of simply existing. Like most moments of personal discovery atop or because of Mount Washington, the connection between what once was, what is and what could be turns out to be inviting, direct and repeated over and over.

Most of the steampunk attendees I speak to insist Sylvester would be thrilled to see such a festival taking place on his railway line, that he'd relish any movement that paid such deep respect toward and so deeply appreciated the gears and pipes, and the steam that gave him such joy. Even Wayne nods.

"Any group that so loves my invention, makes my life's work worth it," he says, speaking to me as Sylvester.

For a brief moment there at the summit a thin mist blows up and over the top, cloaking the train and the Victorian gentlemen and ladies in a blurry veil of time. Peering through that hazy looking glass is haunting, a second's flash of ghostly shadows of the past.

And then it's gone. The air clears, the pizza and hot dogs appears, the tourists in sneakers and shorts mingle with those in top hats, and somewhere down the track, a single Cog Railway whistle blows to herald the old age and the new age. The cog wheel turns, the mountain stands.

CHAPTER NINE

Kindred Spirits

Seeing Mount Washington through the Eyes of the Artists

Is my soul's pleasure; and it sure must be
Almost the highest bliss of human-kind,
When to thy haunts two kindred spirits flee.
—John Keats

In his now-classic work on the Appalachian Trail, *A Walk in the Woods*, author and travel writer Bill Bryson spends some time thinking about a famous painting by the New Jersey born artist Asher Brown Durand.

In 1849, when Durand painted *Kindred Spirits*, he was a member of the burgeoning group of artists that would create a style that would come to be known as the Hudson River School. The founder of that school, Thomas Cole, had just died, and Durand wanted to honor Cole's memory with the painting. In it, Cole and his friend, the poet William Cullen Bryant, are standing high on a ledge, wearing formal overcoats and cravats, looking down into a deep valley. Cole is holding what appears to be a paint brush.

Far in the distance, below the friends, is a waterfall called the Kaaterskill. Like much of the Hudson River School, the landscape is idealized; there is not a place in the Catskill Mountains that looks like that.

But Bryson doesn't dwell on that. Instead, he's mesmerized by the temptation of the scene, the draw created by the juxtaposition of the two explorers in fancy clothes—the artist and the poet—against the hostile but beautiful background.

"I can't tell you how much I would like to step into that view," Bryson writes. "The scene is so manifestly untamed, so full of an impenetrable beyond, as to present a clearly foolhardy temptation. You would die out there for sure."

Bill is not alone. Nearly two hundred years later, those early paintings of the Catskills, Adirondacks, and the White Mountains and Mount Washington—in the early days of tourism—are as powerful a draw now as when tourists in wool skirts and top hats braved a trip to explore the scenes they saw in those paintings.

Over the years, I had the great fortune of exploring some of those wild places, of being able to drop myself into the fantastical landscapes depicted by the great artists of that time—the Emerald Pool, Elephant Head, Cathedral Ledge and, of course, the craggy top of Mount Washington.

I knew what it felt like to explore places I'd seen in glorious landscape paintings. I understood the powerful draw those artists created—celebrating the majesty and danger, the power and awe, of my beloved mountain.

But I didn't know how they did it. I hadn't put brush to canvas since, perhaps, elementary school. I couldn't draw. I couldn't cartoon. How could paint on cloth serve as inspiration? How were artists able to sway your soul?

I planned on finding out, and to do that I needed to become an artist. Which made my current situation all the more perplexing.

I'd come to Bartlett, New Hampshire, to learn to paint, but here I was tromping through the undergrowth alongside a highway trying not to get my feet wet.

My plan was to immerse myself in the goings-on of the twenty or so artists from around the region who annually descended on the Bartlett Inn for four days of workshops, discussion and landscape painting.

As I traveled backward into the history of Mount Washington, it became clearer and clearer that it was the artists of the mid nineteenth century, with their wildly imagined landscapes of the rough and rugged wilderness of the White Mountains, that first made upper-crusters from around the world curious about just what the heck was going on in that little known, distant state anyway.

Landscapes from what became known as the Hudson River School of Art started showing up in exhibits in Philadelphia, Boston, San Francisco and in Europe, with their romantic images of the valleys of Conway, the deep and impenetrable notches and the towering spires of Mount Washington. And before long, those folks began showing up in White Mountains, searching for those views.

Tourists had already started trickling in by the 1830s, but those paintings opened the floodgates.

I wanted to see what they saw, feel the inspiration of those mountains myself. I wanted to gaze upon Mount Washington and be inspired to do something I'd never yet done; paint her.

But first, with my coffee in one hand and my notebook in the other, I had to find Byron Carr. Based on information from a quick cell phone call, I had parked my car near an overpass along Route 302 in Bartlett, just about two hundred yards down the state highway where the artists held their retreat. Byron had already left that morning to set up near the water before the sun got too high.

I trotted across the road and walked to the middle of the bridge before seeing him standing on a rock in the middle of Albany Brook. Now, after some scrambling through the weeds, I manage to make it down myself. He hears me coming, thrashing through the undergrowth.

"Hey, you found me," he calls out, eyes never leaving his canvas.

This isn't our first meeting. Byron had been the one who invited me to come to this retreat, and weeks earlier I had visited his studio in Contoocook where the first steps in my landscape education had begun. But this was the real stuff—a single painter in work boots, facing the curve in the river where the late morning sun best hit the leaves and fired them into brilliant reds and golds, easel on a rock, palette in hand, his eye an organic camera. Byron makes a few long strokes and steps back to eyeball the canvas.

"Not bad," he says to me, "looks like I managed to cover up all the numbers!"

And just like that, the veneer of artist as romantic is broken. Byron smiles, and I find a rock near the painter on which to get comfortable enough to drink my coffee and take some notes. Byron is a working man's artist—like an in-demand studio musician who has been in the business long enough to call his own shots and not be beholden to any of the rock stars he works for. Byron is steady and sure, and he'd be my guide for the two days I was planning on spending with the artists.

My artist guide got a late start on his creative career, beginning to paint seriously when he turned forty; he's sixty-seven now. At the time, he explains, he daughter was two and a half, and he wanted to write and illustrate a children's book for her.

"That got me thinking that at one time in my life, I meant to be an artist," Byron says. "But life just got in the way. So I thought, what the heck?"

Byron spent a few months reviving his creative muscles and learning how to be an artist. At first, he'd simply walk around town, setting up easels alongside the road to make sketches of some of his favorite trees.

"I felt awkward and self-conscious," he says. "I almost quit a few times."

But some advice from fellow New Hampshire artist Stapleton Kearns gave Byron a boost in those early days. The advice appeals deeply to my own sense of the aesthetic of geography coming from a career in journalism. Kearns told Byron to pursue and be aware of the difference between reporting and poetry. Like those early painters gazing at Mount Washington for the first time and understanding that their painting would also be the first time others saw the mountain, the artistic pursuit is often about capturing impressions, or feelings, rather than the fact of a scene. That's what elevates the art.

In the meantime, I notice Byron has a second canvas, blank, at his feet.

"How many paintings do you try to create over the course of a retreat?" I ask.

He shrugs. "I don't try to get a certain number. I just try to get good ones."

Then, sensing my follow up question, he says. "This place, I've driven by here a hundred times, but today for some reason the light appealed to me, so that's what I'm focusing on."

He's using oils down here, easier than acrylics when in the field. The late morning sun is spraying light down through the trees near the brook bend he's painting. With the birches and maples already red and yellow, the serrated sunlight makes the whole section of the stream pop.

It's easy to be distracted down here. Watching artistic creation is not the same thing as creating. I can't imagine what it would be like watching me write.

I keep being pulled away from the canvas: the babble of the brook, the movement of bright red leaves in the currents, the walnuts that drop like tiny bombs out of trees around us. All these things draw my eyes and ears. Where I'd like to be is in Byron's head.

Lost in thought, he moves back again. "I don't know about that background."

He's referring to the fact that a bank of clouds has blocked some of the rays of light. It occurs to me that a mountain artist is never actually going to capture the original view they saw—that the landscape here is always fluid. Nowadays, some artists will take a picture and then work off that later in their studio. But the preferred method of the Bartlett artist group—and indeed of the Hudson Valley School—is called en plein air painting, or painting outdoors. The act of working with natural light became important to Impressionists like Monet and Renoir, and that work ethic carried over to the Hudson School artists.

Only about thirty yards behind us, a motorcycle tears by on the road, the muffler echoing loudly in the trees, as though to punctuate the fact that en plein air artists have more to deal with than just changing weather.

"Hey, I'm trying to paint down here!" Byron yells over his shoulder.

I laugh, and he lifts an eyebrow.

"What?" he says. "I can be focused and still aware of my surroundings."

The morning slips by like the brook nearly under our feet. I find myself relaxing into the task of being a spectator. After a while, the image on the canvas begins to take form, and I try to focus on what's on the canvas—the rocks, trees, light—and compare that to the actual scene.

Finally, Byron steps back a few feet again and takes a long pause. He smiles.

"Well, I haven't screwed up yet!"

The more time I spend with Byron, the more I begin to appreciate why artists of all stripes have worked so hard over hundreds of years to tame Mount Washington and put the mountain in words, or paint, or photographs: because being here is fun.

Imagine browsing an art gallery in Boston in 1870. You've heard there's a new painting on display, set in the White Mountains. Though you've lived in Bean Town all your life, you've never made the arduous 150-mile journey to the mountains. You've seen a few sketches of the mountains here and there, and heard all the tall tales. And two years ago, in a weekly magazine, you saw an illustration from a young artist named Winslow Homer of a painting called *Bridle Path, White Mountains*. This painting was of a lone rider on horseback, a tourist and a woman! From the looks of it, not only was she independent and confident, but she appeared to be far above the clouds, mountains all around her.

Mountains are on your mind when you turn a corner and come upon a monumental canvas, ten feet wide, bordered by an enormous, gold frame. And yet, for all its grandeur, the painting called *The Emerald Pool*, of a place at the foot of Mount Washington, is intimate and concealed. Despite the towering bulk of the imposing mountain behind the waterfall depicted in the painting, the pool itself is gentle. Deer seem to walk unafraid right out of the woods. Albert Bierstadt's painting makes the idea of visiting a place that in your head seemed distant and dangerous, now suddenly possible. Maybe you can get out of the claustrophobic city, make it up there, take a train or a coach. Maybe you can even get to stand right there, next to that pool. Maybe.

So you tell some friends and bring them to see the painting for themselves. And there are others. That painting, and many others like it, is exhibited in New York, Philadelphia, and Chicago. Bierstadt's painting even wins a medal in Vienna.

That place, the spectacular pool of water under the watchful eye of the towering mountain; you can't get it out of your head. It's time you made a pilgrimage to the White Mountains.

Nineteenth-century artists like Bierstadt were at the vanguard of and eager participants in capturing the wild and unwieldy (and often deadly) wilderness of the White Mountains in sketches and paintings and offering their visions up to eager adventurers around the world. These early artists captured the imagination of a country looking to explore and expand—and soon, the tourists began to come.

What's so extraordinary about much of the work that first brought tourists to the White Mountains is how beautifully unrealistic the paintings actually are. In Bierstadt's famous painting, for example, Mount Washington bolts up from the earth in the background of the pool, giving the scene an epic atmosphere. In reality, no mountain can actually be seen from the real Emerald Pool.

Often times, the artists would exaggerate the heights of the mountains or place cliffs and other features where there were none. This wasn't an attempt to be dishonest, but rather simple artistic license to create scenes that combined a variety of impressions about the geography. Like Byron's attempting poetry instead of reporting.

And at any rate, most tourists didn't care, as the area itself was so exciting and unlike anything they'd ever seen, once they got there, the paintings tended to be forgotten.

While the facts and history surrounding those early years of artistry was interesting, what I was looking for was a way to feel that inspiration myself. Even before I stood near a creek watching Byron at work, I wanted to bear witness to his own source of inspiration, and that meant going to his studio.

Like Groveton to the north, Contoocook is not officially anything. Rather, the tiny village inside the town of Hopkinton is also a census designated place, an asterisk in New Hampshire's lower Merrimack County, swallowed and nearly forgotten by its proximity to the state's capital, Concord.

But for an afterthought, Contoocook is a pretty heavy hitter, history-wise.

It is the birthplace of George Hamilton Perkins, who went on to be a commander in the Civil War. Perkins earned his place in Naval history by being the commander of one of the Union Monitors used to capture the Confederate Ironside *CSS Tennessee* in the Battle of Mobile Bay in August of 1864. News of the battle and capture of the port became crucial boosts for Abraham Lincoln's reelection three months later.

Perkins's birthplace still stands in the cross-roads of downtown Contoocook, though sadly Perkins Manor today is simple apartment housing.

Contoocook's second claim to fame is the river from which the village takes its name. The seventy-one-mile long watercourse flows from Pool Pond and Contoocook Lake near Jaffrey to just north of Concord where it dumps into the Merrimack River. The significance of it? Due to some odd geography in the landscape, it's one of only a couple rivers in the state that flow primarily northward.

And that's where Byron Carr comes in.

To find the artist's house, I travel on a long, rural straightway—not far from where renters now live in Perkins Manor, past a warehouse for amusements rides, past small cottages and large tree-lined front yards, until the road seems to thin and all that's left is grass and sloping hedgerows, a sign that water isn't far. And indeed, Byron's family home sits right along the Contoocook, that great northern flowing river, a perfect spot for an artist—in particular one who got his start by painting the trees that sat right outside his windows.

He's there in the grassy drive as I pull up. "Welcome! It's not much, but it's been home for a long time."

Byron's family has lived out here since 1917 and in this house since around 1930 when it was built by his grandfather. Byron's parents added to it in 1948, and then Byron and his wife, Louise, added to it again in 1990.

The home, low and tucked back from the road, is perfect for a landscape artist who happens to be a couple years away from retirement and looking for solitude and nature. I can faintly hear the river behind the house. It's a warm late summer day, and the rhythmic buzzing of cicadas hum on and off, on and off.

Byron's studio is down in the basement and you have to walk through, literally, a huge hole in a cement wall that was broken through when he expanded the house from its original footprint. His work desk, about half the size of a pool table, sits under two large plate glass windows that overlook the backyard. There's much light. And like every studio of every artist, at first glance it appears a tornado has recently run through the room. There is paint everywhere, of course, and supplies. Sketches on the walls, easels, frames, and piles and piles of paintings.

Byron estimates there are about 250 paintings in the basement. One of the first things he does, within minutes of meeting me, is take me into a small side room.

"Look over here," he says, pointing to a stack of thirty to forty paintings on top of each other. "That's my pile of tears."

He explains that those are discarded works, abandoned in the middle or tossed on the pile when finished because he didn't like them.

Byron is slight of stature; he looks like Captain Picard with a shaggy white beard. But he's fast on his feet and doesn't hold back. Artists in any genre can sometimes be precious about their work, speaking in the loftiest of terms about their muse, about the mystery of inspiration. Byron isn't like that.

"How do you know when a painting is done?" I ask.

He shrugs. "When I get sick of painting it."

To him, painting is a trade, like woodworking or car repair. You read about it, you study the folks who do it well, you do it yourself repeatedly and then you teach it. As Byron explains, a fellow artist gave him the advice that if you want to learn faster, teach. So Byron taught night classes while he was learning himself. And when the offer came to help plan and be part of the Bartlett Artist Retreat, he jumped at the chance. He's been doing it now for twelve straight years.

For nearly thirty years, he's worked at a local real estate management firm doing everything from fixing leaky toilets to renovating office space. But even in that job, he has the chance to express his creativity when he designs and builds storefronts for properties. At the nearby Orange Leaf Frozen Yogurt, all the interior mahogany trim and vestibule was done by Byron.

"So," he says, as we walk back to his work table. "What do you want to see?"

"Teach me to paint," I say, feeling immediately foolish for making such an impossible request.

But he doesn't miss a beat. Byron pulls a clean thick stock paper over to the table, mixes some globs of paint on the side and says, "Hit play on my laptop over there will you?"

He has a YouTube video of the opera *Don Giovanni* cued up. I click play and Byron says, "Okay, watch."

And as the first strains of Mozart's Overture fill the studio, Byron Carr takes a long, deep breath, sets brush to canvas and begins to paint.

I am on my way to the Bartlett artists retreat, driving south through Crawford Notch, on a glorious, warm fall day. There is no wind, and the sky and mountains feel mischievous, like they are keeping a secret. The notch is packed with tourists and hikers, leaf peepers and kids.

Near the southern end of the notch is one of those camera-ready pull-offs: a couple park benches, a nice cleared grassy area, and a straight-shot perfect view of the distant summit of Mount Washington. The day is so clear that the summit towers gleam as clear and bright as polished silver.

Sitting in a red canvas folding chair, under a black and silver umbrella, is an en plein artist plying her trade, painting the long view of the mountain. I slam a u-turn and roll into the pull-off. I'm here this weekend to study and learn about painting the mountains. Despite the fact that I'll be late getting to the retreat, here's a perfect chance to watch a painter at work.

When I approach, she's surrounded by onlookers. Some just watch, others are asking questions. "How long have you been painting?" "How do you decide what to paint?" "How long will it take to dry?" And my favorite, "Is it hard to paint in public?"

She's remarkably patient, answering the questions kindly and handing out business cards in between strokes. I puzzle for a moment about the act of strangers actively inserting themselves into the creative process. I've written at cafes, coffee shops and parks many times, but I've never attracted a crowd. Perhaps it's the visual aspect of actually watching an image appear on the canvas. A friend called it the Bob Ross effect, referring to the American artist and instructor who, for ten years on his popular PBS show, taught viewers about happy little trees and happy little clouds.

After a while, the curious thin out and I manage to introduce myself.

Her name is Leslie Scott-Lysan, she's from Wakefield, Massachusetts, and she's been set up here for about an hour, working on capturing the glowing Mount Washington. The canvas she's using is small, maybe a foot wide, and she takes her time, using small brushes for details.

"How long have you been painting?" I ask.

She shrugs, her eyes never leaving the canvas. "Off and on through my life, but seriously only about seven years ago after a trip to Mohegan Island."

Even to someone clueless about art history, Mohegan Island rings a bell. The tiny island, about twelve miles off the coast of Maine near Boothbay Harbor, is well known as an artist retreat. Samuel de Champlain visited the island all the way back in 1604, and explorers from Capt. John Smith to the famous pirate Richard Nolan have been coming ever since. The island's full-time population has never grown beyond 145, which they hit in 1870. As of 2010, only sixty-nine souls called the island their home.

But that number swells considerably in the summer months. In recent years, Mohegan Island has taken the shape of a popular and inspirational artist resort. An art colony was already established by the 1890s when such luminaries as William Henry Singer and Martin Borgord became early artists-in-residence. Since then, a revolving door of artists—including George Bellows, Edward Hopper, Rockwell Kent and Andrew Wyeth—have made appearances on the island.

There's a museum out there, and a handful of trinket and art supply shops.

And it was at one of those shops, inspired by the colony, that Leslie bought a painting kit—pencils, paper and brushes—and sketched a rusted, white iron bucket full of bright red geraniums. And she's been painting and honing her craft ever since.

She relies on what she calls a "spiritual connection" to the outdoors, and specifically to the White Mountains.

"This is my happy place," she tells me. "Making art for me is all about color, light and working alongside the Creator."

That attitude comes from that fact that her career in marketing was sidelined by the diagnosis of Takayasu's arteritis, a rare autoimmune disease. Once retired, she turned to her art as a form of healing and meditation. Now sixty, she's turned her hobby into a passion.

"What about you," she asks. "Are you an artist?"

"A writer," I say. "I'm heading down to an artist retreat in Bartlett to learn how to paint and write about them."

She laughs. "Well, you're off to a good start."

"What do you mean?"

"Well, that's the retreat I'm attending, I'm one of those artists!" She does put down her brush this time and looks up. "What would you like to know?"

And so, my weekend of art lessons begins in a rest area along a state route in the shadow of Mount Washington.

I've never met him, nor seen a picture of him, but the moment I walk into the art reception for painter Erik Koeppel at the Jackson Historical Society, I know exactly who he is. I know this not based on his art or any description; there's no one standing at a podium. There are likely around seventy-five people in that crowded hall.

I am able to recognize him instantly because of the simple fact that he actually looks like one might expect one of the world's youngest, and foremost authorities in the Hudson River School of Art, to look like.

The thirty-seven-year-old en plein authority is tall and thin, wearing a dark gray suit over an open collar shirt. Black shoes. Clean shaven. And on his head, an ivy cap, sometimes called a driver's cap. He looks as though he could suddenly mount a penny-farthing and peddle through the Jackson covered bridge and into the sunset.

This particular show is a fund-raiser for the Historical Society and is happening on the evening of my first night with the Bartlett artists, whose inn is just up the road. When I asked about the Hudson River School, Byron, Leslie, and several others told me to come here, to meet Erik.

"There is no artist doing what he's doing," Byron said.

"And so young!" said Leslie.

So here I am, on the day before my first art lesson, trying to get into the mind of a master and feeling entirely out of my element.

Up the road, the Bartlett artists are drinking Jack and eating subs, lounging in comfortable, well-worn chairs by a fireplace, telling stories about light and stone walls and cold creeks. Here, the surrounding area's high society is in attendance, eating finger sandwiches and sipping wine—a full cheese and grape spread on the long table down the center of the hall.

The Historical Society has been around since 1977 and resides in a beautifully restored, white Victorian two-story. The old town hall now houses the Museum of White Mountain Art at Jackson and holds receptions like this one throughout the year to celebrate its revolving collection.

In the mid-1800s, Jackson was one of the first places tourists—interested in the White Mountains due to the landscape art of painters like Thomas Cole—were drawn to. The old homes of locals became boarding houses, but in fairly short order, hotels and grand resorts began popping up to accommodate the influx. One of those resorts, The Wentworth Inn still stands, and before coming to this reception, I spent a pleasant half hour in the inn's lavish cafe sipping coffee.

For a better understanding of Jackson's place in the White Mountain economy, one has to look only as far as the Wentworth Inn, a grand hotel built out of a father's love for his daughter. Jackson resident Joshua Trickey had already made a name for himself by becoming one the first residents to build and open an inn for tourists: the Jackson Falls House, built in 1858. But in 1869, his daughter was betrothed to married the popular and famous General Marshall Clark Wentworth. Wentworth had served in the Civil War, and despite the fact that his title of "general" was honorary, Wentworth was a big deal in Jackson, a local boy made good and now coming home.

So, as a wedding gift to his daughter, Georgia, and the general, Trickey built the Wentworth Inn, then called the Thorn Mountain House. The resort changed hands and names a few times over the years and saw its peak in post-World War II when acts like Harry Belafonte, Zero Mostel and Jackie Mason gigged in the four hundred-seat casino.

But like most things in the mountains, history comes full circle. In 1988, the Wentworth was bought by a couple from Oregon who moved to Jackson with their then-eight-year-old son. The couple was Fritz and Diana Koeppel and their son was Erik.

In a place like Jackson, everyone knows each other, and everyone knows Erik, now one of the resort town's most famous residents.

In fact, so well-known is the town's resident master painter that in 2016 an exhibition was given called the Jackson Five, highlighting the five former and current artists with roots in Jackson. Two of those artists—Erik and his partner Lauren Sansaricq—are in the room today.

I grab a handful of finger foods—hummus and jam toasted onto two-inch round slices of rye bread—and decide to have a look at Erik's work before introducing myself. His paintings are lovely and sublime, meeting every bit of the expectations I had going in. The landscapes are dreamy and soft, even the unmistakable foreboding cloud patterns over Mount Washington. In many cases—much like

Cole's work—Erik manages to captures both the awe and the dread of a towering mountain.

How about that, I think; he actually is a master. Poetry over reporting.

Out of the corner of my eye I see one of my favorite historians in all of New England, Bob Cottrell. I angle over to him, feeling better that someone else in the room is wearing flannel. Bob's the curator of the Henney History Room at the Conway Public Library, and he holds an MA from the University of Delaware in Early American Culture. There's nothing about Mount Washington he does not know, and few people involved in any aspect of the history of the mountain are unfamiliar with Bob.

More than a year earlier, as I was just beginning to collect information for this project, seemingly everyone I spoke to—from hikers to CEOs—told me to go talk to Bob. And when I showed up at his door with the half-cocked idea of studying Mount Washington for a year, Bob did two things.

First, he pulled all the original *Among the Clouds* newspapers out of storage for me to read. *Among the Clouds* was the first and only newspaper printed at the summit, quite a feat for 1877.

Second, like a giddy schoolboy with a secret, he unveiled to me the original topographic molds, from the 1920s, built to make some of the original maps of the area. His approach to history is causal, but his enthusiasm is not; it's infectious.

"Fancy finding you here, Bob," I say, finally making my way through the crowd to meet him. He's busy setting up a projector; turns out he's giving a presentation on Thomas Cole as part of the reception.

"Hey Dan, I should have known you'd be here!"

We make small talk, but I'm most interested in his take on Erik's work.

"You can see for yourself that's it's pretty amazing," he says. "The really interesting thing about Erik's work—or Thomas Cole's, for that matter—is this meditative effect that distinguishes greatness from proficiency."

"Like reporting vs. poetry," I say, pretending to be smart.

"That's it!" he says.

We chat some more about the pull of paintings in attracting tourists, and out of nowhere, he lays a memorable factoid on me.

"See how most of the sizes of the paintings are about the same?" I look around the room at Erik's paintings and many of the others. Then I think of Byron's creek work. They are mostly the same size. "Back in the day, artists specifically used a certain size canvas to make it easier for tourist to fit the painting into their steamer trunks for easier transport home."

"Trunk paintings," I say, delighted.

Even then, artists were doing what they could to get a leg up on the competition. You won't buy a painting if you can't get it back on the train for the long ride home.

There's one last thing I'm curious about before meeting Erik himself. The main sponsor of this exhibit, a well-known Hudson River School art collector and philanthropist, Andy McLane, is hobnobbing with attendees, and I'm curious what has drawn him to the Whites all these years.

Though Andy lives down near Boston now and works at a private equity investment firm, he came from more humble beginnings: born in tiny Littleton, he was a member of one of the AMC's Hut Croos and a Peace Corp volunteer in the 1960s.

Today, he and his wife have made their mark on New Hampshire with some well-known philanthropic activity. Dartmouth College has a residence hall named after Andy's father and members of the family that are alumni due to a $9 million gift a couple years ago. And down in Plymouth, a $250,000 gift to the Museum of the White Mountains will go toward an annual fellowship given to Plymouth State University students to integrate museum programs into their classrooms.

Throw in being the sponsor of programs like this one, and owning more than three hundred works from a wide range of Hudson River School artists, and Andy McLane is, perhaps, what the Medici's might have called a living sponsor.

Tall and approachable, Andy sports the look of a north country banker—clean shaven, casual collared shirt, but not stuffy, like he could break out the skis at a moment's notice.

He tells me his love of White Mountain paintings happened accidentally.

"I always enjoy visiting the old hotels in New Hampshire," he says.

"So about twenty years ago, I was in a gallery in Boston looking for a Christmas present for my wife and wanted to buy a painting of an old grand hotel, but couldn't find one."

Instead, Andy settled on a landscape painting. One led to two and three, and without realizing, in time he had become one of the country's foremost collectors of White Mountain art.

When asked about the appeal of the Hudson River School of Art, he's philosophical.

"Well, currently, it's not a terribly popular style, but it's never going to go out of favor," he says. "There are always going to be people who love the mountains so there's always going to be people who appreciate this style of art."

Between Andy's realistic take on the popularity of the Hudson School art and Bob's understanding that proficiency and poetry were mutually exclusive, it was worth considering what Edmund Burke had to say about the art of the sublime.

The eighteenth-century English philosopher was one of the first thinkers to consider the possibility that people could be emotionally, positively moved to awe by nature that could be both lovely and peaceful as well as dangerous and unsettling. In other words, a pastoral valley full of color and tranquility could generate happiness in the soul as surely as a scene of storm and ice above the clouds. Further, to best capture the sublime, regardless of the natural scene, Burke emphasized the importance of the romantic imagination; the role of art as he saw it was to portray an idealized version of nature, thus making its threatening qualities more awe-inspiring and less terrifying.

Thomas Cole picked up on this philosophy and ran with it when he came to visit the White Mountains in the late 1840s. He became the father of the Hudson River School of Art mainly because he was drawn to the harsh qualities of the mountains, and his work often focused on both things at once: the calm and the terror of the mountains.

But that was only one of the pillars in which Erik Koeppel was plying his trade.

In later years, after Cole had passed, the New Ipswich, New Hampshire artist Benjamin Champney came to Conway and turned the landscape art world on its head again. Champney criticized the old masters and sought more realistic settings and truthfulness in his work. To Champney, nothing could beat the actual view of Mount Washington, so why idealize it?

Erik Koeppel's work manages to ride that fine line between the old masters' use of the imagination to transport viewers into sometimes surreal geography, and still keep the scenes fairly true to the actual view. His nods to Cole can be found in the editing of his work; no telephone lines or paved highways can be found in a Koeppel landscape. Meanwhile, his depictions of the weather, clouds and more terrifying aspects of the mountains are vivid, and indeed awesome.

Clearly, I'm a fan. In Erik's work, I can begin to see echoes of what those early travelers sought back then when a trip to Mount Washington could fill you both with bone-chilling terror as well as the joy of being closer to God.

The reception is a success, the finger food picked down to empty plates. As the cool fall of early winter descends onto one of New Hampshire's most visited towns, and Historical Society members begin to fold up chairs and cap the wine bottles, I finally manage to sit with Erik and Lauren.

The two met in 2009 during a fellowship program in New York's Catskill Mountains and have been partners and artists together ever since. They share a studio together in their home just up the road. It's not an exaggeration to say that Koeppel and Sansaricq are the most powerful artist couple in New Hampshire.

When they speak about their work, the themes are the same: nature as a force that pulls humans closer to the divine and the artist being a conduit through which the emotional experience of the natural world can be translated.

"Landscapes are things that are always happening," Erik tells me in a soft, almost shy voice. "Clouds, sunsets, cliffs—these are things that can move you with a depth of experience that's hard to talk about, that's something that's emotional."

Erik thinks about his role as an artist in terms of feeling that emotional connection, translating it onto the canvas and bringing it back to the viewer.

"The difference between what something looks like and what it feels like, that's my role as an artist," he says. "To condense the poetry of the human experience in nature."

This umbilical relationship between poetry and art is referenced over and over throughout pretty much the entire history of the two. Our friend Walt Whitman, of course, had something to say about that relationship. He wrote that "The art of art, the glory of expression and the sunshine of the light of letters, is simplicity." Just like Walt, breaking down the complexity of the creative urge into simple moments of sunshine and expression.

That movement—translating the human experience whether by art or poetry—fits here among the artists. Whether it's Erik, listening to the spiritual muse perched on his shoulder as he translates heavenly glory into colors on canvas, or whether it's Byron standing in a creek spending a couple days away from work, painting the play of light on a birch tree, that pull is as undeniable as it is impossible to ignore.

"I find what moves me," Erik says. And then, "The White Mountains have always moved me."

The pull is irresistible, like gravity is stronger here, like your heart is bigger, like anything is possible. In the shadow of Mount Washington, artists meet their greatest dreams and most terrible demons, and slay them, or allow them to devour their souls. Sometimes both.

Tomorrow morning, I would follow Byron into that shadow and open my heart to the awe and terror, and see what happened.

The morning is bright, though not clear. The clouds near the summit and ridgeline of Mount Washington look fierce and angry. The sun is still low enough to provide a spectacular undercast, bathing the parking lot in a deep orange and yellow glow.

Byron and I are in the far corner of the Glen Trails Outdoor Center parking lot, easels out, facing the occasionally visible summit of the mountain. We are in the same, nearly exact spot, that just a few months earlier I began Alton Weagle Day dressed like Walt Whitman. We are painting.

But try as I may, I just can't focus with the large family from Mumbai watching over my shoulder. Byron wasn't kidding when he talked about being self-conscious when he started painting around town.

Since we began about an hour ago—two easels side by side, facing the road, during one of the busiest, most tourist-heavy weekends of the year—it's like we'd become an attraction in and of ourselves. Some folks are polite, asking permission to come close, being cautious and tentative around the weird guys with the paintbrushes. Others do not care.

"What you boys doing?" says a big man in a cowboy hat with a cigar. Byron, the consummate professional, continues to paint, his eyes focused in concentration, darting up at the mountain and back to the canvas. Me? I can barely figure out which color is red and which is orange, so I do what I always do, I fall back on being a reporter.

"Painting Mount Washington," I say, "or as much as we can see. Want to have a look?"

He does indeed. Turns out, Ben and his wife, Virginia, live in Texas and they are heading north up the coast to Acadia National Park. But first, they stopped to catch a glimpse of Mount Washington, though the mountain hasn't yet fully shown itself this day.

"Well, I must say," the big man says, "what you two are doing is something else. Why, I don't know if I could paint a straight line to say nothing of a whole mountain!"

We chat a little more, and they head out to find more leaves and maybe catch a deal on a gallon of maple syrup.

"Nice people," I say to Byron.

"Who?" he asks. He's a pro, that Byron.

More people come and go, the weather patterns change drastically, sometimes within minutes of each other, and I fear that I ask Byron far too many questions. His initial instruction for me was "do what I do." He set up my easel next to his and then squirted about a half dozen globs of paint onto a makeshift palette for me to use.

My first real lesson in being a painter comes very early in the process. I watch Byron use a lovely royal blue to begin filling in some space above the mountain, a perfect color for the dark cloud banks near the summit. But when I go to do the same, I realize he hadn't given me that color.

"Uh, Byron, can I have some of that dark blue paint?"

"You have to make it," he says.

The puzzled look on my face gives him a chuckle.

"Make it," he repeats to his child protege. "Mix it."

He mixes a bit of black, a bit of orange and some lighter blue together and there appears the perfect royal blue for clouds. My first lesson: put two colors together, and they make a third. That should be simple. Common sense. But in my head, it's not.

There's a popular quote attributed to Thomas Cole that I draw from as I struggle to produce a sky that doesn't simply look like a gray and blue smear. He wrote: "The sky is the soul of all scenery. It makes the earth lovely at sunrise and splendid at sunset. In the one it breathes over the earth a crystal-like ether, in the other a liquid gold."

The wispy clouds near the summit of Mount Washington roll and growl over the ridge, forming and reforming, breaking and reassembling. Sometimes it feels like little pieces of the cloud banks come apart and shower down in the ravines, thin strands of shades of gray. Other times, the blue sky behind breaks through, turning the clouds and valley below into different colors.

I suddenly realize that Byron is asking me to do exactly what the landscape is organically doing right in front of my eyes: follow the colors, the sky changes the valley, the autumn leaves change the clouds, and the wind, like the hand of the painter, moves the geography to create a new picture over and over.

So caught up am I in this new way of looking at the mountain that I don't realize Byron is looking over my shoulder. He cocks his head and says, "Can I give you some advice?"

"Of course!"

"This area down here," he says, pointing to a section of the canvas that's supposed to be a rolling hill, but instead looks like a blobby mound. "If you add some lighter colors down here, it would suck less."

My heart and soul may have had an epiphany about the nature of the landscape, but clearly my head and hand had a lot to learn. I shake the thoughts of Thomas Cole out of my mind, duck my head and focus on what I see, what I could do—what Dan Szczesny is capable of.

And all around me, the tourists gawk, but I ignore them and try to bring color and meaning to my mountain. I try to suck less.

If it is possible to take your art seriously and not seriously at the same time, the Bartlett artists have figured it out.

For four days, the fifteen or so artists have spread out through the White Mountains. Some gravitated toward barns and railroad depots and tractors. Some discovered the fine lines of a fence, or the mystery of a country road drifting into the horizon. All of them have returned on this final day at the inn with at least one landscape, babbling brook, deep valley, or soaring mountain.

They gather each year to walk in the footsteps of the masters, to ply their love for paint and canvas as it was done two hundred years ago and how it continues to be done today. For some, this is art for the sake of art, a brief respite from their daily lives to throw up the gate and let their soul wander. To others, these few days serve as a way to practice their craft and add these works to their catalog to sell or reproduce.

Many nineteenth-century artists made lithographs or prints for tourists. Today, some of these artists make postcards or greeting cards.

As the evening cascades into the relief and melancholy of a long project coming to a close, all the artists make their way into the main sitting room. The Bartlett Inn includes bed and breakfast-style rooms inside the main house, but also a series of tiny cabin rooms. Changed and showered from that day's en plein work, they gather one final time for what they call an end-of-retreat show.

Byron returns with boxes of pizza from down the road, homemade brownies and cookies are offered and the artists sit back in the chairs and couches, sipping wine from boxes.

Leslie brings some tequila and passes the bottle.

They are bawdy and in high spirits, these disciples of Cole, admirers of Koeppel. Byron serves as the emcee for the evening, and as he gets the various paintings ready, the artists tease each other about their work.

"Hey, I saw you on the tracks, but I wasn't sure you'd be able to move fast enough if a train came!"

"That painting has some pretty good bones, but maybe you ought to find it some skin."

Byron sets up a flood light and directs it toward a makeshift shelf he's assembled near the fireplace mantle. He slips on some rubber dishwashing gloves as some of the paintings are still wet.

Then I watch, mortified, as he places the two paintings we did that morning next to each other under the spotlight. To my eye, there is no comparison, it's like if a four-year-old tried to duplicate Byron's painting.

And then they begin.

"Well, let's start with Dan's painting," Byron says, and the room quiets. "As you all know, Dan is writing a book on Mount Washington and he wanted to experience landscape painting." Byron turns to my painting, and I expect a quip or joke. Instead, he says, "This here is the first painting he ever created."

And they all applaud, and there I am in the middle of these creatives, humbled not by the knowledge that I painted well. I didn't. Rather, they applaud, and Leslie claps me on the back, and a couple of them say "good job" and "great work" because that is what true artists do—they build each other up and encourage.

Once the commotion has died down, Byron asks me to speak to the painting. What was I trying to accomplish? How did it feel? What method did I use?

I stumble my way through an explanation about wanting to feel what the great artists felt, about wanting to be able to express my feelings of love for Mount Washington, how inspired I am by it, through a medium that was unfamiliar to me. But the words don't come easy, it's difficult for me to explain a process that I literally experienced for the first time that morning.

"Did you like it?" someone asks.

"I did, yes."

"Would you do it again, do you think painting is a medium you'd like to continue to learn?"

"Yes!" I say automatically, caught in the warm glow that enthusiasm from peers provides, and soon Byron has moved on.

I've thought about that moment quite a bit since then, now a couple months removed. And in retrospect, the proper answer would have been, no.

In an 1896 essay titled "What About Art?" the great Russian literary master Leo Tolstoy himself waded into the debate about the meaning of pursuing or enjoying art. He believed that all art—regardless of medium—was an expression that extended far deeper into the human psyche than mere pleasure.

To Tolstoy, art was "one of the conditions of human life."

"Viewing it in this way we cannot fail to observe," he wrote, "that art is one of the means of intercourse between man and man."

So crucial is the expression of art to humans, thought Tolstoy, that our very ability to express ourselves—through compassion, empathy, joy—is dependent on not just the artist's work, but on the ability of what he called the "receiver" to take in and process the art.

"Every work of art causes the receiver to enter into a certain kind of relationship both with him who produced, or is producing, the art," he wrote, "and with all those who, simultaneously, previously, or subsequently, receive the same artistic impression."

So that painting, whether it be shown in the intimate comfort of the Bartlett Inn or displayed around the world to millions, creates connection between not just the artist and the viewer, but between previous and subsequent generations of artists and viewers. Tolstoy is simply suggesting that art is eternal, and crucial to the human experiment.

Back in Bartlett, Byron gently takes down my first painting and hands it to me with a smile before moving on to the next artist. These beautiful people are gracious and enthusiastic about my work, as I would be to a brand-new writer gathering her nerve to stand and read a poem in front of a room for the first time.

But would I want that painting to be the means of communicating my expressions to humanity? I fear not. Though I'm glad the artists here, at least, don't care.

The evening rolls by, dozens of paintings are lifted to the exalted pedestal under the spotlight. I recognize most places. Some artists have painted three or four—about one a day—over the retreat. Others display seven or eight. One shows four versions of the same scene, a bend in the nearby Saco River. Each painting illustrates different lighting, lighter and darker shades of the water, and in one a section of the bank is eliminated entirely to highlight the rapids—a nod to Thomas Cole's romanticism.

One artist, Sharon Allen, from Derry, New Hampshire spent some time in a hay field in North Conway—a location she and several artists come back to again and again. Sharon's paintings are bright and rich, the bails of hay like yellow cotton balls reflecting the sun, her trees vivid green. Colors explode on her canvas.

Given that she's a native of Bayonne, New Jersey, the vibrancy in Sharon's work makes more sense when placed into the context of her hometown.

"That area is referred to as the armpit of the nation," she says. "Bayonne is literally one mile wide, and a good portion of that is tank farm, by three miles long. At the time that hubby and I escaped to the suburbs, there were sixty thousand people in that three square-miles. Concrete and blacktop all of it, trees a welcomed rarity."

She passed through New Hampshire on the way to Maine in 1966 and decided she'd live here someday. That day came about ten years later when she convinced her husband to move. She took her first art classes in the late 1990s. With memories of all that concrete and steel in her head, the first lessons she signed up for were en plein, and she's been painting landscapes ever since.

Meanwhile, back at the show, Leslie's painting of Mount Washington receives critical acclaim, though she expresses doubt that it's finished or even that it's worth trying to finish.

"Live with it a little while," Byron suggests. "See how you feel later."

And so it goes—the paintings, the wine, the artists laughing there in the heart of the White Mountains. The air is beginning to cool outside as fall begins to take hold, and lights are scarce on the property, except for the spotlight and lamps of the sitting room. From the road, this scene must appear much as it did a hundred years ago, a lone lit window facing the mountains that bring these artists inspiration, warming the night as leaves fall on the cold grass.

As the artists talk about their work, I slip my hand down to the side of the chair where my painting is leaning and touch the top of the still damp canvas. My fingers come back blue and gray and white. I rub them together and create a new color there on my fingertips, my head swimming with the acrylics of creating. A few miles away and a few thousand feet vertically, Mount Washington touches the New England sky, always in repose, always waiting for the next artist to feel the mountain's pull.

Asher Brown Durand's famous painting is inspired by an 1815 sonnet by John Keats titled "O Solitude." In the poem, a forlorn and lonely narrator, feeling trapped by "the jumbled heap / Of murky buildings" wishes that if he must be lonely then at least he wants to be lonely in nature, in the wilderness where he feels he can at least cope better with the solitude.

The middle section of the poem is an ode to the nature Keats longs to seek, "where the deer's swift leap / Startles the wild bee from the fox-glove bell."

But then, in the last six lines, the poem take a hard turn, and Keats realizes that even in nature, being alone is not ideal. The only way to reach the "highest bliss of human-kind" is to be among the mountains with a kindred spirit.

Cole and Durand understood this. From their home in Jackson, Erik and Lauren understand this. And the artists of the retreat, gathering together each year to share camaraderie and inspiration, certainly understand the call for kindred souls.

A few weeks later, as I work in my office, my daughter comes marching in, some sneaky plan on her mind to steal my Post-it notes and undertake a doodling frenzy.

My painting from the retreat happens to be leaning near my desk, and as she walks by, she runs a crayon absently over part of the canvas. I reach out, momentarily horrified, but suddenly, I understand as well.

My kindred soul. All these adventures. For nine months I have worked to understand the meaning of that mountain, and now as the year winds down I will make another trip up. It is time to bring my daughter to the summit.

— CHAPTER TEN —

Ablutions of a Goddess

Mount Washington Meets a Toddler

Today is one of the warmest days I can remember, this late in the season, this high on the mountain. I'm parked in a small pull-over at about the six thousand-foot mark along the auto road. We are above the clouds, which roll in enormous billowing cauliflower formations, pouring up from the west, churning in the madness of a hot fall day.

After nearly ten months of getting to know this place, I am finally introducing Mount Washington to my daughter. And she is happily asleep in the back seat.

Our weekend together has been magnificent. With my wife away on a business trip, we spent the last few days lounging in the mountains. In the unusual heat, I took her to see the Basin—that great cataract formed by the Pemigewasset River, a glorious pothole that has mystified visitors for centuries.

Uma wore a green flowered print dress over bare shoulders, and I wrapped a red bandana over her hair. Seven years ago near this spot, my wife and I with a group of close friends began our trek to the top of

Mount Lafayette where we were married there on the ridge. Each guest was given a bandana with the date of our marriage and a pattern of hiking boots and poles as a memento. My daughter wore one of these bandanas, the words "Dan and Meena's Wedding" across her forehead.

Most can quote Henry David Thoreau from an 1839 trip he took to the Basin where he called the thirty-foot diameter by fifteen-foot-deep swirling hole the "most remarkable curiosity of its kind in New England."

But I prefer the glowing hyperbole penned by the travel writer Samuel Eastman. In his 1858 book, *The White Mountain Handbook,* he writes that the Basin is a "luxurious and delicious bath."

"It is certainly fit for the ablutions of a goddess," Eastman writes.

Perhaps, but our time at the actual Basin was short. Uma preferred the cool and clear pool far above the Basin, a section of mountain water only about half a foot deep and full of pebbles—red, green, and golden. It is a place of far gentler beauty than the rushing torrent of the Basin a hundred feet or so below.

Uma slipped off her sneakers and crunched her feet into the sandy beach. Remarkably, we were alone, and as she waded into the water, my little goddess, it felt like we should be here—like the day and the weather and the mountain that waited for us on the other side of the ridge were content to allow us the transgression of our visit.

She found a muddy glacial pothole in a nearby rock shelf, her own Basin here in the headwaters, and slipped her feet under the mud and silt. My little girl, baptized by the mountain stream, laughed as the earth slid between her toes.

Now, here we are, two wanderers resting on the shoulder of Agiocochook, waiting for the breath of the mountain air to nudge her awake—that same air that helped her drift off on the way up.

It's so warm I turn off the car and gently open the door, letting in a mild, clear breeze. We're in no rush, it's only early afternoon, I have a cooler bag full of snacks and the mountain today is patient.

The cars come and go, the clouds ripple and braid, and a Cog train slowly chugs up the track toward the top, a white passenger car against the blue sky. Riders hang out the open windows, faces turned to the summit. The Cog whistles blow—starting low then becoming shrill, the sound bouncing off the rocks.

I check on Uma, but she's out, her dreams no doubt filled with mystical trains to the stars.

I recline my seat and lean back, watching the few nearby visitors to this part of the mountain. When we pulled in, we parked near a beaten down silver Cherokee Sport. The old SUV was backed in, its back hatch open. I watch as an older couple unpacks lunch from a big red cooler they'd dragged out from the truck bed.

They both wear jeans and flannel shirts. The man pushes a ragged baseball hat higher up his forehead and rubs a bushy white beard. Slowly, like an offering to the mountain, the man pulls a pepperoni stick out of the cooler and begins cutting it into thin slabs. He offers some to the woman, but she shakes her head and climbs back into the front seat of the truck.

She has a long, black brace on her leg, from ankle to thigh, and it takes her a long time to get comfortable and close the door behind her. Some in the outdoor community regard the auto road as an eyesore at best, an environmental disaster at worst. But as I watch her settle into her seat, her eyes never leaving the landscape, I realize without this road she'd be deprived of this wonder. No one should be deprived of this view.

After a while, her eyes droop and she falls asleep, joining my daughter for a mountain-induced rest.

Meanwhile, the man lights a cigarette and takes a long, slow drag, letting the smoke curl up over his whiskers. His face is lost in the smoke for a moment, and when the cloud clears, his eyes are gazing intently out over the Northern Presidentials. I see not an old man smoking but a young explorer, wearing wool perhaps, a staff that he carved—the mountains and the future his. He leans back and pops a slab of salami greedily into his mouth, smiling. This mountain is still his.

"Daddy, where are we?" I hear a little voice behind me.

"Right where we should be, baby, wanna go get some pizza?"

In the parking area below the summit, as I'm bundling her up, an SUV pulls up near us and five kids of varying ages tumble out. They spread across the parking lot and surrounding rocks like spilled milk. Clearly this isn't their first time here. They are loud and joyous and thrilled to be above the clouds.

Uma watches them, watches me, and as I set her down on the gravel parking lot, she seems to really look around for the first time, trying to process what she's seeing. I take her hand to begin the walk up, but she pulls in the other direction. There's a rock wall that serves as the boundary for the parking lot, and beyond that wall is the Carter/Wildcat ridge on the other side of the valley. To the north, it's clear sky seemingly all the way to Canada. To the south, undercast appears to be rolling in, and she's most interested in this.

"Clouds?" she asks, and I realize that aside from the comfort of the window seat of an airplane, she's never been above the clouds, never experienced the tops.

I lift her up onto the rock, and we watch the puffy clouds roll in and around. The journalist and pop philosopher Caitlin Moran wrote that "it's always sunny above the clouds. Always. That every day on Earth—every day I have ever had—was secretly sunny after all."

There's always sun out there somewhere. Always.

Any worries that I may have had about her reaction to the summit fly away in the wind as we crest the top of the long staircase, and Uma reaches down to grab a handful of stones and pebbles. I give her space, wanting her to explore this place on her own, find comfort where she likes.

Big mistake.

Ignoring the hikers and tourists and dogs, ignoring the summit and the wind, she beelines toward the observatory's precipitation collector, and it takes me a moment to realize her plan is to dump her two fistfuls of rocks into the big yellow can. I'm startled nearly to inaction. She's never been here before, never laid eyes on that structure; how does she even know there's an opening at the top?

There's a light chain around it, and a small platform. She gets within ten feet of the thing, and breaks into a run, holding her hands out in front of her—my tiny goddess, the yellow collector her altar, the stones her offering.

She makes it under the chain, her hands just inches from the rim, when I finally catch up and scoop her away. I carry her over to a nearby overlook away from the crowds where we can get a little privacy. We're facing west, and I realize the glorious summit of distant Mount Lafayette is shining bright.

"See that mountain, baby girl?" I point across the valley. "That's where your mommy and daddy got married."

But that concept is lost on her. Instead, she holds out her hands, still heavy with her offering.

"Okay, I'll tell you what, let's just toss those stones, let's just make an offering to the mountain for letting us be here together."

I pick up a few of my own stones, stand her on a high rock and count to three. We toss the handfuls into the wind and the breeze drifts them off and down, my first mountain meditation with my daughter.

"Daddy, I'm hungry."

So we go eat.

In the olden days, back when I actually hiked Mount Washington, hitting that packed cafeteria and waiting in line with the tourists for a bowl of chili or slice of pizza felt revelatory, like I was the one who had earned it. Everybody else, the people who drove or took the Cog, they were posers, that candy bar might as well be stolen for all the effort *they* put in.

Well, those days aren't exactly the past; I do plan on climbing again, with Uma maybe. But that pizza and chili is still there, and this time, I hold my daughter as we wait in line, and in front and behind us are hikers. And I can see that same glow in their faces, that anticipation, that feeling that only exists when you get up at 4:00 a.m. and spend the whole day hiking uphill on rocks, through wind and rain, and you get to this place and your calves feel shredded and you're starving and you crawl to the cafeteria and find yourself in line behind a pudgy dad in jeans holding a toddler. And that dad says to you, "Hey, have a good hike?"

I turn to the couple behind me, mid-twenties, full on Gore-Tex gear complete with ice axes because you can never be too sure, and I look them straight in the face and say, "Hey, have a good hike?"

Always wanted to know how it felt to be on the other side—the side of badly wanting my daughter to be up here regardless by road or train. I want her to feel the power of this place, of these mountains, but I know without the road, that wouldn't be possible yet. Turns out—as we collect our pizza and a nice slice of cheesecake—it feels pretty good.

The crew I spent my week with isn't on duty this afternoon, but observer Tom Padham is there to greet us when I bring Uma to the weather room.

Tom's a good guy, laid back and well spoken; he's often the face of the observatory when the observers do live broadcasts to schools or to media.

After a windstorm where Tom went out onto the deck and was videoed fighting 105 mph winds, the Weather Channel's morning show, *AMHQ*, interviewed Tom about the experience. The veteran observer humored the anchors as they peppered him with classic questions like "Were you afraid?" and "Can just anyone walk up there to experience that wind?"

"Well, this is just part of our job up there," he told them, and the rest of the world who may have tuned in, wondering why anyone in their right mind would try to battle such weather. "Every hour for eighty-five years, observers have been stepping outside to gather information." After a pause and a well-practiced smile, he added, "When you're up here for a week at a time, it helps to have a little fun as well."

Tom greets us and talks a little bit about the weather for the day. I was hoping to get her down into the living quarters and maybe even up into the tower, but she's just not interested in all these devices, buttons and levers. She perks up a bit when we spy Marty lounging in his normal haunts high above the main control area. He gives us a quick once-over before ducking his head back into his snooze. Properly dismissed, and with the weather clear and bright outside, it's time for us to explore the summit.

We begin with the observation deck. The wind is slight, there's no moisture in the air and the crowd has thinned by the time we get up there. It's already about 4:00 p.m., which means the lunch time crowd is gone and not too many more folks will be coming up before the road shuts down at 6:00 p.m. The result is that Uma, for a glorious three minutes, has the whole observation deck to herself.

I let her run, and she does, eager to burn off some of those pizza calories. The clouds at the rail billow up, and she runs to the edge and back, does a few spins and wants to check out the viewfinder. I watch her, this little human, caught up in the vast mountains. I want her to see—really see—the Northern Presidentials, to feel her heart swell when she gazes upon that range. But I'm just projecting, of course.

Her experience here has no context in terms of height, valleys, bad weather and good, temperature and wind. All these things are relative to something else. To her, this is just a place of air and rocks, the observatory deck is a place to run.

So the weather holds, and the clouds stay still and the wind stays mild and everything that can go wrong, doesn't. Near the observation deck, there's a whole section of steep, jangled rocks, and she asks to climb them. I hold her hand as she makes the tentative steps from one slick rock to the next. She loves the rocks, though most in this area are as tall as her.

Some of my fondest hiking memories were those warm summer hikes up on Mounts Adams and Madison, and the feel of these jumbles of rocks, radiating heat into my palms as I scrambled up.

For the longest time, I would have sworn that these rocks were granite, thus our state's ubiquitous nickname, The Granite State.

Alas, the rocks here on Mount Washington are not granite. And since there's no non-geology lesson way of saying this, Mount Washington is made—primarily—of an extremely erosion-resistant schist of the Littleton Formation, a metamorphic rock formation consisting of compressed sea floor sediments.

So, why is New Hampshire the Granite State? Well, that has everything to do with Marie-Joseph Paul Yves Roch Gilbert du Motier de Lafayette. General George Washington just called him Marquis de Lafayette, but around these parts, he was just Lafayette. The French-born aristocrat lent a hand to the rebels during the Revolutionary War, became a major general in Washington's army at the age of nineteen, then went back to France for the most important job of all—getting the colonies money and support. Mount Lafayette, where I was married, is named after him.

Many years later, in June 1825, at the invitation of President James Monroe, Lafayette traveled back to the colonies, now a fledgling country that he helped liberate, and was received with enormous fanfare. On the tour, he visited every single one of the new country's twenty-four states, including New Hampshire.

In Concord, he was treated to an enormous celebration dinner on the state house lawn, in which six hundred guests took part, two hundred of which were Revolutionary War veterans.

During that celebration of speeches, performances, and songs, a particularly pro-New Hampshire ballad stood out, written by Concord lawyer and man-about-town Philip Carrigain. That ballad, which was published in state media as a poem in the weeks after the banquet, contains the line, "He comes by find entreties mov'd / The Granite State to see." The fact that the state's bedrock is granite and was famous for its granite quarries in the nineteenth century helped the nickname along.

And as Uma scrambles over Mount Washington's schist, slowly picking her way to the true summit, Philip Carrigain has one more role to play. A few years prior to Lafayette's visit, Carrigain was part of an engineering party to go up into the Northern Presidentials and other parts of the Whites and draw up a map. Those surveys named or changed many of the peaks to names we now recognize—Franklin, Monroe, Jefferson, Willard—all came out of that work. Lake of the Clouds was called "Blue Pond."

Once done, Carrigain produced his map of New Hampshire. Today, he has a mountain, brook, notch, and pond named after him.

And nearly two hundred years later, to gain the full height of 6,288 feet, a toddler navigates the jagged edges of the non-granite rocks surrounding the mountain Carrigain surveyed.

I see her slip a couple small pebbles into her pocket. She's in the habit of stealing away tiny rocks from places she visits. I suspect this has something to do with her first big mountain climb and my friend of the Minis, Stephen Crossman.

We climbed Mount Major when Uma was a year and half, a small but spectacular mountain along the shores of Lake Winnipesaukee. That's where we met Stephen. I carried her up on my back and we made small talk with a large group who joined us that day. The sky was clear and bright at the top, and Uma wandered at the 1,800 foot summit happily.

At some point, Stephen had found a flat, oval stone, drilled a small hole in the top, and strung a cord through. He presented the tiny stone medallion to Uma, and it has hung near her bed ever since.

Today, there are dozens of stones in her collection, and a day rarely goes by that I don't find an unknown stone in her pocket, under the car seat, or under the bed.

Talisman? A familiar connection to nature from an early age? In any case, despite the principles of Leave No Trace that suggest we take nothing and leave nothing, for this, her first time atop the mountain, I'll overlook the two small pebbles nestled in her pocket.

Slowly, we make our way up to the actual summit, a place that I'd been to dozens of times this past year but yet feels so new and unique this one time—like bringing her caps the first true moment. There's a small line at the summit sign, but we're there quickly.

A kind woman takes a few pictures of us, and I take my daughter's hand in mine and trace the "W" in the sign, much as how I did several times this year. She giggles and smiles and lets me take a selfie with us. Our time together at the summit lasts perhaps two or three minutes, but to me it is a core memory—the highlight of my year and perhaps my time with my daughter in my life.

She's happy, of course, because that's her nature, but whether or not this summit trip makes an impression beyond an afternoon with the sun in the sky, I have no idea. She won't actually remember this trip, not consciously at least. But maybe, somewhere deep in her nerve endings, some part of her identity will be connected to this place, or this day, or maybe just to my taking her here. Maybe, in twenty years, wherever she is, whatever she's become, she'll see a picture of Mount Washington or hear a story about the Observatory and without even knowing why, she'll feel loved. Maybe.

By the time we're leaving, it's late in the afternoon. Being one of the last cars off the mountain gives us the advantage of having the road nearly to ourselves. The weather has changed, it's colder now, and a shimmering mist has begun to rise up from the valley below. I drive us down slowly, even for the auto road. I feel a melancholy about our first trip coming to a close, like it wasn't enough. Maybe I forgot something, left it up there—a memory that I was supposed to reflect upon there in the sun, but now it's lost to the air and Uma will never get to experience it.

I take my time. All those familiar landmarks she missed coming up because she was asleep, I want her to see them now. That long straight-away near the parking lots. Ball Crag. The seven-mile post. The Cow Pasture. The fantastic edge road with the astounding views of Mounts Jefferson and Adams.

"Do you like it here?" I ask, trying to glimpse her reactions in the rear view.

But she's quiet, tired from the excitement and the wind. Her little cheeks are red. I see that her eyelids are drooping.

I sigh, content that she's comfortable, that she's not afraid of heights, and that the day and mountain have been good to us. Revelation isn't something to force, or expect. That's something for another day, or perhaps even another place.

I pull onto the hard-packed cragway and slowly navigate the sharp turn before approaching that glorious half mile or so of thin dirt roadway. And as I do, I finally hear Uma's voice, like a whisper.

"Daddy," she says, "we're going into a cloud."

Sure enough, that mist is about to overtake us. The mist comes in waves from below, like a shimmering wall, up and over the cragway. The cloud is thin at first, but as I drive closer, we seem to come together, the cloud drifting lazily up over the hood and up the windshield until we enter it.

And as the final views of the valley and mountains disappear, and we are fully immersed, Uma lets out a long, deep sigh and says, "Cloud." She reaches out and places a tiny hand on the window and leaves it there. We are a dream, her and I, weary travelers at the end of the day, moving inward. The mountain embraces us until we two are all that remain, us and a few feet of road and scrub along our path. Mount Washington takes away our sight, and we are left with the memory of the day, my baby girl and I.

Here among the clouds, here atop this living rock, here in a place of life and of death, we are free.

By the time I reach the valley, the mist has lifted and we return once again to the hikers, bikers, truckers, and asphalt. Before I turn onto the state road to head south, I take one last peek at my mountains, but the summit is hidden.

And Uma is once again asleep, her hand still resting on the window's edge. The mountain has kissed her eyes and said goodbye.

CHAPTER ELEVEN

The Other Mountain

Finding Connection in the Town Among the Clouds

I end as I began, with a storm on the way.

On one of the final cool but clear days of the season, I find myself standing next to a brilliant orange Volkswagen van, near a concrete statue of the Hindu god Ganesha, staring up into a clear blue sky at a former church where Alice once lived. Alice used to own a restaurant where it was said that you could get anything you want, except Alice of course.

The calendar says early December. The weather forecast says snow is coming, snow I'm racing to beat. I breathe deep, the Massachusetts Berkshire air smelling like damp leaves and rust from the nearby railroads tracks.

I ought to be used to this, I suppose—this feeling of climbing through the windows of opportunity as my mountain presents them to me and finding myself in places seemingly unconnected to Agiocochook. Yet in my heart, at this stage of my journey, I understand that it is *all* connected.

Every spike in every long-lost railroad track. Every curve in a New England mountain road that used to be dirt, that used to be for First

Nations, that used to just be watershed. The stories and the generations and the way a devotee shades his eyes when he looks up at a towering grain mill, or a packed and vibrating football stadium, or at the burning flame of the sun setting behind an ice-covered mountain. Reverence connects us all.

With that in mind, I came to Massachusetts at the invitation of a handful of residents from the tiny town of Mount Washington, in the far southwest corner of the Bay State, to try to understand how the third smallest town in the state, three hundred miles from the mountain, could have come to be nicknamed the "Town Among the Clouds." The locals simply call their town "The Mountain."

But on the way there, I had to drive through Great Barrington, Massachusetts, and that meant the van and the statue and the church and Alice. That meant Arlo Guthrie.

I won't dwell long on the odd happenstance that a book on New Hampshire's Mount Washington led me to the former church where Arlo Guthrie lived in the late 1960s that served as inspiration for the song "Alice's Restaurant," a song so embedded in our popular culture that it's actually become a Thanksgiving tradition.

But, at this point in my year, that mountain was flinging me to and fro over the history and common collective conscience of New England with such flagrant disregard for the strict purpose of writing the book, it was almost as though that pile of rocks up north was making it clear that there was no end to her reach. There were too many loose ends now, too many stories. Around every turn, another and another, peculiar moments in time calling me to hear their tales.

As far as I know, Arlo never set foot on Mount Washington, never wrote about it. But there is one tiny, curious, nearly overlooked fact that seemed to give me permission to mention him here. The famous folk singer—born in New York City, son of Woody, whose song "Massachusetts" is the state's official folk song—lives not far from where I am standing. Arlo currently lives in the town of, wait for it,

Washington, Massachusetts. (Not to be confused with Mount Washington, Massachusetts, a few miles south.)

And so, I gleefully explored Great Barrington a bit, with Arlo in mind. Here's what I found. That full, eighteen-minute-song, actually titled "Alice's Restaurant Massacre," is based on a true incident that took place when Arlo was living in that refurbished church with Alice and Ray Brock. That restaurant was real too, though the name of the place was The Back Room. Alice is still alive, and a painter, living in Provincetown, Massachusetts.

Arlo owns the church building I'm standing in front of. He bought it in 1991, renovated it and renamed it the Guthrie Center at the Old Trinity Church. And if today was Thursday, I'd be able to attend a free hootenanny.

I can't imagine a thing nearly as pleasurable as attending a hootenanny in a cultural center that inspired "Alice's Restaurant" and is owned by Arlo Guthrie. The connections to my mountain were slight, but the joy was immense so I hope I'll be forgiven this detour.

It was time to find the tiny town that brought me here to begin with.

Mount Washington, Massachusetts, is special for a number of reasons, the least of which is its name. In fact, the town is not actually named after the mountain in New Hampshire. Like the mountain, it's named after the first president. The designation of "Mount" to the front of the name highlights the fact that the town sits on a plateau—at about 1,500 feet—surrounded by the Taconic Range and its corresponding mountains. Thus, the Mount.

But in parsing the name of this tiny town, it occurred to me that I never fully understood just how popular the name Washington really is. I spent a full year exploring a place named after the famous George without ever looking into the pedigree.

So, it's worth mentioning that Washington is the most popular place name in our country. I tracked down nearly 40 cities and 88 towns or villages named Washington. Thirty-one of the 50 states have counties named Washington. New Jersey alone has five Washington townships, and Wisconsin has seven towns named Washington.

There are at least five mountains over 4,000 feet, five neighborhoods, three ports, half a dozen major bridges, dozens of high schools and colleges and if you Google "Washington Street" you will get nearly thirty million hits.

There is one town named Washington in New Hampshire, but there is only one street in New Hampshire named Mount Washington, in Derry. Mount Washington Street is about two blocks up the road from where I first lived when I came to New Hampshire.

The first major monument dedicated to Washington to begin construction was the Washington Monument in downtown Baltimore, started in 1815. The first to be completed is a curious thirty-foot high dry-laid stone structure in Boonsboro, Maryland, along the Appalachian Trail. With the nearby Baltimore monument nearing completion, Boonsboro townsfolk gathered en masse at 7:00 a.m. on July 4, 1827 and marched to the site to begin construction and beat their Baltimore neighbors. By the end of the day, the tower was half built and finished later that season.

Washington's enormous head is, of course, joined by three other presidents on the face of Mount Rushmore in South Dakota. There are traffic circles, busts and statues (on a horse and off) everywhere you turn. And a copy of Jean Antoine Houdon's famous marble statue of Washington that currently sits in the Rotunda of the State Capital of Richmond also is on display in Trafalgar Square in London, England.

There is, of course, one of the most popular tourist draws in the world, the Washington Monument in Washington, DC Inside the monument are three commemorative granite stones, all dating from the 1850s, with ties to New Hampshire. One is a gift from the state, one is a gift from Durham, New Hampshire, and one was extracted from the home of General John Stark in Manchester, New Hampshire and presented to the monument commemorative committee by the Ladies of Manchester. Stark, of course, was a good friend and general of Washington's, and the man who uttered the phrase that would go on to become his home state's motto: "Live free or die: death is not the worst of evils."

But my favorite is in an unincorporated area along the Brazos River in Washington County, Texas. Washington-on-the-Brazos State Historical

Site welcomes visitors to the place where, in 1836, while still part of Mexico, the Texas Declaration of Independence was signed. The signers wanted to honor the first American president, but they wanted to make sure the site was in no way associated with that other Washington, the one along the Potomac. Thus, Washington-on-the-Brazos was born. There at the gift shop you can purchase, for $199, a customized signers pen engraved with the signature of whichever of the fifty-nine original signers is your favorite. If I were to buy one of those pens, I most certainly would choose George Washington Barnett.

Incredibly, of all those Washingtons scattered like glitter throughout the country, there are only two towns named Mount Washington. One is where I'm heading.

The other Mount Washington is in Kentucky, a sleepy commuter community of Louisville whose claim to fame happened in 2006 when then-Mayor Francis Sullivan made a memorable appearance on the game show The Price is Right. Mayor Francis did a half break dance, half tumble on stage after being called up by Bob Barker, then managed to give the game show host a key to the city, proclaiming that the next time Bob was in Mount Washington, Kentucky, the key and two dollars would buy him a cup of coffee anywhere in town. (You'd think Bob would be able to catch a pass on the two dollars.) At any rate, the mayor lost the PT Cruiser but did walk away with a cool $183 of winnings to take back home.

So, of all that fame and fortune world wide—the tourists, marble, history, and commemoration—what's so special about a tiny village of 140 people living on the edge of the Taconic Mountains in far southern Massachusetts? Turns out, nothing at all, but everything that matters.

People have lived here on this twenty-two square mile plot of rolling mountain hills a long time. The Mohicans were here first, then the early Dutch settlers. Landowner Robert Livingston bought up much of the surrounding land and got into skirmishes with the Dutch until the folks from the Massachusetts Bay Colony began to arrive.

By the time "The Mountain" had reached its peak population of about 375 in the late 1800s, it had already become an important source of charcoal to the region. The circular remains of charcoal fire pits can still be found strewn throughout the woods in town.

And for such a tiny, out-of-the-way place, Mount Washington packs a big historic punch.

The first celebrity to arrive, in 1781, was Mother Ann Lee, founder of the Shakers. She took up residence in the Benjamin Osborn House, a modest Georgian Cape, and spent nearly two weeks hosting guests and recruiting faithful. The house is now owned by the state and is located inside Mount Washington State Forest.

Next up, a place called Boston Corners—a tiny sliver of 1,200 acres cut off from the rest of the state by a cliff wall of the Taconics—was the site of the first world championship prize fight. Prizefights were illegal in 1853, so Boston Corners was selected specifically because the geography of the area made law enforcement nearly impossible. American Champion Yankee Sullivan fought British champ Jack Morrissey, and crowds came up from New York City via Troy and Albany, New York. Newspaper reports counted the rowdy crowd as swelling to five thousand, surrounding a meadow clearing where the fight took place.

Odds were on Morrissey, who was twenty-three years old. Sullivan was forty. But Sullivan had spiked his boots and led right from the beginning. Incredibly, the fight last thirty-seven rounds until the moment when the fighters' seconds jumped into the ring and a free-for-all broke out. The ref unexpectedly called the fight for Morrissey, who won the $2,000 purse.

Massachusetts took warrants out for the arrest of both men, and each was jailed for a time and fined.

But it's the final celebrity that is still spoken of in hushed whispers in Mount Washington, a man who seemed to have befriended every resident of the tiny mountain town. And to this day, nearly seventy-five year later, still casts a shadow over Mount Washington families.

For it's not every day that your town mascot can be Babe Ruth.

Mount Washington constable David Whitbeck is telling me about

George Herman Ruth, Jr. The town's one elected law officer is a big man with thick, red hands and a wide smile. At fifty-four, with his bushy, gray-streaked beard, David is the kind of guy who knows every house, every trail, and every resident of his town by name. He's been constable since 2004. Before that, his father, Jim Whitbeck, had been constable since 1968.

And before that, David's grandfather, Merv, was friends with the Great Bambino.

"My granddad had a hunting camp back in the day," David tells me. "Babe would come up to The Mountain, do some hunting with the guys, then on the weekend he'd rent out this very hall, the place we're sitting in right now, and throw some pretty wild parties, from what I heard."

The hall David is referring to is the town's community center, city hall and library. Several of the town's more prominent residents have joined us, including David's mother, eighty-four-year-old Margaret "Peg" Whitbeck. Peg sits on the Town Historical Commission and is the secretary of the Historical Society. In her spare time, she also fills in here, at the library—which consists of about eight metal book cabinets along one wall of the meeting hall.

There's an old safe in one corner, apparently containing important town papers, as old buildings like this tend to catch fire a lot. And atop an old file cabinet is an ancient ballot box, the one the town uses for elections. As constable, David is responsible for that box and runs the elections. There's a gold plaque fastened to the front of the box dedicated to David's father.

David spent some time up in North Conway, New Hampshire, at the base of the other Mount Washington. He lived up there for six years a while back during a time when his wife ran a rental company. He skied, hunted, and yes, climbed the Rock Pile. But he knew he'd eventually come back.

It must be difficult to leave a place when your family pedigree is so significant to a town that your surname has been bestowed upon a mountain. Mount Whitbeck is 1,837 feet and sits right at the northern end of town. David's also in construction, which is how he makes his living. The constable gig is more of a generational birthright, though David says he works for it.

"It's just keeping the peace, you know, talking to people," he says. "I'll go out if there's a problem and just talk, get people to calm down."

The current excitement in the town is the fact that just two weeks ago, town hall got an internet hookup for the first time. A tree had downed the line earlier that morning and most of Mount Washington was currently without electricity, but they were still excited about Wi-Fi. Electricity wasn't a thing here either until 1951. And it had been 1919 when the last post office closed down.

In a documentary of the town made by Rachel Maskew in 2003, Jim Whitbeck is extensively interviewed. He spends a fair amount of time talking about the Babe. By the time the film was made, Jim's an older man, but tough and rugged, wearing a thick flannel shirt, unshaven, his voice the gravelly base of a man who has spent his life in the woods.

Jim remembers that time in terms of how the famous baseball star treated the children of Mount Washington.

"Babe was a good guy, he was always good with kids," Jim says, "He'd come and take us off The Mountain into town and he'd foot the bill. Kids knew that car and they'd all come."

Every person I speak to has a story like this, about the town, about the land or about other residents or visitors. A warm connection to this land, to the surrounding mountains, and to their respective families are traits that set this place off nearly as directly as does its remoteness. Even today, in the Berkshires, one of the most well-traveled and tourist-heavy places in the world, Mount Washington feels set off. You don't just stumble upon Mount Washington. You have to make a point of coming here.

"It's just one of those places," Peg says. "Either you like it or you don't."

One of the reasons why tourists come to The Mountain requires 162 steps to get there.

By late afternoon, the sun is already behind the surrounding hills as I begin my trek down to Bash Bish Falls, the primary tourist draw here and the tallest waterfall in the state. The parking lot for the half-mile trail is a straight shot west from Mount Washington Town Hall, and as the road winds down into the Bash Bish State Park and the ravine that holds the falls, the road gets thin and begins to hug the cliffs so close, it starts to remind me of the Mount Washington Auto Road. It's late in the day and late in the season so there's no traffic, but two cars passing each other here would be tricky.

I can hear the falls from the trailhead. From the moment I step onto the trail, I am heading down via both wooden steps and rock steps. The air is raw with moisture, but the wet leaves and dirt smell lovely—the air is full of anticipation, the gray swirling clouds above eager to burst. I quicken my pace to stay warm and also because I feel so fortunate to find myself in this place for my final hike of the year.

Being so far from my mountain doesn't feel unusual. The woods here are steep and thick and bear witness to the same sort of human touch as the national forest around the Rock Pile. From the engineering of the trail to the roar of distant water, this place is familiar even though I've never been here. Bash Bish feels epic, like a destination.

The trail begins to weave its way down, cutting around little creek inlets and around a scramble of downed trees. Above my head and up the ravine wall, I can faintly see the guardrail of the road that pushes through on its way to New York State.

Bash Bish Brook, which begins as a spring above the falls in Mount Washington, weaves its way out of the ravine, into New York and drains into the Hudson River where it will find its way past the Statue of Liberty and out into the Atlantic Ocean. Here in the ravine, the brook drops nearly two hundred feet, cascading over jumbles of rocks until spilling the final eighty feet over the falls.

As much as these falls are visited by huge swarms of crowds in the summer, or perhaps because of that, Bash Bish is neither a gentle nor a particularly safe place. Yahoo Outdoors recently named it one of the most dangerous waterfalls in the country. Since 1900, more than twenty-five visitors have died at this altar to the wilderness, some having drowned, but most having injured themselves rock climbing or diving and then drowning.

Just three months before my visit, a twenty-one-year-old lifeguard from Ghent, New York slipped into the churning cascades above the main falls, was pulled under some rocks, and drowned. Fire and emergency crews worked for days to try to recover his body but had to give up. They fastened a net over the top of the falls and left. A week later a rain storm surged the water flow, dislodged the poor man's body and the net kept him from tumbling down over the ledge.

In situations like that, according to Constable Dave, the state takes over the operation. Though Dave has participated in plenty of lost hiker search and rescues.

As I break out of the woods and walk the final few yards to the overlook above the falls, it's clear that this is not a place to be trifled with. Even this late in the season, the brook flows hard over the top, splitting into two streams on either side of an enormous pointed boulder that looks like a rhino horn. I walk down the final forty or so concrete steps, pick my way to the side of the dark green pool under the falls, and get a better view.

The emerald pool roils and churns. The moss-covered rocks near the shore and along the cliffs of the falls are slick with dripping slime. There are *no jumping* and *no swimming* signs posted everywhere. In the spring, with fresh rain coming down off the surrounding cliffs, Bash Bish must thunder and bellow; I imagine it's quite a sight at high water.

For now, I slip off my gloves and find a dry boulder to sit back on and take part in a custom I've repeated so often in so many places that it feels like a part of me; I uncap my thermos and pour myself a steaming cup of tea. I lean back there at nearly the end of my journey and close my eyes, listening to the slap of falling water while the liquid warms the cup in my hands.

I'm just getting into a decent meditative groove when voices high above jangle me out of my calm. There, at the very top of the waterfall, standing perhaps five or six feet from the edge, are two young men. They are wearing light windbreakers with no gloves or hats. They are wearing sneakers.

I look down at my phone to confirm that I have no signal here, so I begin calculations in my head on how long it would take me to get back to my car and go find Constable Dave.

Like the mountain in New Hampshire, the mythology surrounding Bash Bish Falls is deep and mysterious, and with each passing year the stories seem to expand and inflate, and perhaps exaggerate with each new telling. And like most keystone legends, the story ends with ghosts.

The falls draws its name from a First Nation woman named Bash-Bish who lived in a nearby village. Legend has it that she was kind-hearted, but her extreme beauty provoked a neighbor to accuse her of adultery against her husband. And though Bash-Bish protested her innocence, village elders sentenced her to death. She was strapped to a canoe and set adrift above the falls. But in the moment that the canoe tipped over the falls, an enormous halo appeared above her in the shape of a ring of white butterflies. The canoe was found shattered in the pool below but no sign of Bash-Bish's body was ever found.

Meanwhile, Bash-Bish had left a young daughter, White Swan, who grew into a young woman more beautiful than her mother. Eventually, she married Whirling Wind, the son of the village chief. But the two were unable to conceive, and word went out that this was because Bash-Bish had placed a curse on the village.

Despondent, White Swan ran off to the falls and climbed up to the perch above the pool. Whirling Wind and some other villagers ran to save her, but they were too late. As they approached the falls, White Swan cried from above, "Mother, take me into your arms." And much to the shock of the men, a white-robed women stepped out of the pool and raised her arms to White Swan, who jumped. Whirling Wind dove to save his bride but drowned.

Whirling Wind's corpse was recovered some time later, but, like Bash-Bish, White Swan's body was never found. Today, it is said that if you look closely from the rocks above the falls, the grieving faces of Bash-Bish and White Swan can be seen in the pool below, and if you are careless, they'll lure you to leap to your own demise in the churning waters.

Most academic folklorists suggest that these despair-leap Native American legends are primarily a "romantic" device used at the expense of first peoples to draw Europeans to these highly sought-after locations. One of the most famous of these leap legends is of Chief Chocorua, who leapt to his death at the top of the mountain in New Hampshire now named after him, after being falsely accused of causing the death of a colonist's son.

Just in New England, there is Lovers Leap Park in Bangor, Maine; Purgatory Chasm in Sutton, Massachusetts; and Rock Rimmon City Park in Manchester, New Hampshire, all of which involve Native Americans tossing themselves off a promontory.

In 1883, Mark Twain published one of his most popular and enduring books, the autobiography *Life on the Mississippi*. In it, he writes, "There are fifty Lover's Leaps along the Mississippi from whose summit disappointed Indian girls have jumped."

I kick around deep in my memory, but can't find a Leap Legend associated with New Hampshire's Mount Washington. And I'm relieved to see that the two young men have somehow managed to scramble down off the rocky outcropping above to the pool and are now slipping and sliding across the slimy rocks on their way up and away from the falls. They, at least, won't add to Bash Bish's casualty list today.

I wonder if the spirits of Bash-Bish and White Swan were watching, maybe nudging them away from the edge. From my perch along the shore, I watch the swirling green pool for a while, looking for ghosts, searching for a sign to explain this place. But there's just water, and Bash Bish rolls and drums like it has for centuries. And like the surrounding mountains—like my mountains up north—Bash Bish is only the happenstance of time and gravity; its meaning is personal and relative only to any meaning I choose to ascribe.

My thermos is empty. The shadows are nearly gone. It's time to leave.

Later, as dusk begins to overtake the hills, I'm sitting in a muddy parking area in Mount Washington State Park, not far from Bash Bish, watching a father and son getting ready to hunt. I'm not sure if they will be hunting in the dark, or perhaps hiking in to one of the hunting camps deep in the woods around this area.

They are both dressed alike, orange vest and hats, camo underneath. They both have beards. They both have what appears to be identical rifles. They don't say much, but they move with practiced ease as they get ready, hauling gear and equipment out of a dirt-streaked white Ram pickup truck. Clearly they've done this before.

I think back to a scene in the Mount Washington documentary with Dave and his dad, Jim, hunting in these very same woods. The two men tromp out into the brush, walking side by side, the swirl of autumn clouds hinting at snow, their breath coming in short huffs. Dave's hair has no streaks of gray. Jim would pass away only a year after the scene was filmed.

Jim stays back with the cameraman as Dave swings around a ridge in the hope of flushing some game back toward his father. Jim jokes around a little as they wait, showing the filmmaker the proper way to stand against a tree to blend in, to be one with the forest and the land. There's this moment in the film where Jim is just leaning against a tree, arms cradling his rifle, where he's looking out into the forest. He's not alone of course, but it feels like he is. No one is saying anything. Wind blows some crackled leaves at his feet.

I like this moment, these few seconds. Did he know his time was short? Is he reflecting on his life here, the connections he enjoys to this land and this place? Is he waiting for his son to appear in the woods ahead, two generations coming together one last time across the landscape?

I wish I could ask him. I feel like the entire reason for my being here—hundreds of miles from my own mountain—is buried someplace in that gaze.

The men don't catch anything that day. They shake their heads, clasp each other on the shoulder, talk about next time, talk about the empty woods. It is a scene that has repeated between parent and child for generations, here in a place where the geography is its own certainty, where the future of this land will likely afford the same opportunity to men and women and families over and over.

The father and son in my parking lot tromp off, and I watch their shining vests against the gloaming of the woods until they fade into The Mountain and the sky is more dark than light.

My time here is done. My year is drawing to a close. Soon, the storm will come, and with it snow that will stay, and I'll mark one full rotation around the sun that I have been living and breathing Mount Washington. It feels proper to be here to bookmark the end of that journey, in a place geographically distant from the mountain but surrounded by a connection to the land that feels the same.

I set out to discover a mountain, and instead the mountain sent me out to find family, to span time and generations, and to seek out stories desperate to be told. It's dark now as I come down off the hills surrounding Mount Washington village, and as I turn north to go home to my baby and wife, my headlights light up the first snowflakes of the oncoming storm.

Travels finished, my mountain is calling me back home.

Afterword

That's not all of it. Of course, it isn't.

There's the Abenaki, Maliseet, Passamaquoddy, and the Western Pennacook. Before a single one of our European ancestors ever laid eyes on Mount Washington, the indigenous first peoples had lived in the area for four hundred generations. Their shadows follow us through the Amoskeag, Coos, Merrimack, Nashua, Piscataqua, Chocorua, Winnipesaukee, and the list goes on and on.

There's Darby Field and the scant history of his first adventure to the top of Mount Washington. Which route? Did he go up the Cutler River and approach from the southeast, or maybe he cut over into Maine and headed north up the Saco from Biddeford and popped out around Twin Mountain. And just why did a merchant and ferryman from Portsmouth climb that White Hill anyway? Oh, how I wish I had the time to retrace those steps. Perhaps I still will.

There are the magnificent and dedicated search and rescue teams. There is the Androscoggin Valley Search and Rescue Team, Pemigewassett Valley Search and Rescue Team, the Mountain Rescue Service, the New England K-9 Search and Rescue, the Mount Washington Ski Patrol, the Upper Valley Wilderness Response Team, the White Mountain Swiftwater Rescue team and, of course, the New Hampshire Fish and Game Department.

The heroism and dedication of these, mostly, volunteer groups is beyond reproach and could fill its own book, easily. I would like to write that book. Perhaps I will.

There are organizations that help veterans, kids and disabled athletes reach those heights. Like Adaptive Sports Partners of the North Country. Every year, hundreds of volunteers—what Adaptive Sports calls *mules*—gather at the base of the mountain to accompany, carry, push, and pull those who are not able get to the summit. This is a day of self-lessness designed to give those who can't get up there on their own the same grand views. During my year, the wind and rain was too heavy at the top, so the teams came anyway and lifted their athletes for a stroll through Franconia Notch. I will tell their story next time.

There are the pilots who landed pipers at the summit. And there are the World War II ski regiments who trained in the bitter cold up on those slopes. There are the modern-day veterans who spend a day each year at the summit, connecting in brotherhood over blood and stories. All of them deserve to have their stories told. Perhaps I'll tell one or more of them someday.

There are the founders and the legends, the hikers and the ultra-runners, the scientists and the politicians, the naturalists and the geologists who are up there, somewhere, every day.

During the year that I was on the mountain, Joseph Gray from Colorado Springs ran up Mount Washington in 58 minutes and 57 seconds. Travis Pastrana drove a specialized Subaru up the mountain, setting a new auto road record of 5 minutes and 44 seconds. And Phil Gaimen, a professional road racing cyclist from Hollywood, pedaled up the mountain in 51 minutes and 13 seconds.

Each of these daredevils and record breakers have a story. Maybe I'll tell them sometime.

And finally, in September, on a clear fall day, a sixty-six-year-old University of Maine sociology professor by the name of Rolf Diamon collapsed while hiking up Mount Washington, near a spectacular outcropping of rocks known as Lion Head. Rolf's son, Nick, performed CPR to try to save his father, but couldn't. Rolf will take his place next to Daniel Rossiter and Lizzie Bourne, and the mortal coil will unwind again and again in this place of life and death, of raw emotion and exquisite beauty.

Rolf's story is already told and will be preserved for the ages.

And we all move on. The history of this particular bit of landscape—as hardened and unmoving as it may appear—is actually a living, organic testament to everything that is terrible and everything that is honorable about us.

Give it a chance, and Mount Washington will move you and heal you. She is a song, calling generations to listen to the echoes of their fathers and grandmothers before them. And she is electricity, energizing those who open their hearts to be better humans, better mothers and grandfathers, as they bring the next generation to the rock.

Over the course of my year, I only scratched the surface of the meaning of Mount Washington, only began to understand her relentless reach and her inevitable pull. And now, my year there, and all of your attention, each of us, are part of the mountain's lore.

So many stories waiting to be told. So many stories waiting to happen. The compass of the mountain spins, and we follow; her magnetic pull reflects our own desire and draws us back, back to the place of the great spirit, ever back to the heights of Agiocochook.

Acknowledgments

In the fall of 2015, I sat in the living room of poet and publisher Sid Hall sipping tea. We were talking about the recent release of my collection of short stories (*Sing and Other Short Stories*) when he asked me if I had any other ideas for books. Sid's company, Hobblebush Books, had also published my book, *The Nepal Chronicles* (2014).

I went down a short list of ideas, and then I got to one that I had not made mention of to anyone, except my wife.

"What about a year in the life of Mount Washington?" I said, giving voice for the first time to an idea that had been living in my brain for a decade and was becoming an increasingly louder tenant.

Sid's eyes grew wide, he leaned back in his chair, and said, "Tell me about that one."

The idea of this book felt so simple to me back then. I'd take a year and just do everything there is to do on Mount Washington, and I'd write about my experience. But as always, the simplest ideas are usually the most complex. Little did I know then, over the course of the next three years, that mountain, that glorious, contradictory, maddening, legendary pile of rocks in New Hampshire's White Mountains would send me on a series of pilgrimages far from its lofty height. It was almost as if I needed distance to see the mountain better, to see her as complete.

And so, I begin with Sid. Thanks for saying yes, when even I was saying no.

To Kirsty Walker, who since then has taken over Hobblebush and has held my hand every step of the way. Through her work on the IndieGoGo fund-raising campaign that allowed this project to begin to her enthusiasm, creativity, and support, having your publisher also be your biggest fan is a great gift.

To Kat Maus who, once again, was somehow able to crawl inside my head and illustrate a book cover that I would never have been able to describe but had wanted all along.

To storyteller and New Hampshire treasure Rebecca Rule who actually said yes when I asked if she'd be interested in writing the book's foreword. In a world full of stories and storytellers, to have you provide such wit and charm to the project has given everyone's story within these pages an air of respect and purpose.

To Susan Kennedy, my friend and primary editor, and to our 1:00 a.m. sessions, and to your amazing ability to teach me about commas and dashes and make it all seem fun. Thank you for keeping me honest, calling me out when I got lazy, and making every single bit of it better.

To my editors on the Alton Weagle chapter, Lisa Parsons and Christine Woodside, your work created the tone and shape of the whole project. And to my fact checker and editor Mike Dickerman, thank you for getting me started down this crazy road.

To all the writers, friends, and storytellers who kindly provided blurbs and had such thoughtful advice and insight into the project. Thank you, Arnie Arnesen, Mike Dickerman, Mary Emerick, James Patrick Kelly, Matt Landry, Willem Lange, Mike Morin, Craig Werner, Betsy Woodman, and Christine Woodside.

To George Etzweiler, for giving me the great honor of running at your side and welcoming me into your home and introducing me to your mountain. Knowing you is truly an honor.

And to John Donovan, my guide at the observatory, thank you for helping me not poison the scientists and for being my mentor at the top.

To my dear friend and enthusiastic supporter, Keith Spiro, your boundless energy—not to mention incredible photography skills—were appreciated in ways I can never fully put into words.

As for Mount Washington, I'm grateful for the support, access, and help of the Cog Railway, the Mount Washington Auto Road, and the Mount Washington Observatory to make this book happen. Each of them went all in, despite my pesky phone calls, constant questions, and ridiculous requests. Each is an institution of the highest order.

To Rebecca "Cordelia" Metcalf at the Cog Railway for letting me crash their Steampunk Festival, letting me come and go where I wanted, and never saying no.

To Howie Wemyss, of the Mount Washington Auto Road, you are a one-person powerhouse. I think of you as the "Mayor" of Mount Washington. I likely asked the most questions to and made the most demands of Howie, and he never flinched. Without that road, this book could not have been written.

To Sharon Shilling of the Mount Washington Observatory, it took a lot of trust, new to the job as you were, to open those doors and give me the behind the scenes access to that extraordinary place at the summit. There is nothing like the observatory in the world, and I hope I did it justice. Thank you for all your hard work.

And on the subject of the observatory, mention must be made of the team running the observatory during my stay. It's not easy having a journalist literally living with you for a week and following you around at work, I know. But Adam Gill, Caleb Muete, and Mike Carmen were consummate professionals, patiently listening to every little crazy question I had and explaining their world to me with detail and humor.

There were so very many people who had stories, who helped me with facts and research and who had faith. There were artists, historians, hikers, naturalists, writers and all manner of creative and passionate folks who stepped up. Thank you all!

Among those I would especially like to thank are: Hans Bern Bauer, Ed Bergeron, Wayne Boyce, Samantha Brady, Slim Bryant, Eric Carlson, Byron Carr, Carolyn Choate, John Clayton, Bob Cottrell, Peter Crane, Stephen Crossman, Vanessa De Zorzi, Berta DeDonato, Ann Trainor Domingue, Jason Dubrow, Bob Etzweiler, Eric Feldbaum, Brian Fitzgerald, Herb Fox, Shirley Fye, Jim Gagne, Christine Girouard, Jocelyn Gould, Rob Harrity, Norman Head, Kirk Horton, Rick Howe, Halford Jones, Josh Judge, Erik Koeppel and Lauren Sansaricq, Amy Koski and Mark Laquerre, Kenneth LaCoille, Jr., Amy Lamb, Neil Lovett, Bob MacKenzie, Lisa Matthews, Donald McCasland, Ken McKenzie, Andy McLane, Kevin McNatt, Bill Millios, Ernie Mills, Aaron Mylott,

Janelle Mylott, Kyle Newton and Krissy Guilfoyle, Larry Mruk, Peter Noonan, Sandy Olney, Lisa Parsons, Allmuth "Curly" Penzel and George Penzel, Eric Pinder, Lovel Pratt, Mike Pelchat, Russ Provost, Jeff Rapsis, Barbara Hull Richardson, Leslie Scott-Lysan, Mary Selvoski, Mary Anne Sledzinski, Faithann and Jeremy and Nola Thibeault, Barbara Weagle, Jim Weagle, Brian Wood, and Marty the Cat.

To my sister, Andrea, for all your work and love with Dad, you are my rock.

To my family, John, Ben, Max, Kiran, Rita, and Sandeep, every time I set out on a long journey like this, you shake your heads, smile, and give me your unconditional support. I am truly blessed to be surrounded by you.

Thanks, Mom and Dad.

To my daughter Uma, you are the sun. At the times when I've been the most exhausted or have begun to doubt my resolve, five minutes in your presence lifts any veil of uncertainty. Thank you for being my tyger, tyger, burning bright.

And to my wife, Meenakshi—from the four corners of the earth, to the tops of the world, to the seashore, every step on this journey is filled with wonder; thank you for telling me it would be okay, thank you for recognizing when I needed sleep, and thank you for believing that I could pull this off. We did it!

Thank You to Our Sponsors

from Dan Szczesny and Hobblebush Books

We are extremely grateful for all of the support we received for *The White Mountain*. This book would not have been possible without our sponsors:

- *The Hippo* (Gold)— *The Hippo* is New Hampshire's essential weekly guide to what to do and where to go: food, music, movies, books, family activities and much more. Find us at www.hippopress.com.
- Keith Spiro Media (Gold)—Solves business problems. Be seen, be heard, be found using strategic, creative community building, social and traditional media, and visual journalism connecting cultures and generations.
- Tax Help Associates, Inc. (Silver)
- Althea Haropulos Photographer (Bronze)
- Campo Enoteca (Bronze)
- Cotton (Bronze)
- The Cozy Tea Cart (Bronze)
- Manchester Historic Association (Bronze)
- Redline Guiding (Bronze)
- Republic Cafe (Bronze)
- White Mountain Photography (Bronze)
- Gibson's Bookstore (In-kind)

A special thank you to the Mount Washington Auto Road, the Cog Railway, and the Mount Washington Observatory for granting Dan access for his research.

We'd also like to thank our IndieGoGo perk donors who enthusiastically helped us get this project off the ground:

- The Mountain Wanderer Map & Book Store
- Juggernaut Fitness Adventure Series

- True Peak Crossfit
- Jim Salge Photography
- MooseMan Nature Photos
- Tuckerman Brewing Company
- Conway Scenic Railroad

And to everyone who donated to our IndieGoGo campaign, including those below, before Dan had even written one word of the book—thank you for believing in our vision and sticking with us for two years!

Byron Champlin	Amy Parulis
Patti Chappel	Doran Dal Pra
Kevin Clements	Rebecca Rule
Stephen Crossman	Karl Searl
Bill Herman	Kerry Shetline
Carl & Nancy Mayland	Sally Strazdins
Tim Mayo	Mark Truman
Noreen K. T. McGrath	Jeremy Ward
Christy Morris	Howie Wemyss
Gregory L. Norris	Jean Worster

Bibliography

Adler, C. Ralph and Dave Thurlow, eds. *Soul of the Sky: Exploring the Human Side of Weather*. North Conway, New Hampshire: The Mount Washington Observatory, 1999.

Anderson, John and Stearns Morse. *The Book of the White Mountains*. New York, New York: Milton, Balch & Company, 1930.

Asselineau, Roger. *The Evolution of Walt Whitman: The Creation of a Personality*. Cambridge, Massachusetts: The Belknap Press of Harvard University Press, 1960.

Belcher, Francis C. *Logging Railroads of the White Mountains*. Boston, Massachusetts: Appalachian Mountain Club Books, 1980.

Boardman, Julie. *Death in the White Mountains: Hiker Fatalities and How to Avoid Being One*. Littleton, New Hampshire: Bondcliff Books, 2017.

Burt, Allen F. *The Story of Mount Washington*. Hanover, New Hampshire: Dartmouth Publications, 1960.

Citro, Joseph. *Passing Strange: True Tales of New England Hauntings and Horrors*. Shelburne, Vermont: Chapters Publishing, 1996.

Dickerman, Mike, John Dickerman, and Steven D. Smith. *A Guide to Crawford Notch*. Littleton, New Hampshire: Bondcliff Books, 1997.

Dickerman, Mike. *Along the Beaten Path: Collected Writings from a White Mountain Tramper*. Littleton, New Hampshire: Bondcliff Books, 2000.

Dickerman, Mike. *Mount Washington: Narrative and Perspectives*. Charleston, South Carolina: The History Press, 2017.

Dickerman, Mike. *White Mountains Hiking History: Trailblazers of the Granite State*. Charleston, South Carolina: The History Press, 2013.

Downs, C. Virginia. *Life by the Tracks: When Passenger Trains Steamed Through the Notch*. West Kennebunk, Maine: Phoenix Publishing, 2007.

Early, Eleanor. *Behold the White Mountains*. Boston, Massachusetts: Little, Brown, and Company, 1935.

Gagne, Ty. *Where You'll Find Me: Risk, Decision, and the Last Climb of Kate Matrosova*. Conway, New Hampshire: TMC Books LLC, 2017.

Heald, D. Bruce. *Gypsies of the White Mountains: History of a Nomadic Culture*. Charleston, South Carolina: The History Press, 2012.

Heald, D. Bruce. *The Mount Washington Cog Railway: Climbing the White Mountains of New Hampshire*. Charleston, South Carolina: The History Press, 2011.

Hession, John and Valeria Michaud. *Wildflowers of the White Mountains: A Field Guide to New Hampshire's Wildflowers from Valley to Summit*. Burlington, Vermont: Huntington Graphics, 2003.

Howe, Nicholas. *Not Without Peril: 150 Years of Misadventure on the Presidential Range of New Hampshire*. Boston, Massachusetts: Appalachian Mountain Club Books, 2001.

Jackson Historical Society. *The Jackson Five: The Museum of White Mountain Art at Jackson, New Hampshire*. Jackson, New Hampshire: The Jackson Historical Society, 2016.

Jordan, J. Charles. *Tales Told in the Shadows of the White Mountains*. Lebanon, New Hampshire: University Press of New England, 2003.

Joslin, S. Richard. *Sylvester Marsh and the Cog Railway*. Manchester, New Hampshire: Morgan Press, 2000.

Julyan, Robert and Mary Julyan. *Place Names of the White Mountains*. Hanover, New Hampshire: University Press of New England, 1993.

Kaplan, Justin. *Walt Whitman: A Life*. New York, New York: Simon and Schuster, 1980.

King, Thomas Starr. *The White Hills: Their Legends, Landscape and Poetry*. Boston, Massachusetts: Crosby, Nichols, Lee and Company, 1859.

Koeppel, Eric. *Selected Paintings*. Jackson, New Hampshire: Self Published, 2015.

London, Jack. *The Road*. Lexington, Kentucky: Hubris Society, 2017.

Loving, Jerome. *Walt Whitman: The Song of Himself*. Berkeley & Los Angeles, California: University of California Press, 1999.

Mattheissen, Peter. *The Snow Leopard*. New York, New York: Penguin Books, 1978.

McAvoy, E. George. *And Then There Was One: A History of the Hotels of the Summit and the West Side of Mount Washington*. Littleton, New Hampshire: The Crawford Press, 1988.

McKenzie, A. Alexander. *The Way it Was: Mount Washington Observatory 1934–1935*. U.S.A: Self Published, 1994.

McQuaid, W. Joseph. *Cog Days: A Boy's Life and One Tragic Summer on Mount Washington*. Concord, New Hampshire: Plaidswede Publishing, 2017.

Parkman, Francis. *The Journals of Francis Parkman, Vols. 1 & 2*. New York, New York: Harper & Brothers Publishers, 1947.

Pinder, Eric. *Cat in the Clouds*. Charleston, South Carolina: History Press, 2009.

Pinder, Eric. *Life at the Top: Weather, Wonder and High Cuisine from the Mount Washington Observatory*. Brookline, New Hampshire: Hobblebush Books, 2009.

Pote, H. Winston. *Mount Washington in Winter*. Camden, Maine: Down East Books, 1985.

Putnam, William Lowell. *Joe Dodge*. Canaan, New Hampshire: Sherwin Dodge Printers, 2012.

Putnam, William Lowell. *The Worst Weather on Earth: A History of the Mount Washington Observatory*. Gorham, New Hampshire & New York, New York: Mount Washington Observatory Inc. & The American Alpine Club, Inc., 1991.

Robertson, E. B. and D. K. *Covered Bridges in the Saco River Valley: In Maine and New Hampshire*. Westbrook, Maine: Robertson Books, 1984.

Sanchez, Anita. *The Teeth of the Lion: The Story of the Beloved and Despised Dandelion*. Blacksburg, Virginia: McDonald and Woodward Publishing, 2006.

Sargent, William. *A Year in the Notch: Exploring the Natural History of the White Mountains*. Hanover, New Hampshire: University Press of New England, 2001.

Slack, G. Nancy and Allison W. Bell. *AMC Field Guide to the New England Alpine Summits*. Boston, Massachusetts: Appalachian Mountain Club Books, 2006.

Smith, Bobbie with Green Mac McKenzie. *The Latchstring is Always Out*. Eaton, New Hampshire: Self Published, 1991.

Spahr, Andrew P. *Mount Washington: The Crown of New England*. Manchester, New Hampshire: The Currier Museum of Art, Manchester, New Hampshire, 2016.

Stark Bicentennial Committee. *History of Stark, New Hampshire*. Littleton, New Hampshire: Courier Printing Co., Inc., 1974.

Stier Maggie and Ron McAdow. *Into the Mountains: Stories of New England's Most Celebrated Peaks*. Boston, Massachusetts: Appalachian Mountain Club Books, 1995.

Tarbet, W. David. *Grain Dust Dreams*. Albany, New York: State University of New York Press, 2015.

Turner, Rosemary Howard. *The Mascots of Mount Washington*. West Ossipee, New Hampshire: Woodchuck Meadow Press, 1974.

Underhill, Miriam. *Give Me the Hills*. Riverside, Connecticut: The Chatham Press, 1971.

Vincent, Lee. *Ten Years on the Rock Pile: A Collection of Stories, Some Hilarious, Some Tragic, About Life at the Summit of Mount Washington*. Nebraska: Board of Regents of the University of Nebraska, 2011.

Washburn, Bradford. *Washburn: Extraordinary Adventures of a Young Mountaineer*. Boston, Massachusetts: Appalachian Mountain Club Books, 2004.

Waterman, Laura with Guy Waterman. *Forest and Crag: A History of Hiking, Trail Blazing, and Adventure in the Northeast Mountains*. Boston, Massachusetts: Appalachian Mountain Club Books, 1989.

Weygandt, Cornelius. *The White Hills*. New York, New York: Henry Holt and Company, 1934.

Whitman, Walt. *Song of Myself*. Harmondsworth, Middlesex, England: Penguin Books, 1995.

About the Author

Dan is a longtime journalist and award-winning author living in New Hampshire.

His books include *The Adventures of Buffalo and Tough Cookie*, a hiking memoir about a one year, 225-mile journey through some of New Hampshire's least known wilderness with his ten-year-old foster daughter; and *The Nepal Chronicles*, about a month-long trek to Everest Base Camp and marriage in Kathmandu. In 2016, *The Nepal Chronicles* won the New Hampshire Literary Award and People's Choice award for best work of nonfiction. The award is sponsored by the state library and the New Hampshire Writers' Project.

His first collection of fiction, *Sing and Other Short Stories*, includes a variety of short fiction spanning Dan's twenty-five-year career as a writer and journalist. Dan's short story, "White Like Marble," was a winner in the 2017 Hemingway Shorts contest, sponsored by the Ernest Hemingway Foundation.

His other books include *Mosquito Rain: Alaskan Travel Essays*, an illustrated travelogue of Dan and his wife's journey to discover the true meaning of the Last Frontier, and *Invincible One*, a collection of poetry focused on a trip to India and Turkey with his then ten-month-old daughter.

Dan is also the editor of the three-volume Murder Ink series, an anthology collection set in New England and based on pulp fiction stories in or around the newsroom. Volume three was released in February 2018.

Dan began his career in Buffalo, New York. Since then, he has written for a wide variety of regional and national publications, including the *Main Line Times, Philadelphia Weekly, Princeton Packet, Pennsylvania Magazine, Yahoo Parenting, Huffington Post, Take Magazine, AMC Outdoors* and *Appalachia* journal.

In 2000, he moved to New Hampshire to cover the presidential election. In 2001, Dan became associate publisher of *The Hippo*, now the state's largest arts and entertainment journal.

He's a member of the Appalachian Mountain Club's 4,000-footer club and has written extensively about the outdoors and hiking. He has camped in the Grand Canyon, hiked England's Coast to Coast Trail, and trekked to Everest Base Camp in Nepal. Dan was a hiking guide and naturalist for Blue Hill Observatory and Science Center in Milton, Massachusetts.

Dan calls Manchester, New Hampshire his base camp where he lives with his wife, Meenakshi, and daughter, Uma. For more information on Dan or his writing, visit www.danszczesny.com.

Also by Dan Szczesny

Invincible One, Poems
(EKP Books, 2017)

Mosquito Rain, Alaskan Travel Essays
(Folded Word, 2016)

Sing, and Other Short Stories
(Hobblebush Books, 2015)

*The Nepal Chronicles: Marriage, Mountains
and Momos in the Highest Place on Earth*
(Hobblebush Books, 2014)

The Adventures of Buffalo and Tough Cookie
(Bondcliff Books, 2013)